under the walnut tree

under the walnut tree

ANNA BERGENSTRÖM   FANNY BERGENSTRÖM

contents

introduction

When we first started working on this book we had a completely different one in mind, but along the way our ideas took another path. Instead of the book we planned to write on entertaining, it turned into a book about a little bit of everything, with recipes based on some of our favourite ingredients. We named it *Under the Walnut Tree* simply because most of the book was created at our summer house in the countryside. There we have an old walnut tree right outside the kitchen door, and in the soft light that seeps through its branches we took photographs, exchanged thoughts and ideas, and shared inspiring meals with friends and family. In the nearby kitchen we tested recipes and photographed even more.

The title also reflects the fact that the book embraces such a wide variety of topics. We ended up with seventeen chapters, including tomatoes, herbs, chillies, citrus, cardamom, pears and chocolate... All beautiful ingredients with their own individual characters, scents and flavours — some quite robust and others with more delicate personalities. The walnut tree, and its delicious nuts, also inspired a whole chapter on nuts and seeds.

Since most of the ingredients can be used in so many different ways, you will find recipes for both savoury dishes, desserts and baked goods within the same chapter. You may also find a recipe from Provence on one page and something from India on the next, or a hint of Sweden alongside South American flavours; all reflecting our family's culinary influences and the way we like to cook. With Scandinavian cuisine as our backbone and a substantial culinary heritage from the south of France, we have always enjoyed cooking simple, honest food that crosses many culinary borders. In recent years we have also been greatly inspired by the Chilean part of our family, as well as by extensive travels both near and far.

It may all seem like a bit of an eclectic mix, but we hope that this book will provide ideas for both everyday cooking and special occasions, and that it will inspire and entice you to embark on a few new culinary adventures. Perhaps you will even rediscover flavours and aromas that may have fallen by the wayside. That, and a bit more, is what we hope you will find *Under the Walnut Tree*.

Anna & Fanny

a few more thoughts...

ENJOY THE SEASONS: Cooking with ingredients in season makes a great difference to a meal. Nothing can really compare to the freshness and taste of newly harvested fruits and vegetables, especially if organically grown. Of course — and in particular for those of us living up here in the north — it's also nice to savour ingredients from far-off lands on occasion, but choosing mainly sustainable produce just feels right. We try to choose organic dairy products, eggs, vegetables, fruit, free-range chicken and other meat from animals that have been raised with care. Using beautiful, seasonal ingredients inspires our cooking and gives a more rewarding overall experience.

FOR FLAVOURING: Nothing balances flavours like salt. We prefer mild sea salt flakes for seasoning, and use a fairly coarse, grey French salt, *sel gris*, for cooking. A couple of good olive oils are also a must; we keep a fine extra-virgin olive oil to drizzle over salads and greens, and a more robust, less expensive one for cooking and frying. A flavourful vinegar is equally important; day-to-day we mostly use red wine vinegar, but keep a sweet, aged balsamic vinegar, as well as a full-flavoured sherry vinegar for occasional use. Garlic, black pepper, thyme, rosemary, lemons and a jar of freshly made ají (a truly versatile chilli in oil, see page 124) are also indispensable to our cooking.

WHAT EVERY KITCHEN NEEDS: A large chef's knife, a small paring knife and a serrated bread knife are essential to any kitchen. When properly cared for, quality knives last for years and years; just wash them by hand and sharpen them regularly. A sturdy mortar and pestle is a fantastic tool for grinding and pounding, which brings out flavours in a unique way. Hand-held stick blenders are superb for mixing soups, and a flat grater is unrivalled for grating citrus zest, ginger and cheeses. Lastly, a large roasting tin and a good-quality heavy-based casserole dish inspire effortless cooking with fabulous results. We often cook 'one-pot' dishes in the oven; it's such a simple way to get lovely dinners to practically make themselves. You will find several such recipes in this book.

Right: Walnuts from our old walnut tree. Overleaf, from left to right: A simple feast; Oranges, mandarins and figs; Roast chicken with chorizo, page 141; Lamb skewers with rosemary, page 113

avocado

nature's perfect fast food

A perfectly ripe avocado is one of the best things there is. Its smooth texture and nutty flavour make it one of our favourite ingredients. An avocado is a small meal on its own, turned into a delicacy just by adding a touch of sea salt and a few drops of vinegar and oil. In our family, we eat avocado in one way or another nearly every day. The kids mash it on their breakfast bread or tortillas, and we enjoy it in salads with crisp lettuce leaves, on toasted sourdough with sliced tomatoes and fresh coriander, or simply drizzled with a bit of sesame and soy dressing. The avocado is such an excellent standby in the kitchen, and with a few ripe avocados on hand you can always prepare a delicious snack or salad within minutes. Add some rocket leaves, crusty bread and sliced salami or jamón serrano and you'll have scrumptious sandwiches for unexpected guests. Or make an easy avocado salad with crumbled soft goat's cheese and toasted pine nuts, as pictured here on the left. The creamy avocado flesh is also perfect for flavourful salsas and such – all it needs is to be cut in half, diced, mashed and seasoned.

What's more, aside from being so delicious, this savoury fruit is actually very wholesome. Avocados contain high amounts of the best possible fat – monounsaturated fat – which is beneficial to both the heart and the arteries. The avocado is one of the healthiest fruits around and, being loaded with vitamin E, folate, potassium and magnesium, it is considered one of the 'super foods'. In other words, an avocado not only tastes great, it is also good for you.

Left, clockwise from top: Avocado halves; Churrasco – Chilean steak sandwich, page 27; A fresh avocado salsa for barbecues, page 21; Our easy salad deluxe (with avocado, chèvre and toasted pine nuts), page 22

There are many varieties of avocado, but only three original species within the family. The Mexican avocado is quite small with smooth, green, purple or almost black skin. A larger variety from Guatemala has thicker, pebbled skin that turns blackish-green when the fruit matures. The West Indian variety is the largest, yielding round, light-green fruits that can weigh up to a kilogram. Common types found in stores are Hass, Fuerte, Ettinger and Reed.

A RIPE AVOCADO should feel firm yet slightly soft, and yield to the gentle squeeze of your hand. Unripe avocados can be placed in a bowl with some apples, as the ethylene gas they give off will speed up the ripening process. Alternatively, put unripe avocados in a paper bag for a few days — the trapped ethylene gas will hasten the ripening process.

TO PEEL AND CUT: A good way to dice an avocado is to cut the ripe fruit in half lengthwise, remove the stone, then gently slide a tablespoon between the flesh and the skin to carefully scoop out the flesh. That way you will have a nice, neat avocado half to slice or dice. If using the avocado in a salad, the easiest thing is to simply scoop out small chunks of avocado flesh directly into the bowl.

A SQUEEZE OF LEMON OR LIME JUICE prevents the avocado flesh from darkening as quickly as it normally would when exposed to air. Leaving the stone with the avocado pieces in a salad or salsa is also said to have the same effect.

a brief history of the avocado

The avocado, *Persea americana*, is, botanically speaking, a berry from a large tree belonging to the same family as bay laurel and cinnamon. These days avocados are cultivated in many parts of the world, but the fruit is thought to have originated in Mexico, where the avocado was very significant to the Aztec people. They named it *ahuácatl* (testicle), which in turn gave rise to our modern 'avocado'. Archaeological findings have uncovered avocado remains in Mexican tombs dating back more than 7000 years, yet it took a long time before the avocado spread to the rest of the world.

Right: Fuerte is a quite large, somewhat glossy, bright green avocado; Hass is smaller, with pebbled skin that turns purplish black when ripe; Avocado oil has a lovely green hue, and is considered just as wholesome as olive oil

Green Goddess dressing

This dressing goes well with crudités, bean salads, crisp lettuce or green asparagus. It's also lovely with poached salmon, prawns or roast chicken served with early spring vegetables.

SERVES 4:
1 shallot
1 small garlic clove
1 tablespoon white wine vinegar
1 tablespoon fresh lemon juice
3 anchovies
2 small avocados
a handful of assorted fresh herbs, such as parsley, dill,
  chervil, coriander, mint, basil and chives
4 tablespoons whole egg mayonnaise
5 tablespoons thick Greek yoghurt
sea salt + freshly ground black pepper

• Peel and finely chop the shallot and garlic. Place them in a bowl and add the vinegar, lemon juice and anchovies. Halve the avocados and remove the stones. Scoop out the flesh and add to the bowl. Mix with a hand-held stick blender.
  Roughly chop the herbs and add to the bowl along with the mayonnaise and yoghurt. Mix into a smooth dressing. Season with salt and pepper; taste and adjust the seasoning if needed.

Quick avocado salad

This is a great little salad to accompany lamb chops or grilled chicken.

• Peel and dice an avocado and place the pieces in a bowl. Sprinkle with a pinch of sea salt, then add a splash of red wine vinegar and some olive oil. Add a handful of chopped fresh coriander and toss gently to combine. All done!

Guacamole

A freshly made guacamole is great with barbecued meats, tortilla chips or crusty bread.

SERVES 4-6:
½–1 fresh jalapeño chilli (optional)
1 medium tomato
½ medium red onion
2 avocados
1–2 tablespoons fresh lime juice
a pinch of sea salt
1 garlic clove, minced (optional)
4 tablespoons chopped fresh coriander leaves

• Slice the chilli lengthwise and carefully remove the seeds, then finely chop with a sharp knife. Finely chop the tomato. Peel and finely chop the onion.
  Halve the avocados and remove the stones, then scoop out the flesh straight into a bowl. Add the lime juice and sprinkle with salt. Mash the avocado with a fork, then add the finely chopped ingredients. Add the garlic, if using, then fold in the coriander. Taste, and adjust the seasoning if necessary.

Avocado mash from Chile

This plain avocado mash is a staple in the Chilean part of our family, where it's served with sandwiches for evening tea, as well as at dinner with a steak and greens.

• Halve a perfectly ripe avocado and remove the stone. Scoop out the flesh into a bowl and mash it with a fork. Season with a bit of sea salt, a few drops of fresh lemon juice and a touch of corn oil or vegetable oil. Serve freshly made as a side to pretty much anything.

A fresh salsa for barbecues

This easy salsa is full of flavour and is a great side dish for a barbecue. (Photo, page 16)

SERVES 5-6:
2 avocados, diced
a handful of fresh coriander leaves, chopped
2 tablespoons fresh lemon or lime juice
3 tablespoons finely chopped spring onions
4-5 drops Tabasco sauce
  or ½-1 fresh red chilli, deseeded and finely chopped
a pinch of sea salt

• Gently combine the avocado with the coriander and lemon or lime juice in a bowl, then add the spring onion. Stir in the Tabasco sauce or the chilli. Season with sea salt to taste.

Zesty avocado dip

YOU WILL NEED:
2 avocados
1 tablespoon fresh lemon juice
1 garlic clove, minced
a pinch of sea salt
freshly ground black pepper
½-1 teaspoon ground cumin
1 teaspoon finely grated lemon zest
5 tablespoons thick Greek yoghurt
a little olive oil, to serve (optional)

• Halve the avocados and remove the stones, then scoop out the flesh straight into a bowl. Mash the avocado with a fork and then stir in the lemon juice. Add the rest of the ingredients and combine until smooth.

  Serve the dip freshly made, drizzled with a bit of olive oil. Serve with wedges of toasted pita bread or colourful crudités on the side.

Avocado and grapefruit salad

A delightful salad with tart pink grapefruit and smooth avocado, topped with rocket leaves.

YOU WILL NEED:
2 teaspoons mild vinegar
1 teaspoon honey
1 shallot, finely chopped
sea salt + freshly ground black pepper
2 tablespoons olive oil
1 pink grapefruit
2 avocados
a small handful of rocket leaves

• Combine the vinegar, honey, shallot, salt, pepper and olive oil in a small bowl. Peel and segment the grapefruit, making sure you remove all the bitter white pith.

  Halve the avocados and remove the stones, then cut them into fairly thick slices. Arrange the grapefruit and avocado on a plate, pour over the dressing and scatter the rocket leaves on top.

Tito's avocado and celery salad

Avocado and celery is a nice, somewhat unusual combination, teamed here in a tangy salad.

• Wash and trim half a head of celery. Cut off the finest top leaves and set them aside.

  Slice the celery stalks and place them in a bowl. Halve 2 avocados and remove the stones, then dice the flesh and add to the bowl. Squeeze the juice of 1 small lemon over the salad and add a splash of mild olive oil.

  Season with sea salt and freshly ground black pepper, and carefully toss to combine. Garnish with the reserved celery leaves. Serves 4-6

Pea, farro and avocado salad with mint

This is a full-flavoured salad to serve alongside lamb chops, chicken or pan-fried haloumi, or just on its own with crumbled feta cheese on top. Farro has a pleasant, nutty flavour, but the cooking time varies depending on the type of farro. We prefer to use semi-pearled, which cooks in about 25 minutes. You can also make the salad without grains, but then a bit less dressing is required.

SERVES 4:
200 g cooked farro or burghul (about 70 g uncooked)
200 g small green peas
100 g baby English spinach, rinsed
2 ripe avocados, diced
a small handful of fresh mint leaves, chopped

DRESSING:
1 shallot, peeled and thinly sliced
2 teaspoons finely grated lemon zest
3 tablespoons fresh lemon juice
1 teaspoon honey
sea salt + freshly ground black pepper
4–5 tablespoons good olive oil

• Cook the farro or burghul until tender, then drain well and set aside in a salad bowl. Cook the peas in lightly salted boiling water for 2–4 minutes. Rinse them in cold water in a colander, then drain well and set aside.

Combine all the ingredients for the dressing. Pour the dressing over the grains in the bowl and stir gently. Add the peas, spinach leaves, diced avocado and half of the mint. Fold gently to combine, then garnish with the rest of the mint. Let the flavours develop for 30 minutes or so before serving.

Nobis salad with croutons and roasted Parma ham

Roasting wafer-thin slices of Parma ham makes them crisp and simply exquisite – a perfect addition to this lettuce and avocado salad.

• Start by making the Nobis dressing on page 60, and then make the croutons on page 63. Use 2–3 slices of Parma ham per person. Line a baking tray with baking paper and then spread out the ham slices on the tray. Bake the ham at 190°C/375°F for about 8 minutes, or until crisp. This can be prepared ahead of time.

Arrange fresh, tender lettuce leaves (rinsed and carefully dried or spun in a salad spinner) in a wide salad bowl. Place large cubes of avocado on top and spoon over the dressing.

Break the crisp Parma ham into pieces and sprinkle them over the salad. Finally add a handful of small croutons and garnish with chives. Serve the salad at once.

Our easy salad deluxe

This is one of our favourite salads to serve with roast lamb or grilled or barbecued chicken, or as a small starter. (Photo, page 16)

• Cover a platter with nice, tender lettuce leaves (perhaps some rocket or little gem). Top with large cubes of avocado, crumbled soft goat's cheese and toasted pine nuts (page 234).

Season with a pinch of sea salt, and finish off with a few drops of red wine vinegar and a drizzle of mild olive oil.

Right: A salad with roasted Parma ham, about to be served with Nobis dressing

John's avocado salad

Our friend John serves this elegant salad with grilled chicken or oven-baked salmon, but it is also delectable on its own.

SERVES 6:
2 heads of cos lettuce or other crisp lettuce
2 perfectly ripe avocados, diced
50 g parmesan cheese, shaved
snipped chives for garnish

DRESSING:
1 garlic clove, finely chopped
3 tablespoons red wine vinegar
2 egg yolks
150 ml vegetable oil
sea salt + freshly ground black pepper
50 g parmesan cheese, grated

· Start by separating and rinsing the lettuce leaves. Spin them in a salad spinner or gently pat them dry with a tea towel. Place them in the fridge for now, to make them extra crisp.

Make the dressing (this is easiest in a food processor). Place the finely chopped garlic (in this case, the garlic is better chopped than pressed in a garlic crusher) in the processor bowl, then add the vinegar and egg yolks. While the food processor is on, slowly pour in the oil in a thin stream. Stop the machine and season with salt and pepper, then add the grated cheese. Whiz briefly again (if the dressing is too thick, dilute it with just a little water).

Now arrange the lettuce leaves on a plate, top with the avocado and drizzle over the creamy dressing. Sprinkle with the shaved parmesan and garnish with snipped chives.

Tuna salad from Mallorca

These simple ingredients of tuna, white beans and chunks of perfectly ripe avocado make a pleasant summer salad.

SERVES 2-3:
1 large bunch rocket or 1 cos lettuce
  or other green leaves
vinaigrette (page 60)
300 g home-cooked white beans (about 125 g
  dried beans) or 400 g tin white beans
3 medium tomatoes
½ cucumber
1-2 shallots
1 tin tuna in oil (about 160 g)
1 large avocado
fresh basil leaves for garnish
100 g soft goat's cheese (optional)
freshly ground black pepper

· Start by rinsing the lettuce leaves and spinning them in a salad spinner, or patting them dry with a tea towel. Make a nice, mild vinaigrette (perhaps the one on page 60).

If using the tinned white beans, place them in a colander and rinse well in cold water. Drain well. Cut the tomatoes into bite-sized pieces and the cucumber into half-moon slices. Peel and finely chop the shallots.

In a large bowl, combine the lettuce, beans, tomatoes, cucumber, shallots and tuna. Halve the avocado and remove the stone, then scoop out the flesh in chunks into the bowl. Gently pour the vinaigrette over the salad and garnish with a few torn basil leaves. Crumble the goat's cheese on top, if using, and finish with a good grinding of black pepper just before serving.

Avocado salsa with prawns and lime

Serve this flavourful salsa with tortilla chips, or as canapés on toasted white bread rubbed with half a garlic clove. Nice nibbles for a party.

SERVES 4:
500 g cooked prawns, unpeeled
½–1 mild red or green chilli
2 spring onions
a handful of fresh coriander leaves
2 avocados
2 tablespoons fresh lime juice
a pinch of sea salt
freshly ground black pepper

· Peel and roughly chop the prawns, then set them aside. Halve, deseed and finely chop the chilli. Shred the spring onions and chop the coriander. Cut the avocados in half, remove the stones and then dice the flesh. Combine the diced avocado with the lime juice, prawns, chilli and spring onions, then season to taste with the sea salt and a bit of black pepper. Add the chopped coriander and serve.

Our friend's egg and avocado starter on crispbread

Try this recipe, even though it may not sound all that remarkable. It is quite a delicious little starter, served on toasted Danish rye bread or crispbread, with a glass of cold beer.

SERVES 3-4:
2 medium eggs
2 avocados
1 tablespoon fresh lemon juice
2 tablespoons finely chopped onion
1 teaspoon Dijon mustard
1–2 tablespoons snipped dill
1 tablespoon mild olive oil
a pinch of sea salt
freshly ground black pepper
a few small sprigs of fresh dill for garnish

· Bring a small saucepan of water to the boil, then lower the eggs into the water and boil for 8 minutes. Rinse with cold water and set aside to cool. Peel and finely chop the eggs.

Cut the avocados in half, remove the stones and then scoop the flesh straight into a small bowl. Add the lemon juice and mash roughly with a fork. Add the onion, mustard, snipped dill, olive oil and chopped egg. Carefully combine everything, then season to taste with the sea salt and black pepper. Serve on crispbread and garnish with the dill sprigs.

Churrasco – Chilean steak sandwich

This rustic Chilean dish is made with a grilled or fried slice of entrecôte or minute steak, and served in a piece of crusty bread with avocado, tomatoes, homemade mayonnaise or aioli and a touch of chilli. (Photo, page 16)

• Finely chop or thinly slice a tomato. Peel and mash an avocado, then add some sea salt and a few drops of fresh lemon juice (or simply slice the avocado). Rinse a few small rocket leaves or other lettuce.

Grill or fry a slice of entrecôte or minute steak, then season with salt and pepper. Spread a really tasty mayonnaise on a piece of baguette or toasted sourdough. Now add the warm meat, then the tomato, avocado and lettuce leaves. Drizzle with a bit of ají verde (the green chilli mix on page 124) and serve at once.

Completos – chorizo in bread

Another scrumptious Chilean classic. This is tastiest when you use authentic chorizo or longaniza, or other quality savoury sausage.

• Place barbecued chorizos in pieces of crusty bread. Top with some mashed avocado, a little whole egg mayonnaise and a generous amount of pebre (the tomato salsa with fresh coriander and chilli on page 38).

Left: Quesadillas with guacamole, sour cream and salsa

Quesadillas with red capsicum, coriander and guacamole

Serve these quesadillas with mashed avocado seasoned with a little sea salt, or with guacamole, sour cream, tomato salsa and, for the chilli lovers, perhaps with a few drops of the ají on page 124.

SERVES 6:
8 tortillas (about 20 cm in diameter)

FILLING:
175 g finely grated cheddar or other cheese
1 large red capsicum (pepper), finely chopped
4–5 tablespoons chopped fresh coriander leaves
1–2 fresh chillies (red or green), deseeded and finely chopped
4–5 spring onions, very thinly sliced

ACCOMPANIMENTS:
avocado mash or guacamole (page 20)
cinnamon chipotle salsa (page 125) or pebre (page 38)
sour cream

• Combine all the ingredients for the filling and spread it on half of the tortillas. Place the remaining tortillas on top and press them together with your hand.

Heat a non-stick frying pan over medium heat. Dry-fry one double 'tortilla pancake' at a time for 1–2 minutes on each side. Stack the quesadillas on a plate and cover with a tea towel while you continue to dry-fry the remaining quesadillas. Finally, use a sharp knife to cut each one into 6–8 pieces. Serve at once with the accompaniments.

Superb club sandwich with avocado and chicken

This is a classic double-decker sandwich (three layers), which has been enhanced by adding sliced avocado to the traditional chicken and bacon. You can use a bought barbecued chicken if you like, but the sandwich is even tastier if you cook the chicken yourself. The chicken can be prepared ahead of time, but the sandwich should be served freshly made.

FOR 2 CLUB SANDWICHES:
1 tablespoon olive oil
1 tablespoon butter
1 chicken breast fillet
sea salt + freshly ground black pepper
1 small garlic clove, crushed (optional)
4 bacon rashers
1 medium tomato
1 small avocado
6 slices of white sandwich loaf or sourdough bread
about 6 tablespoons whole egg mayonnaise
lettuce leaves, rinsed + a few extra leaves for garnish
4 wooden skewers

TO COOK THE CHICKEN: Preheat the oven to 200°C/400°F. Heat a non-stick frying pan over medium heat, then add the oil and butter and brown the chicken for a few minutes on each side. Season with sea salt and black pepper. If using the garlic, sprinkle it over the top of the chicken, then transfer the chicken to a small ovenproof dish and bake in the oven for 13-14 minutes. Remove from the oven and set aside to cool.

NEXT: Slowly fry the bacon until crisp, then remove from the pan and place on paper towels to drain. Cut the cooked chicken into thin slices. Thinly slice the tomato. Halve the avocado and remove the stone, then slice the avocado and set aside.

THE BREAD: Toast all 6 bread slices. Cut 2 of them diagonally into triangles and set aside for later.

Spread some mayonnaise on the remaining 4 bread slices. Take out 2 plates and place one bread slice (mayonnaise-side up) on each plate. Cover the bread with crisp lettuce leaves, then place the sliced chicken on top. Cover with a second bread slice (mayonnaise-side up), then add the lettuce leaves and bacon (2 strips on each sandwich), as well as a few slices of tomato and avocado.

FINALLY: Put the 2 reserved bread triangles on top of each sandwich. If you like, you can spread mayonnaise on them as well; if so, place them mayonnaise-side down. Press the sandwiches together. Using the pre-cut bread triangles as a guide, cut the sandwiches in half diagonally.

Secure the sandwiches with the wooden skewers, and serve at once, garnished with a few extra lettuce leaves on each plate.

Avocado sandwich with turkey, sesame seeds and chilli

This is one of the tastiest sandwiches we know. When we are many at the table, we place everything on separate platters and let everyone assemble their own sandwich.

YOU WILL NEED:
whole egg mayonnaise
sourdough or rustic country bread
smoked turkey or ham in thin slices
tomato slices
avocado slices
a pinch of sea salt
toasted sesame seeds (page 234)
ají (page 124) or another chilli oil
rocket leaves

• Spread some mayonnaise on the bread. Add a few thin slices of smoked turkey or ham, and then add a few thin tomato slices and some sliced avocado. Sprinkle with a pinch of sea salt and toasted sesame seeds. Add a few drops of ají — the marvellous chilli in oil that goes wonderfully with this sandwich — or use a little store-bought chilli oil. And finally, top the sandwich with some rocket leaves.

Danish rye with rocket, mozzarella and avocado

This is a lovely sandwich with sun-dried tomatoes, avocado, rocket and mozzarella cheese on toasted Danish rye bread.

• Spread a little butter on some toasted Danish rye bread. Cover with thin slices of (buffalo) mozzarella cheese. Add a few avocado slices and some chopped soft sun-dried tomatoes (in oil). Sprinkle with a pinch of sea salt, cover with tender rocket leaves and some toasted sesame seeds (page 234) as well. Serve at once, ideally with a cold beer.

Tuna and avocado baguette

These baguettes are perfect for outdoor picnics. They are filled with tuna and avocado, which is such a great combination.

• Mix one tin of tuna (200 g) with about 100 ml whole egg mayonnaise. Season to taste with sea salt, some freshly ground black pepper and a few drops of good olive oil.

Halve a baguette lengthwise and lightly butter both sides. Cover the bottom half of the baguette with sliced tomatoes and avocado. Spread the tuna mixture on top, then add thinly sliced red onion and perhaps a little extra black pepper. Top with small, crisp lettuce leaves. Put the top half of the bread in place and use a sharp knife to cut the baguette into suitably sized pieces. Wrap each filled baguette in greaseproof paper.

Anna's avocado soup

Sometimes we serve this soup in small bowls as a little starter, simply adding a few chives and thinly sliced radishes on top, and serve it with a couple of Parmesan breadsticks. Other times we add a spoonful of lightly whipped cream and some sesame salt (see page 234), or a few small chanterelles sautéed in butter. Or a little whitefish roe with crème fraîche and prawns is another great topping.

In other words, there are many ways to serve this easy-to-make soup, which should be prepared no more than one hour in advance and served lukewarm.

AS A STARTER FOR 6-8:
150 ml pure (whipping) cream
1 litre chicken or vegetable stock
3 large ripe avocados
1 teaspoon sea salt, or to taste
some freshly ground white or black pepper
a small pinch of Herbamare
*   or other herb salt (optional)*
a handful of chives, snipped

ACCOMPANIMENTS:
300 g cooked prawns, unpeeled
*   or 150 ml crème fraîche + 60 g whitefish roe*
*   or 20 radishes*
*   or 100 g small chanterelles*

TO PREPARE THE ACCOMPANIMENTS: Peel the prawns and combine the crème fraîche with the roe, then cover and place in the fridge. Thinly slice the radishes. Trim and clean the chanterelles (just before serving, quickly fry them in a knob of butter).

THE SOUP: Lightly whip the cream, then set aside. Heat the stock in a saucepan, let it simmer for a few minutes and then set aside. Cut the avocados in half, remove the stones, then cut the flesh into chunks. Mix the avocado flesh until smooth using a hand-held stick blender or a food processor. Add the stock, a little at a time, to the mashed avocado. Stir and season the soup with salt and pepper, and some herb salt if you like. Gently fold in the whipped cream.

Serve the soup sprinkled with chives, and with the accompaniments of your choice.

Easy parmesan breadsticks

These cheesy breadsticks are prepared using ready-made sheets of puff pastry, and are great with all kinds of creamy soups or with a pre-dinner drink.

· If using frozen puff pastry, let it thaw at room temperature for 15-20 minutes. Meanwhile, preheat the oven to 200°C/400°F.

Use a rolling pin to roll out the puff pastry just a little (use a bit of flour if needed). Transfer to a baking tray lined with non-stick baking paper. Brush the pastry with lightly beaten egg and sprinkle with grated parmesan cheese. Using a blunt knife or dough scraper, carefully cut the pastry into 2 x 10 cm strips and separate them. Bake for 12-15 minutes, or until golden.

Left: Avocado soup with parmesan breadsticks

tomatoes

tomatoes ripening in the sun

In the wintertime in Scandinavia, it is easy to forget what 'real' tomatoes can taste like: the ones that have ripened in the sun and have a rather sensual scent and that indefinably strong yet sweet flavour, with a perfect balance between sweetness and slight acidity. Such tomatoes often have a supple, elastic skin that practically bursts when you bite into it — a far cry from the sad tomatoes that are grown under fluorescent tubes and sold in supermarkets. When buying tomatoes off-season, we personally feel that small organic ones on the vine are the tastiest choice. They may be a bit on the expensive side, but you only need a few to enliven a salad or snack. In the countries around the Mediterranean, fabulous tomatoes grow all year round: large, uneven, exciting varieties, often with many 'chambers' and an extraordinary aroma. No wonder tomatoes are so fundamental to Mediterranean cooking.

But when tomatoes are in full season, you often find wonderful varieties from local growers at home as well. This is the time to indulge in tomatoes with that genuine flavour; not to mention the pride of picking tomatoes that you have grown yourself. Each year we have a few tall vines growing against a south-facing wall, which yield enormous quantities of lovely, fairly small tomatoes. We harvest them all the way into October, and then end up nipping off the plants that are still full of green tomatoes. We tie the plants with raffia and hang them upside down in the kitchen window, and the tomatoes continue to ripen little by little for yet another month or so.

Left: A simple tomato salad with shallots and herbs

a golden apple – un pomo d'oro

Botanically speaking, the tomato is actually a berry, belonging to the same plant family as potatoes and eggplants (aubergines). It is said to originate from Peru and Ecuador, where it still grows wild. Yet it was the Mexican Aztecs who, in the early 16th century, gave tomato seeds as a gift to the Spaniards, who in turn introduced the tomato to Europe. However, the Europeans regarded it with scepticism, and for a long time many believed that it was poisonous. For a while it was thought to be an aphrodisiac and was sometimes called the 'apple of love' or 'apple of gold' (*pomo d'oro*). There is an Italian cookbook from Naples dated 1755 that contains a recipe for 'Spanish' tomato sauce: a sauce that is now considered the most Italian thing there is...

TOMATOES OF ALL SHAPES AND COLOURS. Nowadays there are hundreds of different tomato varieties: red ones, of course, but also pink, yellow, orange, brownish black, striped and green ones. Enjoy making colourful tomato salads and salsas, or slowly roast the tomatoes in the oven. Roasting or cooking tomatoes helps to release lycopene, an essential antioxidant.

STORING TOMATOES. Don't store tomatoes in the fridge, as they lose their flavour pretty much immediately if stored at cold temperatures. Really ripe tomatoes only last a few days at room temperature, seldom more. When we happen to have too many ripe tomatoes at home, we often prepare a delicious tomato sauce and freeze it – lovely to serve on steaming hot pasta or in a lasagne when you don't have the time to cook a dinner from scratch.

GOOD TOMATOES MAKE THEIR OWN SALAD. When tomatoes are full of sun and flavour, they really don't need any accompaniments. Just slice them, fairly thickly, and sprinkle with a bit of tasty sea salt. Let them stand and soak up the salt for roughly half an hour or so. Drizzle with a fruity olive oil and perhaps a few drops of balsamic or red wine vinegar. That's all. Or top the tomato salad at the last minute with a handful of crunchy garlic croutons and some basil leaves; or simply with chopped flat-leaf parsley and freshly ground black pepper, or a few tender rocket leaves.

Pebre — a fabulous tomato salsa

Pebre is a superb, fresh Chilean salsa that goes with almost anything: barbecued lamb, beef or fish, sausages, or simply with a piece of bread. (Photo, page 44)

SERVES 5-6:
1 large onion, chopped
1 garlic clove, chopped
4–5 medium tomatoes, diced
1 large bunch fresh coriander, finely chopped
½–1 mild green chilli, deseeded and chopped
2 tablespoons vegetable oil
1 tablespoon red wine vinegar
a pinch of sea salt

• Place the onion, garlic, tomatoes, coriander and chilli in a large mortar and pestle and lightly pound together, or whiz quickly in a food processor. Add the oil, vinegar and sea salt. Taste, and add more chilli if desired. Tip the pebre into a small bowl and let the flavours mingle for an hour or so before serving.

Light summer dressing

YOU WILL NEED:
3 medium, ripe and juicy tomatoes
1 small garlic clove, finely chopped
about 1 tablespoon fresh lemon juice
½ teaspoon honey
1–2 tablespoons olive oil
sea salt flakes + freshly ground black pepper

• Cut a small cross in the base of each tomato. Add the tomatoes to a pan of boiling water and simmer for I minute; transfer to a bowl of cold water. Drain and peel, then cut the tomatoes into wedges. Core and discard the seeds. Put the tomatoes and remaining ingredients in a blender and mix until smooth. Season to taste.

Sun-dried tomato pesto

The easiest way to prepare this flavourful tomato pesto is to use a food processor, or you can finely chop the sun-dried tomatoes and combine everything by hand. Enjoy the pesto with pasta, on bruschetta or in minestrone soup.

FOR ABOUT 250 G TOMATO PESTO:
150 g soft sun–dried tomatoes in olive oil
50–75 g pine nuts
75 g parmesan cheese, grated
100–125 ml olive oil
2 garlic cloves, crushed
about ½ teaspoon sea salt flakes
freshly ground black pepper

• Finely slice the sun-dried tomatoes and place them in a food processor. Whiz briefly, then stop the machine and scrape down the pieces that have climbed up the side of the bowl. Add the pine nuts and grated parmesan, then whiz briefly again (whether the pesto should be coarse or smooth is a matter of taste). Add the olive oil, pouring it in a little bit at a time through the tube while the machine is on. Season with crushed garlic, sea salt and pepper.

If making the pesto by hand, finely slice and then chop the tomatoes. Combine with the ground pine nuts, grated parmesan and crushed garlic. Add the oil and season to taste.

The tomato pesto makes a great pasta sauce. Reserve a little of the hot cooking water to loosen the pesto. Combine with the pasta, add some chopped fresh herbs and toss really well. Serve with extra parmesan and black pepper.

TIP: For a quick starter, spread some red pesto on small pieces of toasted sourdough. Top with buffalo mozzarella, a small drizzle of olive oil, freshly ground black pepper and basil leaves.

Tomato salad with basil

This is a wonderful tomato salad. Adding a touch of both salt and sugar can make even the most mundane tomatoes quite aromatic.

SERVES 4:
1 garlic clove, peeled and halved
500 g sweet, ripe mixed tomatoes
a small pinch of caster sugar
½ teaspoon sea salt flakes
freshly ground black pepper
3 tablespoons olive oil
1 tablespoon red wine vinegar
croutons (optional, page 63)
15–20 fresh basil leaves

· Rub the inside of a salad bowl with the halved garlic clove. This provides a perfect hint of garlic, without being too intense.

Rinse the tomatoes, then cut them into chunks and place them in the bowl. Sprinkle with the sugar, sea salt and black pepper. Combine the olive oil and vinegar and drizzle it on top of the tomatoes. Toss together gently and let stand for at least 15 minutes, then add the croutons, if using. Top the salad with some torn basil leaves.

French salade de tomates

Serve this classic tomato salad with plenty of bread to soak up the lovely juices.

· Slice 4 large, ripe tomatoes. Place the slices on a platter and sprinkle with some sea salt flakes. Finely chop 2 small shallots and sprinkle them over the tomatoes. Drizzle with 2 tablespoons of really good olive oil and about 2 teaspoons of red wine vinegar. Season with freshly ground black pepper and garnish with chopped flat-leaf parsley. Serves 2–3

Ensalada Chilena

This salad is practically a national dish in Chile, and a given side for barbecues. The key is to first soak the thinly sliced onion in cold water, which makes it extraordinarily mild.

SERVES 4–6:
1 large onion
4–5 large, ripe tomatoes
1 small bunch fresh coriander
about ½ teaspoon sea salt flakes
a pinch of freshly ground black pepper
3 tablespoons corn oil or other vegetable oil
2 tablespoons red wine vinegar

· Peel and thinly slice the onion and place it in a bowl of cold water. Let stand for 1 hour, then drain the onion in a sieve.

Cut the tomatoes into small wedges and chop the coriander leaves.

Layer the tomatoes wedges, sliced onion and coriander in a serving bowl. Lightly season with sea salt and black pepper and drizzle the oil and vinegar over the top. Gently toss to combine, then let the flavours infuse for 30 minutes. Serve the tomato salad with barbecued lamb or other meats.

Indian tomato kachumber

Try this refreshing little side salad with an Indian curry or tandoori chicken. Delicious!

· Finely chop 2 large tomatoes. Peel and finely chop ½ cucumber and 1 medium red onion. Deseed and finely slice 1 fresh green chilli. Place everything in a small serving bowl and squeeze the juice of 1 lime on top. Add a handful of chopped fresh coriander leaves. Combine everything and season with sea salt. Variation: Add ½ teaspoon ground cumin.

Slow-roasted cherry tomatoes with herbs

Roasting tomatoes slowly in the oven enhances and deepens their flavours. Serve the tomatoes alongside grilled chicken or fish, or as part of a buffet. Or just enjoy them on their own, on crusty bread with a drizzle of olive oil.

TOMATOES FOR 4-6:
30 cherry tomatoes
  or about 20 slightly larger ones
3 tablespoons olive oil
some fresh thyme and rosemary
1 teaspoon sea salt flakes (perhaps a bit more)
¼ teaspoon freshly ground black pepper

• Preheat the oven to 150°C/300°F. Cut the tomatoes in half if large or leave them whole, and put them in a bowl. Pour over about half of the olive oil and scatter with some thyme and rosemary. Season with sea salt and black pepper and carefully combine.

Drizzle the remaining olive oil in a baking dish and arrange the tomatoes (cut-side down if halved) in the dish. Bake in the middle of the oven for 1-2 hours, depending on the size of the tomatoes. They may sag but shouldn't turn brown. The tomatoes will keep in the fridge for about 3 days.

Left: Slow-roasted cherry tomatoes with herbs

Antonia's roasted tomato and mozzarella salad

A flavourful salad to serve as a light meal, with just a piece of bread and a glass of wine.

SERVES 4:
20 quite small tomatoes
2 tablespoons olive oil
½ teaspoon raw (demerara) sugar or caster sugar
½ teaspoon sea salt flakes
2 small shallots
15-20 small black olives
300 g mozzarella cheese
2 tablespoons white balsamic vinegar
  or white wine vinegar
extra 5-6 tablespoons olive oil
extra ½ teaspoon sea salt flakes
freshly ground black pepper
a handful of fresh basil leaves

• Start by roasting the tomatoes. Preheat the oven to 200°C/400°F. Halve the tomatoes and place them, cut-side up, in a lightly oiled baking dish. Drizzle the olive oil on top and sprinkle with the sugar and sea salt. Roast in the oven for 30 minutes or so. Let the tomatoes cool. Meanwhile, chop the shallots finely.

Arrange the tomatoes on a platter and sprinkle with the shallots and olives. Tear the mozzarella into pieces and scatter on top.

Combine the vinegar and extra olive oil and drizzle over the salad. Season with the extra sea salt and black pepper. Garnish with torn basil leaves and serve at once.

Salsa di pomodoro

The Mediterranean countries have an abundance of tomato varieties, and as they are left to ripen in the sun, they taste fabulous. This is a family recipe from Tuscany for a tomato sauce with lots of sunny flavour.

SERVES 4:
2 shallots
4 garlic cloves
2–3 tablespoons olive oil
750 g–1 kg sun–ripened tomatoes
plenty of fresh basil leaves
1 small sprig of fresh rosemary
100 ml dry white wine
sea salt flakes
a pinch of caster sugar
freshly ground black pepper

· Peel and chop the shallots. Peel and thinly slice the garlic cloves. Heat the olive oil in a saucepan and carefully sauté the shallots and garlic in the oil without colouring.

Cut the tomatoes into chunks. We don't peel them; we just halve them, remove the stems and cut them into large pieces.

Add the tomatoes to the shallots and slowly raise the heat until the sauce starts to bubble, stirring constantly. Add lots of finely chopped basil but just a touch of rosemary. Pour in the white wine and season with sea salt, a pinch of sugar and black pepper.

Bring the sauce to the boil, cover and simmer for 15 minutes. Remove the lid, then simmer for another 5–10 minutes to thicken the sauce, stirring occasionally. Season to taste and finish off by adding a little more chopped basil.

A simple tomato sauce

This is a very versatile tomato sauce. Sometimes we top it with crumbled feta cheese and lots of basil or flat-leaf parsley, and serve it with pasta or couscous. It is also an excellent tomato base when making pizza or lasagne.

SERVES 5-6:
2–3 garlic cloves
2 tablespoons olive oil
2 x 400 g tins sieved tomatoes (passata)
  or 1 tin passata and 1 tin chopped tomatoes
about 1 teaspoon sea salt flakes
some freshly ground black pepper
a small pinch of caster sugar
1 bay leaf
1–2 tablespoons tomato paste (concentrated purée)
  (optional)
10–15 fresh basil leaves

· Peel and finely chop the garlic. Heat the olive oil in a saucepan, then add the garlic and sauté for about 1 minute, without browning. Pour in the tinned tomatoes and season with sea salt, black pepper and a pinch of sugar. Add the bay leaf, the tomato paste if using, and then fold in some shredded basil.

Bring to the boil and then slowly let the sauce simmer, uncovered, for about 15 minutes, stirring occasionally. Discard the bay leaf. Taste and then season with salt, pepper and perhaps a touch more sugar if needed.

Creamy tomato soup

This mild tomato soup is very easy to prepare and is nice as a small starter, perhaps topped with some crispy garlic croutons.

SERVES 4, OR 8 AS A STARTER:
8 large, sweet and ripe tomatoes (1 kg)
1 large onion (about 120 g)
3 garlic cloves
2 tablespoons olive oil
500 ml chicken or vegetable stock
  (perhaps a bit more towards the end)
1–2 tablespoons tomato paste (concentrated purée)
about 1 teaspoon sea salt
½ teaspoon caster sugar
a pinch of freshly ground black pepper
100 g crème fraîche
fresh basil leaves
croutons (optional, page 63)

• Start by halving the tomatoes. Core and roughly chop them and set aside. Peel and chop the onion and finely chop the garlic.

Heat the olive oil in a saucepan and gently sweat the onion and garlic for 3–4 minutes without colouring. Add the tomatoes, stock, tomato paste, sea salt, sugar and black pepper, and bring to the boil. Lower the heat, cover and slowly simmer for 30 minutes or so.

Use a hand-held stick blender to whiz directly in the saucepan if you want a smooth soup (we almost always do). You can prepare the recipe up to this point ahead of time.

Reheat the soup, add a dollop of crème fraîche and stir in a handful of finely sliced basil. Season to taste and serve garnished with a few small basil leaves and some croutons if you like.

Zucchini and tomato soup

This soup is somewhat similar to a Spanish gazpacho, and is just as tasty whether served warm, lukewarm or cold. (Photo, page 44)

SERVES 3–4:
1–2 medium onions
2–3 tablespoons olive oil
4–5 medium tomatoes
3 small zucchini (courgettes) (about 500 g)
2–3 tablespoons tomato paste (concentrated purée)
800 ml vegetable stock
  (perhaps a bit more towards the end)
some freshly ground black pepper
about 1 teaspoon sea salt
a small pinch of caster sugar
1 garlic clove, peeled
chopped fresh flat-leaf parsley, to serve

• Peel and roughly chop the onions. Heat the olive oil in a saucepan and lightly sauté the onion. Halve, core and cut the tomatoes into fairly small pieces, then add to the pan. Cut the zucchini in half lengthwise, then into quarters and finally into thin slices. Place them in the pan, then add the tomato paste and stir.

Pour in the stock, then add the pepper, salt and sugar. Bring to the boil, then lower the heat, cover and simmer slowly for 20 minutes. Crush the garlic into the soup and simmer for another 3 minutes. You can prepare the recipe up to this point ahead of time.

Measure out about 200 ml of the soup and set aside. Purée the rest of the soup until it is more or less smooth, then pour in the reserved soup. Stir, and dilute with about 100 ml extra stock if needed. Serve the soup warm or cold, sprinkled with some chopped parsley, and place the pepper mill on the table.

Pebre — a fabulous tomato salsa, page 38

Zucchini and tomato soup, page 43

Salsa di pomodoro, page 42

Creamy tomato soup, page 43

Chickpeas for Lorna

These fragrant, Indian-inspired chickpeas make an excellent vegetarian meal. We like to serve them with plain basmati rice, some refreshing thick yoghurt and a green salad on the side.

SERVES 4:
600 g home-cooked chickpeas (about 250 g dried
  chickpeas) or 2 x 400 g tins chickpeas
2 onions
3 garlic cloves
5 cm piece fresh ginger
1 fresh red chilli or ½ teaspoon chilli powder
3 tablespoons vegetable oil
1–2 teaspoons brown mustard seeds
½ teaspoon ground turmeric
1 teaspoon ground cumin
1 teaspoon garam masala (optional)
1 small cinnamon stick
1 large bay leaf
2 x 400 g tins chopped tomatoes
1 teaspoon sea salt
a pinch of raw (demerara) sugar

· Rinse the chickpeas well, particularly if tinned. Drain and set aside. Peel and finely chop the onions and garlic. Peel and grate the ginger. Deseed and finely slice the fresh chilli, if using.

Gently heat the oil in a large frying pan. Add the onion, garlic, ginger, chilli, all the spices and the bay leaf. Sauté for about 2–3 minutes over medium heat while stirring. Add the tomatoes, sea salt and sugar, and bring to the boil. Let the tomato sauce slowly simmer for 15 minutes, stirring occasionally.

Lastly, add the chickpeas and heat them in the sauce for a few minutes. Season to taste.

Red lasagne with green leaves

This is a truly delicious, satisfying vegetarian lasagne prepared with silverbeet or spinach, pesto, ricotta cheese and a tasty tomato sauce.

SERVES 4:
1 batch of a simple tomato sauce (page 42)
400 g tender silverbeet (Swiss chard) or English spinach
500 g ricotta or cottage cheese
5–6 tablespoons pesto (page 84)
a pinch of sea salt + freshly ground black pepper
a small pinch of grated nutmeg
100 g parmesan cheese, grated
12 lasagne sheets
200 ml full-fat milk

· Start by preparing the tomato sauce, and then carefully pick through and rinse the silverbeet or spinach. Preheat the oven to 190°C/375°F.

In a saucepan, bring a bit of water to the boil. Add the silverbeet to the pan and blanch for 2 minutes (but only 30 seconds if using spinach). Tip the leaves into a colander and rinse immediately with cold water. Drain well, squeeze the leaves with your hands and roughly chop.

Combine the ricotta cheese with the chopped leaves, pesto, salt, pepper and nutmeg. Lastly, stir in about half of the grated parmesan.

Spread a thin layer of the tomato sauce in an ovenproof dish. Alternately layer the lasagne sheets, the green cheese mixture and the tomato sauce, finishing with a layer of tomato sauce. Carefully pour the milk along the sides of the dish. Sprinkle the rest of the parmesan on top.

Bake in the oven for about 40 minutes. Serve the lasagne warm or slightly cooled, with a fresh green salad.

Alex's tomato chicken with basil

This quick and easy chicken turns out much nicer than you might expect just from reading the recipe. It's simple everyday cooking!

SERVES 2:
5 medium, ripe tomatoes
2 large garlic cloves
1 tablespoon olive oil
1 tablespoon butter
2 chicken breast fillets
sea salt + freshly ground black pepper
plenty of fresh basil leaves

· Start by halving the tomatoes, then core and cut each tomato half into about 6 pieces. Peel and finely chop the garlic. Set the tomatoes and garlic aside.

Heat a frying pan (one with a lid) and add the olive oil and then a little knob of butter. Add the chicken to the pan and brown the chicken over fairly high heat for about 3 minutes on each side. Season with salt and pepper.

Add the garlic and let it fry gently alongside the chicken for no more than 30 seconds. Then add the tomato pieces and let everything simmer; they will soon turn soft and pulpy. Cover and cook for 5 minutes. Remove the lid and turn the chicken over, then cook for another 12 minutes uncovered. Make sure that the chicken is cooked through.

Sprinkle generously with finely chopped basil and serve straight out of the frying pan, ideally with some oven-roasted potato wedges and a green salad, or simply with plain pasta.

Lamb patties with lemon

These small lamb patties are seasoned with lemon zest, garlic and herbs, and simmered in a tomato sauce.

SERVES 4:
3 tablespoons dried breadcrumbs
125 ml beef or lamb stock, or water
500 g minced lamb
1–1½ teaspoons sea salt
½ teaspoon freshly ground black pepper
2 tablespoons finely grated lemon zest
1 egg
a large handful of fresh flat-leaf parsley or dill, chopped
1 garlic clove, crushed
fresh thyme, parsley or dill for garnish

TOMATO SAUCE:
1 large onion, chopped
2 tablespoons olive oil
400 g tin chopped tomatoes
sea salt + freshly ground black pepper

· Place the breadcrumbs in a bowl and pour in the stock or water. Let stand for a few minutes, then stir. Add the mince, salt, pepper, lemon zest, egg, chopped parsley or dill, and garlic. Mix well and chill while preparing the sauce.

Sauté the onion in the olive oil in a casserole dish. Add the tomatoes and season with salt and pepper. Bring to the boil and simmer, uncovered, for 5-6 minutes.

Shape the mince mixture into 12 patties. Lower them into the tomato sauce in the casserole dish, cover and gently simmer for 15 minutes. Sprinkle with the herbs, and serve the patties with rice, couscous or tagliatelle.

Pizza, page 50

Spanish tomatoes

Pizza with roasted capsicum, olives and rocket

A savoury tomato bread, page 51

Pizza our way

The best pizzas are made with fresh toppings and a really good dough. Pizza dough should be kneaded vigorously and preferably be allowed to rise twice in order for it to become nice and elastic (although we are often too impatient and just let it rise once!). The dough makes 2 large or 4 individual pizzas.

DOUGH:
15 g fresh (compressed) yeast
½ teaspoon salt
200 ml lukewarm water
3 tablespoons milk
2 tablespoons olive oil + 1 tablespoon extra
290 g plain flour + about 15 g extra

TOPPING:
½ batch of a simple tomato sauce (page 42)
400 g mozzarella cheese
sea salt + freshly ground black pepper
3 tablespoons olive oil
a large handful of tender rocket leaves

THE DOUGH: Crumble the yeast into a large bowl or food processor and add the salt. Pour in some of the water and stir to dissolve the yeast. Add the rest of the water, milk, olive oil and flour, and then combine until the dough comes together. Work the dough (in the bowl) for 5-6 minutes using a wooden spoon, or whiz it quickly until smooth in the food processor. Add the extra flour if needed.

Shape the dough into a large ball and place it in a clean and lightly oiled bowl. Brush some of the extra oil on top of the dough, cover and set aside to rise for at least 40 minutes, or until the dough has doubled in size.

When the dough has risen (and if you have the time), use your fist to gently push the risen dough back into the bowl, and let it rise again. That is how real pizza bakers do it.

TOP AND BAKE: Preheat the oven to 260°C/500°F. Knead the dough on a lightly floured surface and divide it into 2 or 4 pieces. Knead each piece and roll out into quite thin pizza bases. Place the pizza bases on baking trays lined with non-stick baking paper.

Spread a thin layer of tomato sauce almost all the way to the edges of the dough. Top with torn pieces of mozzarella and season with sea salt and freshly ground black pepper. Bake the pizzas (one tray at a time) in the middle of the oven for about 10-12 minutes (a bit longer for larger ones). Drizzle with a little olive oil and scatter with rocket leaves. Serve straight away.

WITH ROASTED CAPSICUM AND PROSCIUTTO: Spread the tomato sauce over the base and scatter with the mozzarella, as above. Top with a few wide strips of roasted red or yellow capsicum (pepper) (page 246) and some sautéed onion. Top with a few slices of prosciutto or salami, and sprinkle with a handful of black olives. After baking, garnish with a few basil leaves.

WITH VEGETARIAN TOPPING: First spread a layer of tomato sauce over the dough, then add a few slices of roasted zucchini (courgette) (page 92) and roasted capsicum (pepper) (page 246). Add halved tinned artichoke hearts, olives, sliced mushrooms and pieces of mozzarella. Season with salt and pepper. Bake and serve topped with rocket and a small handful of basil leaves.

Tomato bruschetta

A carefully made bruschetta is one of those things that is always appreciated, and is a perfect starter to almost any meal. Toasted country bread, some fruity olive oil and sun-ripened tomatoes are a lovely combination. (Photo, page 32)

SERVES 6:
5-6 medium tomatoes
sea salt + freshly ground black pepper
1 tablespoon olive oil
1 teaspoon white balsamic or red wine vinegar
6 slices of country bread
1 large garlic clove, peeled
2 tablespoons olive oil for the bread
6-8 large fresh basil leaves, shredded

· Start with the tomatoes. Cut them into halves and then into quarters. Discard the cores, stems and seeds. Finely chop the tomato flesh and place in a bowl. Sprinkle with some sea salt, a couple of grinds of black pepper and drizzle with the olive oil and vinegar. This can be prepared a few hours ahead of time.

Toast or grill the bread slices. Cut the garlic clove in half and rub one side of the bread with the cut garlic, then drizzle with olive oil. Place the chopped tomatoes on top and sprinkle with the shredded basil leaves. Grind over some more black pepper and serve immediately.

A savoury tomato bread

This rustic bread with sun-dried tomatoes and black olives is perfect picnic food – perhaps with some feta cheese, thinly sliced red onion, rocket leaves and cold cuts in the basket as well. (Photo, page 49)

YOU WILL NEED:
15 soft sun-dried tomatoes in olive oil
30 g fresh (compressed) yeast
1 heaped teaspoon salt
2 tablespoons honey
500 ml lukewarm water
200 g thick Greek yoghurt
2 tablespoons olive oil
75 g pitted Kalamata olives
690 g plain flour + 100 g extra

· Cut the tomatoes into small pieces. Set aside. Crumble the yeast into a bowl and add the salt and honey. Pour in about half the water and stir to dissolve the yeast. Add the yoghurt and olive oil. Stir again and then pour in the rest of the water. Add the tomatoes, olives and, lastly, the flour. Knead lightly until the dough comes together, then cover with a tea towel and set aside to rise for 1 hour.

Preheat the oven to 250°C/480°F. Line a baking tray with non-stick baking paper. Sprinkle some of the extra flour on the work surface and tip the dough on top. Knead lightly with floured hands, shaping it into a round loaf. Place on the baking tray and set aside to rise for about 30 minutes. Score the bread with a sharp knife.

Bake the bread for 10-12 minutes, then lower the heat to 150°C/300°F and bake for 1 hour. Let the bread cool under a tea towel.

leafy greens

a salad of mixed lettuce leaves…

… some sweet-tasting and others slightly bitter, dressed with a vinaigrette or just with a good olive oil and a splash of lemon juice is a simple treat.

To us, a daily green salad is essential, whether plain or with a variety of leafy greens with different tastes and textures. Adding a peppery note of watercress, some bright green pea shoots or tiny, purplish amaranth leaves can liven up the salad. Our favourite olive oil for lettuce is a mild, grassy olive oil from Tuscany, which beautifully complements the delicate flavours of any leaves.

TO WASH LETTUCE: Pick through the leaves and remove any wilted ones. Separate the lettuce leaves and snip off the ends of the stems to get nice clean cuts. Rinse the leaves thoroughly, ideally in a large bowl of cold water, swirling the leaves around with your hand to remove any grit or soil. Drain in a colander.

THE MAGIC SALAD SPINNER: Place the rinsed leaves in a salad spinner: nothing removes excess water better without bruising the leaves. Spin the lettuce in small batches – it's done in no time. If you don't have a salad spinner, gently pat the leaves with a tea towel. The dressing will cling much better to fairly dry lettuce leaves.

FOR EXTRA CRISP LETTUCE: Loosely place the rinsed, dried leaves in a damp tea towel or in a large plastic bag. Place the lettuce in the fridge for a few hours or overnight to make them extra crisp.

TO DRESS A SALAD: Prepare the dressing of your choice. If making a vinaigrette, let the garlic or shallots macerate with the vinegar and a touch of salt for about 10 minutes before adding the oil. Dress the salad just before serving, but in moderation: the dressing should never overpower the salad. Toss gently to lightly coat the leaves, and bring the salad to the table.

VINEGARS AND OILS: It is truly worthwhile to invest in good-quality vinegars and olive oils; there are so many lovely varieties that can really lift a salad. We like to use a mature red wine vinegar, and we always keep a bottle of good extra-virgin olive oil reserved for salads and such. As a nice variation, we also keep a small bottle of fresh walnut oil; its wonderful nutty flavour pairs magnificently with escarole or other chicories.

rocket, cos, escarole or little gem...

Making beautiful salads is easy when you have lovely, fresh lettuce leaves to choose from. Combine flavourful varieties, both bitter and sweet.

COS LETTUCE is oval-shaped with long, succulent leaves. It is excellent in salads with creamy dressings, and also with fried chicken, salmon or other warm ingredients. Cos lettuce is often used in Caesar salads.

LITTLE GEM LETTUCE is also known as heart lettuce. It is a small, compact variety of cos lettuce, with beautiful, mild-tasting leaves.

ROCKET or rucola is truly a versatile salad leaf, with its nutty, sometimes even peppery taste. It grows wild in southern France and is included in the salad mix, mesclun, along with young dandelion leaves, chervil and others.

OAK LEAF LETTUCE is a loose-leaf lettuce with green serrated leaves, sometimes with red edges. Oak leaf must be rinsed thoroughly, as grains of sand often get stuck between the tightly packed leaves.

MÂCHE LETTUCE is also called lamb's lettuce and has tiny green leaves growing in a rosette. It's a great little lettuce in combination with other leaves.

ROUND LETTUCE also known as head, cabbage or bibb lettuce, grows in loose, chubby heads. It's a nice, mild variety, which can easily be forgotten among all the more popular ones.

WATERCRESS has tiny, bright green leaves with a delicious, peppery flavour. Use it as the sole accompaniment to a piece of barbecued salmon or steak, or in a salad with sweet oranges.

WITLOF (CHICORY OR BELGIAN ENDIVE) has small, narrow, pale yellow or almost white leaves, and is common during the winter season. Witlof is grown in the dark, which explains why it is so pale. There is also a red variety. Filled witlof is great as finger food for cocktail parties, or it can be boiled, braised or baked *au gratin* or served just with a drizzle of walnut oil.

RADICCHIO is a small red and white type of chicory. It is related to witlof, and is also slightly bitter but still very tasty. Radicchio is best when combined with other, milder leaves. Treviso radicchio is another wonderful variety.

FRISÉE (CURLY ENDIVE) looks like a scruffy little bush with narrow, spiky and slightly bitter leaves. The paler leaves in the centre are usually a bit milder. Frisée leaves work well in combination with more neutral-flavoured leaves.

ESCAROLE is another bushy type of lettuce with jagged leaves. Related to the frisée, but not as bitter.

BABY GREENS OR BABY LEAF SALAD is a mix of different baby green leaves (such as baby English spinach, mizuna, oak leaf lettuce and pea shoots).

LOLLO ROSSO AND LOLLO BIONDA are fringed, crinkled loose-leaf lettuces with delicate reddish-brown or green leaves, which easily become a bit floppy in a salad with dressing. Grains of sand can hide in the frizzy leaves, so always rinse lollo lettuce very carefully.

ICEBERG LETTUCE has long been considered a bit boring, but the leaves are both durable and crisp. For a nice variation, boil the iceberg lettuce in large wedges and serve them warm with lemon, salt and butter (see page 72).

and a few asian leaves...

KANGKUNG OR WATER SPINACH is a delicious leafy green, widely used in Southeast Asian cooking. The narrow leaves and thin stalks can be quickly stir-fried or steamed. Kangkung is also known as morning glory.

MIZUNA is a lovely little leaf that suits most types of salads, and is also quite easy to grow in the garden. The tender leaves are bright green and serrated.

BOK CHOY OR PAK CHOY is a mild Chinese cabbage with green leaves and wide, pale stalks. It is great for stir-frying, steaming or braising. A smaller variety is called baby bok choy.

growing leafy greens

It's easy and inspiring to grow your own lettuces and other leafy greens, and the outcome is truly rewarding. Sow the lettuce seedlings a few at a time, with a few weeks in between plantings; this way you can enjoy perfectly fresh leaves throughout the season. Once the plants have grown to about 3 cm, it's usually time to start a new crop. In our small kitchen garden, we sow the first lettuce seeds early in the season, as we are always eager to pick those new, tender rocket and little gem leaves. Later, we add the chicories and other winter lettuces. We also sow some marigolds and peppery nasturtiums among the salad plants; they flower so prettily and their petals add a nice splash of colour to green salads.

AN EASY-TO-GROW SELECTION: Rocket, mesclun mixes, oak leaf, little gem, round lettuce, cos, mizuna, mâche, chicories, spinach, silverbeet (Swiss chard) and bok choy.

Right, clockwise from top: A fresh Asian-style salad to go with the sesame dressing on page 61; Baby English spinach leaves are wonderful when steamed; Kangkung (water spinach); Bok choy

Nobis dressing

This is a truly versatile dressing. It will keep for a few days in the fridge, and is wonderful with all kinds of salads or as a dipping sauce for witlof or a platter of crudités. We often include it on buffets, or serve it with briefly boiled or grilled asparagus.

SERVES 6:

1 egg, at room temperature
2 teaspoons white wine vinegar
about 1 teaspoon Dijon mustard
¼ teaspoon salt
a pinch of freshly ground black pepper
250 ml sunflower oil
½ garlic clove, crushed
4 tablespoons finely snipped chives

· Carefully lower the egg into a small saucepan of boiling water and boil for 3 minutes: no more, no less! If the egg cracks, you have to start over with a new egg — it's important that the egg is truly soft-boiled. Remove and rinse with cold water. Halve the egg and use a teaspoon to scoop the egg out of the shell straight into a food processor or blender. Add the vinegar, mustard, salt and pepper. Whiz to combine, then slowly pour in the oil while the machine is on. Stop the machine, season with just a little of the garlic and the snipped chives. Briefly mix again and season to taste.

The sauce is thick and best served separately in a jug or bowl. You can dilute it with a little water if you wish.

Everyday dressing

Instead of making a proper vinaigrette, just splash a little fresh lemon juice over nice, crisp lettuce leaves, sprinkle with sea salt and finish with a drizzle of really good olive oil.

Our vinaigrette

There are hundreds of ideas on how to make the perfect vinaigrette. Lately, we prefer to make our dressing this way.

VINAIGRETTE FOR 6-8:

1 garlic clove
a pinch of sea salt
freshly ground black pepper
2 tablespoons red wine vinegar
½ teaspoon honey
½ shallot, finely chopped
6 tablespoons olive oil

· Peel and lightly bruise the garlic clove (don't use a garlic press or the flavour will be too acrid). Place the garlic in a small bowl with the salt, pepper, vinegar and honey. Add the finely chopped shallot and set aside to macerate for 10 minutes, then stir in the olive oil.

Remove and discard the garlic clove. Briefly whisk the dressing and season to taste. Drizzle the vinaigrette over lettuce leaves, toss gently to lightly coat the leaves and serve.

Creamy mustard dressing

Follow the recipe for the vinaigrette (on the left). Omit the garlic if you like, but add 1 tablespoon coarse-grained mild mustard just before adding the oil.

Whisk or stir the dressing; the mustard makes it a bit creamy. Serve with mixed lettuce leaves, salads with cheese or in a potato salad.

Sesame dressing

In a small bowl, combine 2 tablespoons mild rice vinegar, 2 tablespoons Japanese soy sauce, 1 tablespoon caster sugar, 1 tablespoon sesame oil and 4 tablespoons water. Add 3 tablespoons toasted sesame seeds (page 234).

This is a perfect dressing for avocado, Asian noodle salads, over fine (julienne) strips of carrot, or for crispy green leaves topped with diced cucumber and red capsicum (pepper).

Cranks' excellent dressing

Combine equal parts vinaigrette and thick Greek yoghurt. This will result in a creamy, extraordinarily appetising dressing suitable for leafy green salads, grated carrots, cold boiled eggs and bean salads.

This is one of our all-time favourite dressings, which we came across during a few memorable days behind the scenes at Cranks, the legendary London restaurant.

Vergé's dressing

This dressing is named after culinary legend Roger Vergé. The dressing is splendid on plain green salads, with freshly boiled snow peas (mangetout), wax beans or salads with cannellini or other beans. Top with herbs such as thyme, chervil, parsley and chives.

· Combine 2 egg yolks with 1 tablespoon Dijon mustard, the juice of ½ lemon, ½ teaspoon honey, a pinch of sea salt, some freshly ground black or white pepper, 2-3 tablespoons oil (walnut oil, if possible) and 4-5 tablespoons thick (double) cream.

Lemon dressing

Combine 2 tablespoons fresh lemon juice, 1-2 teaspoons grated lemon zest, ½ teaspoon honey, a little sea salt and freshly ground black pepper. Lastly, add 3-4 tablespoons good olive oil. This dressing is fabulous on thinly sliced fennel with shaved parmesan cheese, or for a salad with salmon or seafood.

Old-fashioned cream dressing

Combine 5 tablespoons pure (whipping) cream with 1-2 tablespoons fresh lemon juice, a pinch of salt and a small amount of white pepper. Stir vigorously. Round off with a pinch of sugar, if desired. Lovely on mixed green leaves.

Embellish the salad

A plain green salad immediately becomes a bit more festive when topped with some nuts, pieces of mozzarella cheese or a handful of crunchy bread croutons. Here are a few ideas for how to adorn a salad:

PARMESAN is a fabulous cheese to use in green leaf salads. Shave it into thin flakes using a potato peeler, or grate it directly over the salad bowl just before serving.

GRUYÈRE AND EMMENTAL are two other cheeses that work really well in a green salad. Cut the cheese into thin strips or small cubes and dress the salad with a creamy mustard vinaigrette.

CRUMBLED SOFT CHEESES such as goat's cheese, blue cheese or feta quickly turn plain leaves into a feast. Soft cheeses crumble more easily when refrigerator-cold. Chèvre (with the rind removed) goes well with all kinds of salad leaves (ideally with pine nuts or walnuts as well), while feta cheese often requires something extra on the side, such as thinly sliced red onion or a few black olives.

ROASTED PARMA HAM is deliciously crisp and nice to scatter over a salad. You can also sprinkle the roasted ham over a potato salad or a hearty potato and leek soup.
Use 2 wafer-thin slices of Parma ham per person. Preheat the oven to 180°C/350°F. Spread out the slices on a baking tray lined with non-stick baking paper and bake for about 8 minutes. Allow to cool.

AVOCADO is, of course, great in salads, and you will find plenty of tips in the chapter on avocado, starting on page 14.

CROUTONS are great to sprinkle over a green leaf salad or on top of a fish soup. They can be made 1-2 days in advance and stored in an airtight jar.
For 4-5 serves: Cut off the edges of 4 slices of day-old white bread. Then cut the bread into small squares the size of sugar cubes. Fry them until crisp in 2 tablespoons mild olive oil and add ½ crushed garlic clove. Stir to combine. Let the croutons cool on a plate.

NUTS AND SEEDS such as pine nuts, hazelnuts, sesame seeds or sunflower seeds become tastier if you toast them before sprinkling over salads. Spread out the seeds or nuts in a warm dry frying pan, and gently toast while stirring. Larger nuts, such as cashews or hazelnuts, can be roughly chopped before toasting. Peanuts, preferably unsalted, are great in Asian salads. Toast them and then rub off the brown skins. Walnuts and pistachios, on the other hand, often taste fantastic as they are. For more on nuts and seeds, see the chapter starting on page 224.

POMEGRANATE SEEDS are beautiful to sprinkle on salads. Just make sure to remove all the bitter, whitish-yellow membrane in which the seeds are embedded. Pomegranate is a great match with blue cheese and crispy salad leaves.

NECTARINE SLICES or fresh figs in wedges are both pretty and delectable in salads. Serve with wafer-thin slices of Parma ham and a vinaigrette, or with a mild balsamic vinegar and a drizzle of olive oil. Perhaps also with soft goat's cheese or buffalo mozzarella.

Left: Sliced nectarines in a green salad; Pomegranate, mâche lettuce, baby English spinach leaves and blue cheese

Caesar salad

Pick the freshest lettuce leaves you can find, ideally cos or little gem lettuce. You can also add a few baby English spinach leaves if you wish. Caesar salads often include grilled chicken (see Superb club sandwich on page 28) or sometimes grilled salmon, but the original salad is said to have been completely green.

You can prepare most of this salad beforehand, but serve it freshly assembled.

SERVES 4:

3 slices of day-old white bread
2 tablespoons vegetable oil
½ garlic clove for the croutons
2 small heads little gem lettuce
  or cos lettuce
baby English spinach (optional)
½ garlic clove for the salad bowl

DRESSING:

1 egg
1 tablespoon red or white wine vinegar
1 tablespoon fresh lemon juice
1 teaspoon Dijon mustard
2 teaspoons Worcestershire sauce
  or 3 mashed anchovies
½ garlic clove, crushed
sea salt + freshly ground black pepper
100 ml vegetable oil
3 tablespoons grated parmesan cheese
  + extra to serve

THE CROUTONS: Cut the bread slices into cubes. Fry the cubes until crisp and golden in the oil. Crush a little garlic on top and stir until combined, then remove from the pan and leave to cool on a plate.

THE LETTUCE LEAVES: Separate and rinse the gem or cos lettuce well, leaf by leaf, and drain. Rinse the spinach well, if using. Spin in a salad spinner or gently pat dry with a tea towel. Tear the gem lettuce into large pieces. Place the salad leaves in an airy plastic bag in the fridge for a few hours, to make the leaves extra crisp.

THE DRESSING: Bring some water to the boil in a saucepan, lower the egg into the water and cook for exactly 2 minutes. Remove and rinse immediately with cold water. Halve the egg and use a teaspoon to scoop the runny, soft-boiled egg directly into a food processor. Add the vinegar, lemon juice, mustard, Worcestershire sauce or anchovies and garlic. Season with salt and pepper. Mix for 20 seconds or so.

Slowly pour in the oil in a thin stream while the machine is on. Add the grated parmesan cheese and mix once more. Season to taste.

LAST OF ALL: Rub the inside of a salad bowl with the halved garlic clove, which gives a pleasant whisper of garlic. Add the lettuce leaves. Drizzle the dressing on top and add some extra parmesan cheese. Scatter croutons over the top and serve.

A big birthday salad

This generous salad is great with creamy Nobis dressing and freshly baked bread. It's easy to make a larger batch when catering for a crowd.

SERVES 5-6:
various kinds of lettuce leaves, such as rocket, radicchio,
  round lettuce, baby English spinach or mâche
2 eggs
1 small barbecued chicken
100 g bacon rashers, sliced
100 g blue cheese
2 avocados, in cubes
1 bunch radishes, sliced
75 g walnuts, roughly chopped
Nobis dressing (page 60)

· Rinse the lettuce leaves well, gently pat dry or spin them in a salad spinner. Place in airy plastic bags and refrigerate until needed. Boil the eggs for 7-8 minutes.

Remove the chicken skin and bones and cut the meat into pieces.

Slowly fry the bacon over medium heat until crisp, then remove from the pan and drain on paper towels. Cover the base of a salad bowl with the mixed lettuce leaves. Distribute the chicken pieces and crumble the blue cheese and bacon on top.

Add the cubes of avocado, sliced radishes and roughly chopped walnuts. Cut the boiled eggs into wedges and arrange on top of the salad. Serve with Nobis dressing in a jug on the side.

Baked salmon on spinach

This is an incredibly simple way to serve salmon — baked on a bed of tender spinach leaves. The recipe originally comes from Swedish chef and restaurateur Nils Emil Ahlin.

SERVES 4:
800 g skinless salmon fillet
1 tablespoon olive oil or soft butter
200 g baby English spinach
1 heaped teaspoon sea salt
freshly ground white pepper
300 ml thick (double) cream
100 ml dry white wine
4-5 tablespoons grated parmesan cheese

· Trim the salmon if necessary, remove any small bones with tweezers, then cut the salmon into 4 pieces. Grease an ovenproof dish with the olive oil or soft butter.

Pick through and rinse the spinach leaves well. Gently pat them dry or spin them in a salad spinner. Arrange the spinach in the greased dish. Place the fish on top and season with salt and white pepper.

Carefully pour a mixture of the cream and wine over the salmon and then sprinkle the grated parmesan on top. Bake at 175°C/345°F for 20-25 minutes. Serve with boiled potatoes.

Honey-roasted goat's cheese on baby greens

Use nice, tender baby lettuce leaves for this salad, with perfectly fresh walnuts and a really tasty soft goat's cheese. Sometimes we add a couple of pear slices too, or fresh figs in halves.

AS A SUGGESTION FOR 4:
250 g mixed baby lettuce leaves
vinaigrette (perhaps the one on page 60)
a handful of walnuts
350 g soft goat's cheese in 4 thick slices
2 tablespoons olive oil
1 tablespoon fresh thyme leaves
  or 1 teaspoon dried thyme
2-3 teaspoons honey

· Rinse and carefully pick through the lettuce leaves, then gently pat dry or spin them in a salad spinner. Prepare the vinaigrette about 15 minutes in advance, to let the flavours develop. Chop the walnuts roughly.

Preheat the oven to 250°C/480°F. Place the goat's cheese slices on a baking tray lined with non-stick baking paper. Drizzle with the olive oil and sprinkle with the thyme. Drizzle the honey over the top. Bake for 4-5 minutes.

Meanwhile, tip the lettuce leaves into a bowl, pour the vinaigrette on top and toss gently to coat the leaves. Arrange the lettuce on individual plates. Place the warm goat's cheese on top, scatter with the walnuts and serve right away.

Portobello bruschetta with pecorino and rocket

This is a small meal on its own. Toasted sourdough is topped with fried portobello mushrooms, a little bit of pesto, rocket leaves and shaved pecorino or parmesan. It's easy to make and simply scrumptious.

MAKES 4 BRUSCHETTAS:
4 large portobello mushrooms (caps only)
2 tablespoons olive oil or 1 tablespoon butter
sea salt flakes + freshly ground black or white pepper
2 large slices of sourdough bread
½ garlic clove
4-5 tablespoons pesto (page 84)
rocket or baby English spinach leaves
shaved pecorino or parmesan cheese

· Start by frying the whole mushroom caps (without stems). Fry them slowly on both sides in the olive oil or butter. Season lightly with salt and pepper.

Toast or grill the bread slices. Rub one side of each slice with the cut side of the garlic clove, and then cut the bread in half. Place the bread, garlic-side up, on individual plates.

Spread some pesto on each piece of bread, cover with a mound of rocket or spinach, and finally a warm mushroom. Scatter with the pecorino or parmesan shavings and serve while warm, perhaps with a drizzle of olive oil and freshly ground black pepper.

Spring rolls from Hanoi

These Vietnamese-style spring rolls (*nem*) are fantastic on an Asian buffet or as a starter. Enjoy them wrapped in crisp lettuce leaves with fresh mint and nuoc cham, a flavourful dipping sauce. (Photo, page 75)

FOR 25-30 SMALL SPRING ROLLS:
about 250 g frozen spring roll pastry
30 g glass noodles
250 g minced pork
2 spring onions, shredded
1 small carrot, julienned
1 shallot, finely chopped
2 tablespoons grated fresh ginger
2 garlic cloves, finely chopped
1–2 fresh chillies, deseeded and finely chopped
2 tablespoons soy sauce
½ teaspoon caster sugar
2 teaspoons cornflour (dissolved in 2 tablespoons
  cold water) + extra as 'glue'
about 400 ml peanut or neutral oil for deep-frying
about 30 large crisp lettuce leaves
1 large bunch fresh mint leaves
Nuoc cham dipping sauce (page 126)
  and/or Thai sweet chilli sauce

THE NOODLES: Thaw the spring roll pastry. In the meantime, put the glass noodles in a saucepan of lightly salted boiling water. Remove from the heat and let the noodles stand for 3-4 minutes, or according to the cooking instructions on the packet. Strain the noodles through a sieve and rinse with cold water. Drain and set aside.

THE FILLING: Sauté the minced pork until browned, then add the spring onions, carrot, shallot, ginger, garlic, chilli, soy sauce and sugar. Simmer for 7-8 minutes.

Dilute the cornflour in the cold water, and add to the pan. Cut the cold glass noodles into pieces using kitchen scissors, and then stir them into the mince and allow to cool.

THE SPRING ROLLS: Gently fold out the spring roll pastry and cut into 12 cm squares (if not using pre-cut pastry). Place 1 heaped tablespoon of the filling close to one corner. Fold over the corner closest to the filling, then fold over the two side flaps and roll into a tight roll (rolling towards the last corner). Seal the pastry using a little extra cornflour dissolved in water as 'glue'.

DEEP-FRYING: Slowly and carefully heat the oil in a large saucepan. Deep-fry a few rolls at a time for 3-4 minutes, or until golden brown. Remove with a slotted spoon and drain on paper towels.

TO SERVE: Place the spring rolls on a large platter with the lettuce leaves and the mint. At the table, let everyone wrap their spring rolls (with a few mint leaves) in lettuce and dip in nuoc cham sauce or in store-bought Thai sweet chilli sauce. It's nice to have both sauces in small bowls on the table.

Small mushroom quiches

We used funnel chanterelles here, but you can use any fresh mushroom.

FOR 6-8 SMALL QUICHES:
100 g butter
140 g plain flour
¼ teaspoon baking powder
¼ teaspoon salt

FILLING:
200 g funnel chanterelles or other mushrooms, wiped clean and roughly chopped
2 tablespoons butter
salt + freshly ground white or black pepper
a handful of rocket leaves, chopped + extra leaves to serve
300 ml full-fat milk
3 eggs
150 g cheddar cheese, grated
shaved parmesan or pecorino cheese, to serve

· Melt the butter in a saucepan over low heat, then set aside and let it cool slightly. Combine the flour, baking powder and salt in a bowl, then add to the melted butter in the pan and work into a dough. Using a floured thumb, press the dough into 6-8 small ungreased fluted pie tins. Place them in the fridge for 20 minutes.

For the filling, sauté the mushrooms in a dry frying pan for 5 minutes, then add the butter and sauté for a few more minutes. Season lightly with salt and pepper. Add the rocket and take the pan off the heat.

Bake the pastry-lined pie tins at 175°C/345°F for 8-12 minutes, then remove from the oven. Combine the milk, eggs and cheddar cheese. Season with a pinch of salt and pepper. Stir in the mushrooms and rocket. Increase the oven to 200°C/400°F. Fill the pie shells with the mushroom filling and bake for 15-20 minutes. Serve topped with rocket and shaved parmesan.

Crispy feta cheese pastries

These appetising pastries are filled with feta cheese, thyme and spinach (or you could use rocket). Serve them with a fresh green salad, thinly sliced red onion, a few black olives and a splash of mild balsamic vinegar.

MAKES 8 PASTRIES:
4 rectangular sheets frozen puff pastry
100 g baby English spinach or rocket leaves
200 g feta cheese, crumbled
2 tablespoons butter, melted
1 garlic clove, crushed
4 tablespoons chopped fresh thyme leaves
3-5 tablespoons chopped fresh flat-leaf parsley
a pinch of freshly ground black pepper
1 egg, lightly beaten

· Let the puff pastry thaw at room temperature for 15 minutes.

Meanwhile, pick through and rinse the spinach leaves or rocket. Pat dry or spin them in a salad spinner, then finely chop the leaves. Combine the spinach with the crumbled feta, melted butter, garlic, thyme, parsley and pepper. Set aside.

Preheat the oven to 200°C/400°F. Roll out the puff pastry and cut into 10 cm squares. Place some spinach and cheese mixture in the centre of each square. Brush the edges with a little beaten egg, fold into triangular 'packages' and press the edges together with a fork. Brush with the beaten egg.

Place the pastries on a baking tray and bake in the middle of the oven for about 25 minutes, or until golden. Serve the pastries just cooled, accompanied with fresh green leaves.

Left: Small mushroom quiches; Crispy feta cheese pastries

Tourte de blettes chard pie

The only downside with this delectable pie is that the silverbeet darkens quite a bit, but that's just the way it is with our French family recipe…

SERVES 6-8:
175 g plain flour
1 tablespoon caster sugar
80 g butter, in cubes
1 egg + 1 tablespoon cold water + 1 teaspoon white vinegar

FILLING:
300 g silverbeet (Swiss chard)
1 onion, chopped
2 tablespoons olive oil
1 tablespoon balsamic vinegar
4 tablespoons pesto (page 84)
4 tablespoons sultanas
½ teaspoon salt
freshly ground black pepper
200 g soft goat's cheese, crumbled
3-4 tablespoons pine nuts

· Put the flour and sugar in a bowl, add the butter and combine with your fingers. Whisk the egg lightly with the water and vinegar, and add to the flour mixture. Mix into a dough, then press it into a non-stick 24 cm springform tin. Refrigerate for 20 minutes.

Rinse the silverbeet well, pat dry and then roughly shred the leaves. Sauté the onion in the olive oil, then add the silverbeet and sauté for 3 minutes. Stir in the vinegar, pesto and sultanas. Season with salt and pepper. Set aside and allow to cool.

Preheat the oven to 190°C/375°F. Bake the pastry shell for 15 minutes. Add the filling and sprinkle with the goat's cheese and pine nuts. Bake for about 40 minutes. Serve the pie just cooled, with a green salad.

Rocket frittata

A frittata is a rustic Italian omelette, made here with green peas, rocket, mint and lots of shaved parmesan.

SERVES 4:
100 g baby English spinach
1 small onion
4 eggs + 2 tablespoons water
a scant ½ teaspoon salt
freshly ground black pepper
2 tablespoons butter or olive oil + 1 tablespoon extra
200 g frozen baby green peas
1 bunch rocket
6-8 fresh mint leaves
50 g parmesan cheese, shaved

· Rinse the spinach leaves, pat dry then roughly shred them. Peel and thinly slice the onion. Lightly combine the eggs and water in a bowl, and season with the salt and pepper.

Heat a non-stick frying pan, then add the butter or olive oil. Sauté the onion for a few minutes, then add the peas and spinach. Sauté for a few minutes more, then pour the egg mixture on top. Cook the frittata over medium heat. Lift the egg mixture here and there with a fork, just like when frying a regular omelette. Put a large plate over the frying pan and flip the frittata onto the plate.

Add the extra butter or oil to the pan, and then carefully tip the plate so that the frittata can slide back into the pan; cook for a few minutes on the other side. Serve the frittata slightly cooled, topped with the rocket, mint and shaved parmesan.

Right: Frittata with rocket, green peas and parmesan

Warm iceberg wedges

We love this tasty and simple French classic, served with lemon and butter.

• Remove any wilted leaves from 1 large head of iceberg lettuce, and cut into 4 large wedges.

Bring 1 litre of water to the boil in a saucepan. Add 1 heaped teaspoon salt and 2 teaspoons butter. Lower the lettuce wedges into the boiling water, then cover the pan and cook for just 3 minutes, no longer. Remove the wedges with a slotted spoon, drain and serve immediately with lemon juice, sea salt flakes and a knob of butter, or with a mild vinaigrette (page 60).

Tender cabbage with lemon

Pointed-head (oxheart) cabbage is an excellent spring vegetable, with mild, tasty leaves. It is very good when boiled and served warm with fresh thyme, lemon juice and butter. Or perhaps with the summer sauce on page 85, or the yoghurt cheese with herbs on page 87.

• Remove the outer leaves of 1 head of pointed-head cabbage. Cut it into large wedges. In a large saucepan, bring lightly salted water (1 teaspoon salt for 1 litre of water) to the boil and add the cabbage. Cover and simmer over low heat for about 10 minutes. Remove with a slotted spoon, drain and serve straight away.

Braised baby bok choy

This is a quick and easy way to prepare bok choy. It is delicious as one of many dishes in a Chinese meal, or to serve with stir-fried pork and steamed white rice. You can prepare everything in advance and then cook the bok choy at the very last minute. (Photo, page 74)

SERVES 4:
400–500 g baby bok choy
1 litre water + 1 teaspoon salt
2 tablespoons peanut or vegetable oil
1 large garlic clove, thinly sliced
1 tablespoon grated or thinly sliced fresh ginger
a scant teaspoon sesame oil
1 teaspoon brown sugar
2 tablespoons oyster sauce

• Lightly trim and tail each bok choy, then halve each one lengthwise. Bring the water and salt to the boil in a large frying pan and add the bok choy. Cover and cook for 2–3 minutes, or until tender but still a bit springy. Remove with a slotted spoon, drain quickly and set aside.

Heat the oil in a wok or frying pan. Add the garlic and ginger and stir-fry for 30 seconds or so, then pour in the sesame oil, brown sugar and oyster sauce and stir until the sugar dissolves. Add the bok choy to the wok and braise for just a minute more. Arrange the bok choy on a serving platter and pour the lovely cooking juices over the top. Serve immediately.

Kangkung Javanese-style

This is a tasty stir-fry using water spinach or kangkung, as it is called in Indonesia. It is wonderful served alongside fish, crab or meat, but also great for a vegetarian meal. Serve with steamed white rice. (Photo, page 74)

YOU WILL NEED:
150 g kangkung (water spinach)
60 g unsalted peanuts (about 5 tablespoons)
2 tablespoons peanut or vegetable oil
2 garlic cloves, finely chopped
1 tablespoon grated fresh ginger
1 fresh red chilli, deseeded and finely chopped
2 tablespoons oyster sauce

• Pick through the kangkung. Trim the stems and rinse the leaves well in cold water. Shake off the excess water and cut the spinach into 6–7 cm pieces. Set aside.

Toast the peanuts for 5–6 minutes in a dry frying pan, stirring frequently. Allow to cool a little and then rub off the brown skins if necessary. Roughly chop the nuts and set aside.

Heat the oil in a wok or frying pan, then add the garlic, ginger and chilli. Stir-fry briefly, or just until the garlic is lightly golden, then add the oyster sauce and kangkung. Stir-fry for another 2–3 minutes until the spinach is slightly softened but still a bit crispy and green. Arrange the kangkung on a platter and sprinkle with the chopped peanuts. Serve at once.

Tofu and spinach stir-fry

Use firm tofu for this dish, so that the pieces don't fall apart in the wok. Serve with jasmine rice. (Photo, page 75)

SERVES 3–4:
300 g firm tofu
1 tablespoon light soy sauce
2 tablespoons peanut or vegetable oil + 1 tablespoon extra
1 tablespoon grated fresh ginger
100 g cashew nuts, roughly chopped
2 garlic cloves, finely chopped
1–2 teaspoons sambal badjak or sambal oelek
150 g snow peas (mangetout), topped and tailed
150 g baby English spinach, rinsed and drained
1–2 tablespoons kecap manis (sweet Indonesian soy sauce)

• Cut the tofu into 3 cm cubes. Combine the soy sauce, oil and ginger in a small bowl. Gently fold in the tofu, coating it with the sauce, and set aside to marinate for about 30 minutes. Meanwhile, toast the cashews in a dry frying pan until golden.

Heat a wok or frying pan, then add the tofu and marinade and sauté for 2–3 minutes. Carefully transfer the tofu to a plate, cover and set aside for now.

Add the extra oil to the wok, then add the garlic, sambal and snow peas. Stir-fry for a few minutes before adding the spinach, which should only just wilt but still keep its colour and freshness. Lastly, stir in the kecap manis and return the tofu to the wok. Gently fold to combine, then arrange on a platter. Sprinkle generously with the toasted cashews and serve.

Kangkung Javanese-style, page 73

Braised bok choy, page 72

Spring rolls from Hanoi, page 67

Tofu and spinach stir-fry, page 73

herbs

imagine cooking without herbs...

Parsley, so natural in parsley butter or in a salsa verde; the summery scent of dill on top of piping-hot new potatoes; and leafy green basil, which best releases its flavour when the leaves are pounded in a mortar or roughly torn over a salad — fresh herbs bring so much joy to cooking and they instantly make you a better cook. Their fragrance alone can raise your spirits, and their extensive historical heritage is a link backwards through time. Not to mention the fact that fresh herbs make food more appealing to the eye.

At our house (or respective houses, that is), we always keep a few pots of basil, thyme and rosemary in the kitchen window. We are also fortunate enough to be able to grow lots of herbs in the garden, and we use them fresh as long as the season allows: mint for the teas, sage for lamb and flatbreads, and lots and lots of fresh coriander, flat-leaf parsley and thyme, which go so well with almost anything. Herbal plants also make a great addition to any garden because of their beauty, and many of them are truly charming as cut flowers. In the wintertime, when our garden is covered in snow, we still enjoy some of the summer herbs that we dried and stored in the pantry. When dried, herbs become more concentrated in flavour, making dried thyme and rosemary perfect for fish soups, roast lamb or slow-cooked casseroles, while oregano and marjoram go into bean salads, soups, tomato sauces and much more. Yet somehow, we still feel that fresh herbs are beyond compare, as they provide such genuine inspiration to cooking all year round.

Above: Mini pizzas with herbs; A simple salad with chickpeas, red onion, lots of parsley and a vinaigrette.
Left, clockwise from top: Pesto, page 84; Thai basil; Lemon and parsley; One-pot Parma chicken, page 109

the magic mortar and more

Do you have a mortar and pestle? Mortars are unrivalled when it comes to grinding and pounding all sorts of herbs, spices, chillies and salsas. It isn't just a question of mixing and blending, but rather to slowly crush, mash and pound the ingredients to bring out the flavours. Pesto sauce made in a mortar tastes fabulous, and so does a freshly made tomato salsa. You can always use a hand-held blender or a food processor, but it's never quite the same. A mortar is a truly wise investment, and it's actually practical to have two: a smaller one for dried spices and a larger one for salsas and such.

CHOPPING HERBS: Use your best kitchen knife and preferably a wooden chopping board. The herbs should be dry (so gently pat or shake them first, if rinsed beforehand), and any coarse stalks should be removed. Basil and mint leaves should always be chopped at the very last minute before using, or the cut edges will turn black and unappealing. A good way to finely chop basil leaves is to roll several leaves together into a hard little 'cigar' then slice them very finely (making a chiffonade). Or just roughly tear the leaves over a salad.

FINES HERBES is a French fresh herb mixture of finely chopped parsley, chervil, tarragon and chives. This combination is marvellous on top of omelettes, or with veal scallops, poached salmon and more.

BOUQUET GARNI is a small bundle of fresh herbs tied with a piece of kitchen string (or placed in muslin). The classic French combination contains stalks of parsley, thyme, bay leaf and a piece of leek or a couple of celery leaves, although the ingredients may vary. Bouquet garni is added to stocks or slowly cooked dishes.

a brief word on growing herbs

It's lovely to have a small herb garden of your own, whether it's just a few pots with your favourite culinary herbs on the balcony, or a larger plot with more varieties. Herbs are very easy to cultivate, and most herbs will be happy with only a few hours of sun a day. Ideally, the soil should be humus-rich and porous, and not heavily fertilised.

   Alongside the most common kitchen herbs, some nice additions could be sweet cicely, hyssop, savory, sweet bergamot, marsh mallow, lemon balm and different varieties of lavender, for the occasional use and their sheer beauty.

some favourite herbs

THYME, *Thymus vulgaris*, is a firm favourite of ours. We use lots of it, both fresh and dried. Thyme works wonders in such a multitude of dishes: with roasted vegetables or chicken, with lamb and other red meats, in bean or lentil salads or simply scattered over cubes of feta cheese drizzled with fruity olive oil. Lemon thyme, *Thymus citriodorus*, has somewhat larger and shinier leaves. It is also nicely fragrant and very tasty; try it with fish or in potato salads, or in a yoghurt-based summer sauce alongside smoked trout or salmon.

OREGANO, *Origanum vulgare*, is at its most aromatic when dried. The low-growing variety, *Origanum v. compactum*, has a deep, intense flavour. Oregano is great for pasta dishes, grilled chicken or lamb, pizza, baked eggplants (aubergines), tomatoes and much more. You can use both leaves and flowers for seasoning and garnishing. And the flowers are beautiful in a bouquet as well.

ROSEMARY, *Rosmarinus officinalis*, is a bushy plant with light-blue flowers. It's a herb with a long medicinal history, and has been highly appreciated for its antiseptic benefits throughout the ages. Rosemary has a wonderful yet somewhat dominant flavour, and is perfect for grilled lamb or pork, and in stews. It is also delicious in herb butter or on top of roasted potatoes or root vegetables, or with olives and mild sea salt on focaccia bread.

SAGE, *Salvia officinalis*, is a small perennial plant with greyish-green leaves. The tender new leaves are the most flavoursome. Sage works very well with pork, lamb, veal, in herb butters and in tomato dishes. It's the classic herb in an Italian saltimbocca, and a few sage leaves quickly fried in olive oil make a tasty garnish for lamb chops or a frittata.

MINT comes in countless varieties. The leaves are mainly added when the dish is nearly or completely done. Fresh mint (spearmint), *Mentha spicata*, is great for herbal teas, yoghurt dips, fresh cream cheese and bean salads, as well as with cucumber, roasted lamb, melon and much more. A variety of spearmint is the Moroccan mint, which is famously used for teas. Asian mint, *Mentha asiatica*, is commonly used in Asian dishes but you can just as easily use fresh mint leaves. Peppermint, *Mentha piperita*, isn't all that great in cooking (it tastes too much like candy canes), but is suitable for herbal teas. Most types of mint are very easy to grow, but they have a tendency to spread out, so give them a corner of their own. When harvested, dry the mint leaves in an airy place (out of direct sunshine), and then store them in an airtight jar.

BASIL, *Ocimum basilicum*, gives you a taste of summer all year round. Basil leaves, from the common variety *Genovese*, are the backbone of Italian pesto sauce, and are great in tomato and pasta dishes, and for salads. Basil originated in India, and there are lots of different varieties – cinnamon basil, globe basil, lemon basil and Thai sweet basil, to mention just a few – with tiny or huge, violet or wrinkled leaves.

CORIANDER, *Coriandrum sativum*, also known as cilantro or Chinese parsley, is a truly versatile, annual herb. The tender leaves are perfect for stews, salads, barbecued meats and vegetables, Indian curries, South American salsas and many kinds of Asian dishes. In Thailand and India, the roots are also used for cooking, giving a deeper flavour to curries and soups. Coriander seeds, which resemble Seville oranges in flavour, are used in Scandinavia in bread and with salmon, and are included in Indian spice mixes such as garam masala. Coriander can be grown in a pot on the balcony, or in the garden.

DILL, *Anethum graveolens*, is a given ingredient in classic Scandinavian dishes such as herring, new potatoes, crayfish, sour cream sauces and cured salmon. Dill is also frequently used in Greece, Turkey and the Middle East, and occasionally in Indian cooking. Fresh dill is very fragrant and often best when added at the end of the cooking time.

FLAT-LEAF PARSLEY, *Petroselinum neapolitanum*, has a lovely flavour that works really well with almost anything. Lemon and parsley is a splendid combination used in dishes such as Middle Eastern tabbouleh and Italian gremolata. Add the parsley leaves towards the end of the cooking time, or when the dish is done. You can also add the stems to the pot when boiling meat or fish.

FRENCH TARRAGON, *Artemisia dracunculus*, is a perennial herb that becomes milder and more aromatic when dried. Use fresh tarragon in moderation – the flavour is so intense that only a few leaves are needed. Tarragon is perfect with eggs, chicken, in tomato salads and is essential in a Béarnaise sauce.

CHERVIL, *Anthriscus cerefolium*, is a modest annual herb with delicate, light-green leaves resembling those of tender parsley. Chervil has a gentle flavour suited to omelettes or mild-tasting, creamy soups. It is one of the components in the French fines herbes mixture.

Right: A plate with a bit of everything: Couscous with fresh mint and sliced nectarines; Wine-marinated shallots with thyme, page 92; Crispy feta cheese pastries, page 69; Sliced figs, olives and peperoncini

Salsa verde

Salsa verde is an exceptionally versatile green sauce. Because of its concentrated flavour, you just need a few tablespoons per person. It is delicious with roast beef, seafood, vegetables and grilled fish or chicken.

SERVES 6-8:
50 g fresh flat-leaf parsley
3 anchovies
1-2 tablespoons capers
1 large garlic clove
200 ml olive oil
½ teaspoon sea salt, or to taste
a pinch of freshly ground black pepper
about 1 tablespoon fresh lemon juice or vinegar

IN A FOOD PROCESSOR: Remove any coarse parsley stalks. Place the leaves in the food processor with the anchovies and capers and let it run for a few seconds. Stop the machine, scrape down the side of the bowl and then run for a few seconds more. Add the peeled and roughly chopped garlic clove, then slowly pour the oil through the tube while the machine is on.

Season sparingly with salt (the anchovies are quite salty) and pepper. You can prepare up to this point a few hours ahead. Don't add the lemon juice or vinegar until you are ready to serve: that way the sauce will keep its bright green colour for longer.

BY HAND: Finely chop the parsley with a sharp knife, and then finely chop the anchovies, capers and garlic. Combine everything in a small bowl, pour in the olive oil a little at a time, then stir in the lemon or vinegar and season to taste.

Pesto

The tastiest pesto is made the traditional way: by pounding the pine nuts and garlic in a mortar, then pounding the basil leaves as well before slowly adding the olive oil and, lastly, the parmesan. But you can also make a great pesto using a food processor or hand-held blender.

Pesto is best when served freshly made, but will keep for a few days in the fridge. If storing the pesto, cover the surface with a thin layer of olive oil.

YOU WILL NEED:
1-2 garlic cloves
40 g pine nuts
sea salt + freshly ground black pepper
40 g fresh basil leaves
about 150 ml olive oil
50 g parmesan cheese, grated

USING A MORTAR AND PESTLE: Peel and chop the garlic cloves. First pound the pine nuts and garlic with a bit of salt. Add the basil leaves a few at a time and pound them as well, adding a few drops of olive oil if needed. Stir in the parmesan and, lastly, the rest of the olive oil. Taste and season with salt and pepper.

USING A HAND-HELD BLENDER: Place everything except the garlic, salt and pepper in a deep bowl, and mix until creamy and smooth. Season with mashed or crushed garlic, the sea salt and a bit of pepper.

PESTO WITH PARSLEY: Substitute the basil leaves with flat-leaf parsley (and the pine nuts with walnuts, if you like).

Simple summer sauce

This lovely sauce perfectly complements many different dishes, such as smoked fish and new potatoes, grilled meat or tender vegetables.

SERVES 4-5:
200 g crème fraîche
3 tablespoons whole egg mayonnaise
½ teaspoon mild Dijon mustard
1 garlic clove, crushed
2 tablespoons each of snipped dill and chives
sea salt flakes + freshly ground black pepper

· Combine all the ingredients and season with salt and pepper. Cover and chill the sauce for about 30 minutes, to let the flavours mingle.

Our favourite basil sauce

SERVES 5-6:
1 litre water + 1 teaspoon salt
200 g baby English spinach
a good handful of fresh basil leaves
200 g whole egg mayonnaise
200 g crème fraîche
sea salt + freshly ground black pepper

· Bring the water and salt to the boil in a large saucepan. Add the spinach and boil for just 1 minute, no longer. Tip the spinach into a colander and rinse with cold water. Squeeze the spinach dry and then mix with the basil and mayonnaise using a hand-held blender or food processor. Stir in the crème fraîche and season with salt and pepper. This sauce is really good with potato wedges, salmon, warm or cold roast lamb and spring vegetables.

Green herb oil

A few drops of herb oil can work wonders in soups, with prawns, smoked salmon and grilled fish, or just to dip some chewy country-style bread in. You can use basil, parsley, dill, coriander and a variety of other herbs.

However, please remember that herb oils have a short shelf life, and can develop harmful toxins if left standing too long. But a fresh and well-seasoned herb oil is one of the tastiest things there is.

YOU WILL NEED:
1 litre water + 1 teaspoon salt
60-70 g fresh herb leaves such as basil, dill,
   coriander or flat-leaf parsley
10-15 ice cubes (important)
200 ml good-quality, mild olive oil
½ teaspoon salt
freshly ground black pepper

· Bring the water and salt to the boil in a large saucepan. Place the herb leaves in a metal sieve, and lower the sieve into the boiling water for just 20 seconds. Remove and immediately lower the sieve into a bowl of cold water filled with the ice cubes.

Lift the sieve, squeeze the leaves dry with your hand and then place them in a food processor or deep bowl. Add the olive oil, salt and pepper, and mix in the food processor or with a hand-held blender. Let stand for about 1 hour.

Next, strain the oil by pouring it through a coarse sieve and then discard the leaves. Pour the strained oil into a clean bottle or jar and seal with a lid. Store the oil in the fridge and use within 4-5 days.

Tzatziki with dill

We often make a tzatziki, the refreshing Greek yoghurt sauce, with snipped dill instead of fresh mint. Tzatziki is a splendid side dish on a buffet or barbecue, or simply served with crusty bread and black olives. (Photo, page 89)

SERVES 4-5:
1 medium cucumber
½-1 teaspoon salt
400 g thick Greek yoghurt
1 garlic clove, crushed
a pinch of freshly ground black pepper
1 tablespoon olive oil + extra to serve
4 tablespoons snipped fresh dill

· Rinse, peel and coarsely grate the cucumber. Place the cucumber in a sieve, sprinkle with the salt and combine. Set aside to drain for about 20 minutes, and then use your hand to squeeze the liquid out of the grated cucumber.
  Place the cucumber in a bowl. Combine with the yoghurt, garlic, pepper, olive oil and most of the dill. Allow the flavours to develop for an hour or so, then drizzle with a little extra olive oil and sprinkle with the reserved dill before serving.

Indian raita with mint

Raita is a classic Indian side dish that comes in many varieties, like this simple one.

· Season 400 g thick Greek yoghurt with sea salt flakes, freshly ground black pepper, 2 tablespoons finely chopped fresh coriander and 1-2 tablespoons finely chopped fresh mint leaves. Add ½ teaspoon ground cumin, if desired. Serves 4-6

Fresh mint labneh

Labneh is a Middle Eastern yoghurt cheese that is great with wedges of pita bread, hummus, tabbouleh, olives or other meze dishes. You can also drain and shape the labneh into delightfully creamy cheese balls, but we like to enjoy it as a smooth dipping sauce instead.

· Combine either thick Greek yoghurt or store-bought labneh with finely chopped fresh mint or crumbled dried mint. Season with sea salt flakes and a few drops of fresh lemon juice. Add a touch of harissa (chilli paste), which gives a slight but pleasant heat. Stir to combine, then tip the labneh onto a plate. Drizzle with olive oil and serve sprinkled with a pinch of sumac or paprika.

Feta cheese cream

Delicious as a starter with chewy bread, or to accompany potato wedges, beetroot, barbecued meat and more.

SERVES 4-6:
300 g feta cheese
4 tablespoons finely chopped fresh thyme
  or 2-3 teaspoons dried thyme
4 tablespoons chopped fresh flat-leaf parsley
100-150 ml olive oil
a pinch of freshly ground black pepper

· Put the feta cheese in a bowl and mash with a fork, then combine with the herbs and olive oil (or use a food processor to mix until smooth). Season with pepper and let the flavours meld for 30 minutes.

Creamy fresh yoghurt cheese

Making your own fresh cheese is easy, and this is a simple version that we often serve with freshly baked bread. Let the yoghurt drain for a few hours to give the cheese a fine consistency, and then season it with garlic and the herbs of your choice. If you don't drain the yoghurt, you'll get a thick herb sauce that goes perfectly with cold cuts, poached salmon or smoked fish.

FOR ONE BATCH:
500 g thick Greek yoghurt
200 g crème fraîche
1 garlic clove, peeled
20 g chopped fresh herbs, such as parsley, chives,
  basil, thyme, lemon thyme and oregano
mild sea salt or herb salt, to taste
freshly ground black pepper

· Combine the yoghurt with the crème fraîche, and drain for 2-3 hours in a coffee filter cone with a paper filter, or in a piece of muslin. Pound the garlic with the herbs in a mortar, or chop everything finely by hand. In a bowl, combine the drained yoghurt with the garlic and herbs; season to taste. Cover and allow the flavours to develop for a few hours in the fridge.

Chèvre and thyme dip

Use a fork to gently mash 200 g soft goat's cheese (rind removed). Combine with 200 g crème fraîche, 1-2 teaspoons honey and 1-2 tablespoons chopped fresh thyme. Season with sea salt and freshly ground black pepper. Set aside for 1 hour before serving with roasted capsicums (peppers), toasted sourdough or cooked beetroot.

Garlic herb butter

Adding a bit of garlic herb butter takes your oven-roasted vegetables to a whole new level. Just place a few knobs of the butter on the half-done vegetables and continue cooking in the oven. Herb butter is also a real classic on a steak. (Photo, page 76)

SERVES 8-10:
a large handful of fresh flat-leaf parsley (no stems)
a large handful of fresh mixed herbs, such as thyme,
  oregano and lemon thyme
250 g fridge-cold butter, in large cubes
½ teaspoon salt
freshly ground black pepper
2-3 teaspoons balsamic vinegar
½ teaspoon crumbled dried tarragon
1-2 garlic cloves, crushed

· Put the parsley and mixed herbs in a food processor and whiz or pulse until chopped.
  Add the cubes of cold butter, as well as the salt, pepper, balsamic vinegar and tarragon. Mix swiftly, then add the crushed garlic last. The key is not to let the garlic overpower the butter and herb flavours. Mix until combined.
  Use greaseproof paper to shape the butter into a roll and refrigerate. Once chilled, the herb butter is easy to slice.

Jean's thin savoury flatbread, page 90

Artichoke hearts with garlic, thyme and chilli, page 92

Minty green pea dip, page 93

Tzatziki with dill, page 86

Potato and herb galette

This herbed potato galette is surprisingly good – almost elegant – despite its simplicity. Cut into pieces and serve with a glass of wine.

DOUGH FOR 2 GALETTES:
15 g fresh (compressed) yeast
1 teaspoon honey
½ teaspoon salt
200 ml lukewarm water
3 tablespoons milk
3 tablespoons olive oil
280 g plain flour

ON TOP:
5-6 medium potatoes
2-3 tablespoons olive oil
2 teaspoons dried oregano or thyme
1½-2 teaspoons sea salt
freshly ground black pepper
fresh thyme leaves
fresh rosemary

THE DOUGH: Crumble the yeast into a bowl. Add the honey and salt, pour over some of the water and stir to dissolve the yeast. Add the rest of the water, milk, olive oil and, lastly, the flour. Knead the dough in the bowl using a wooden spoon or an electric mixer with dough hooks. Cover and let rise for at least 40 minutes.

PREPARE THIS WAY: Preheat the oven to 250°C/ 480°F. Line two baking trays with non-stick baking paper. Knead the dough briefly, then divide it into two portions. Roll out each piece into a thin circle, then transfer to the trays.

TOP AND BAKE: Peel and slice the potatoes into really thin slices. Arrange them over the dough, overlapping them slightly like roofing tiles. Drizzle with the olive oil.
Sprinkle with the dried herbs (not the fresh ones yet), salt and pepper. Bake one tray at a time for about 12 minutes. Scatter with fresh herbs when 3-4 minutes of the baking time remains. Serve the galette just cooled or cold.

Jean's thin savoury flatbread

Our friend Jean serves these tasty flatbreads topped with thinly sliced zucchini (courgette), tomato, herbs and sea salt. You can use the same kind of dough as for the galette. (Photo, page 88)

• Make one batch of the galette dough (recipe on the left), and set aside to rise. Carefully tip it onto a lightly floured surface and knead gently. Divide the dough into four portions, and then cut each portion into four pieces.
Preheat the oven to 250°C /480°F. Line two baking trays with non-stick baking paper. Shape each dough piece into a ball. Use a rolling pin to flatten each ball into 'tongues', about 5 mm thick. Place them on the trays.
Brush with olive oil, then add thin slices of zucchini (courgette) and tomato, plenty of dried herbs, whole sage leaves and a good pinch of sea salt flakes. Bake for 8-9 minutes.

Right: Potato and herb galette

Garlic and herb-roasted zucchini

Thin slices of zucchini turn out really well when roasted with garlic and herbs. Serve them as a small starter with some bread and mixed olives. (Photo, page 413)

SERVES 4:
2 medium zucchini (courgettes)
½–1 teaspoon sea salt flakes
2 garlic cloves, finely chopped
1 tablespoon dried thyme, oregano
   and/or rosemary
   or 3 tablespoons fresh herb leaves
2–3 tablespoons olive oil

• Preheat the oven to 230°C/450°F. Top and tail the zucchini, and slice them diagonally into thin slices, approximately 4-5 mm thick. Arrange in one layer on baking trays lined with non-stick baking paper.

Sprinkle with the sea salt flakes and finely chopped garlic (crushed garlic will be too acrid). Scatter the herbs over the top and drizzle over the olive oil.

Bake the zucchini in the middle of the oven for 10-15 minutes, or until lightly golden. Serve either just cooled or cold.

Jazzed-up feta with herbs

Cut feta cheese into 3 cm cubes and place in a serving bowl. Drizzle with a little olive oil and sprinkle plenty of fresh or dried thyme on top. Add a pinch of freshly ground black pepper if desired. Perfect with salami, olives or other quickly assembled finger food.

Artichoke hearts with garlic, thyme and chilli

So very easy to make and a great feature on a buffet. You can also marinate olives or pieces of feta cheese the same way. (Photo, page 88)

FOR A LARGE BOWL:
2 x 400 g tins artichoke hearts
½–1 mild red chilli
2 garlic cloves, finely chopped
1 tablespoon dried thyme
fresh thyme leaves (if desired)
about 2 tablespoons olive oil
a scant ½ teaspoon sea salt flakes

• Drain the artichoke hearts in a colander and place them in a bowl. Deseed, finely slice and sprinkle the chilli into the bowl. Add the garlic and herbs, then drizzle over a little olive oil. Sprinkle with the sea salt flakes. Gently toss to combine and allow to sit for at least 30 minutes.

Wine-marinated shallots

Another tasty and versatile side dish for buffets. (Photo, page 83)

• Peel about 250 g shallots and place them in a saucepan. Combine 2 tablespoons tomato paste (concentrated purée), 200 ml white wine, 3 tablespoons olive oil, 1 tablespoon honey, 1 tablespoon balsamic vinegar, 1 teaspoon salt and 2 teaspoons dried thyme, and pour it over the shallots. Bring to the boil, lower the heat, then cover and simmer slowly over low heat for 15 minutes. Season with salt. Serve chilled.

Minty green pea dip

This fresh-tasting dip is delicious in pita bread with sliced grilled chicken, or as a dipping sauce for toasted pita wedges. (Photo, page 89)

YOU WILL NEED:
250 g frozen baby green peas
about 2 tablespoons olive oil
9–10 fresh mint leaves, shredded
1–2 tablespoons fresh lemon juice
sea salt flakes

· Bring lightly salted water to the boil in a saucepan and boil the peas for 3 minutes (or follow the instructions on the packet). Pour them into a colander and rinse immediately with cold water.

Mix the peas using a hand-held blender or food processor. Add the olive oil and mint. Mix until more or less smooth, and season with lemon juice and sea salt to taste.

Tabbouleh

We never tire of this summery Middle Eastern salad with lots of flat-leaf parsley, lemon and a touch of mint.

· Put 75 g burghul in a bowl of cold water and soak for 30 minutes, rinse in a sieve, drain and place in a bowl. Add 4 finely chopped spring onions, 3 ripe tomatoes in small cubes, lots (about 120 g) of very finely chopped fresh parsley and 10–15 chopped fresh mint leaves. Add 3–4 tablespoons lemon juice and 100 ml mild olive oil, then season with sea salt and pepper. Toss to combine. Serves 4

Elsa's burghul salad

Enjoy this salad on its own, or with barbecued lamb or chicken, ideally with a dollop of the fresh yoghurt cheese or labneh on pages 86–87.

SERVES 6–8:
600 ml chicken or vegetable stock
2 tablespoons butter or olive oil
200 g burghul
½–1 cucumber, diced
3 tender celery stalks
15 cherry tomatoes, halved
5 spring onions, finely shredded
100 g fresh flat-leaf parsley, finely chopped
100 g fresh dill, chopped
finely grated zest and juice of 1 organic lemon
1–2 teaspoons honey
1 teaspoon salt, or to taste
freshly ground black pepper
about 5 tablespoons olive oil
10–15 fresh mint leaves

· Bring the stock to the boil with the butter or oil. Add the burghul, then cover the pan and boil for 4 minutes. Set aside and let stand for 10 minutes with the lid on. Fluff up the grains with a fork, and allow to cool a little.

Prepare all the vegetables and herbs. Try peeling the celery with a potato peeler to remove the stringy bits, if you wish, then cut the celery stalks into small cubes. Put the still-warm burghul in a large bowl with the halved tomatoes and the remaining prepared vegetables and herbs (except the mint).

Combine the lemon zest, juice, honey, salt, pepper and olive oil, and pour it over the salad. Gently toss and season to taste. Shred the mint and scatter it on top before serving.

Coriander mushroom salad

Try this simple salad with barbecued lamb or other meat. Be generous with the coriander.

· Trim chubby white mushrooms, only rinsing them if absolutely necessary (if so, dry them carefully). Thinly slice the mushrooms and place them in a bowl.

Add a few drops of mild red or white wine vinegar and pour a little good-quality olive oil on top. Season with sea salt flakes and fold in plenty of chopped fresh coriander. Serve freshly made.

Galvarino-style green peas

It's easy to forget how appetising plain old green peas can be. This is how our Chilean aunt Marta serves them.

· Cook frozen or freshly picked green peas by covering them with lightly salted cold water. Bring to the boil and cook for 2-3 minutes. Add a glass of cold water, take the pan off the heat and place it on a wooden chopping board for 5 minutes with the lid on. Drain the peas in a colander and allow to cool.

Tip the peas into a serving bowl and fold in a good handful of chopped fresh coriander. Add a dash of red wine vinegar and vegetable oil, and season with mild sea salt.

Previous page: Lentil salad from Arles; Pasta salad à la Gina

Pasta salad à la Gina

This pasta salad is full of flavour, and handy when serving a large crowd or going for a picnic. (Photo, page 95)

SERVES 4-6:
dressing (see below)
300 g penne or other pasta
4 shallots, thinly sliced
20 sun-dried tomatoes in olive oil, sliced
100 g black olives, pitted and split
1-1½ tablespoons dried thyme
sea salt flakes, to taste
freshly ground black pepper
400 g mozzarella cheese
5 tablespoons tender fresh thyme leaves, chopped
150 g prosciutto or salami, sliced
1 large bunch rocket
a good handful of fresh basil leaves

THE DRESSING: Combine 2 roughly mashed garlic cloves with a scant teaspoon sea salt, 3 tablespoons mild red wine vinegar and 1 teaspoon honey. Let sit for 15 minutes. Discard the garlic and stir in 90-100 ml good-quality olive oil.

THE SALAD: Cook the pasta in plenty of salted water until just barely al dente. Rinse it quickly in cold water in a colander and drain well. Tip the pasta into a salad bowl and pour the dressing on top. Add the shallots, sun-dried tomatoes, olives and dried thyme. Season to taste with sea salt flakes and a good grinding of black pepper.

Add the mozzarella cheese torn into pieces, the fresh thyme and the prosciutto or salami. Scatter roughly torn rocket and basil leaves on top before serving.

Lentil salad from Arles

In Arles, in the south of France, we once came across a pleasant Puy lentil salad with roasted capsicums, which served as a model for this version. Puy lentils are very tasty and keep their shape when cooked. (Photo, page 94)

SERVES 6-7:
400 g Puy lentils
2 roasted red capsicums (peppers) (page 246)
1 litre mild chicken or vegetable stock
2 teaspoons dried thyme
3 celery stalks, thinly sliced
2 red onions, finely chopped
a large handful of fresh flat-leaf parsley, chopped
½–1 teaspoon sea salt flakes
freshly ground black pepper
2 tablespoons fresh lemon juice
4 tablespoons olive oil, or to taste

· Soak the lentils in cold water for 1-2 hours. Meanwhile, roast the capsicums. Once the capsicums are done, peel off and discard the skin, then dice them and set aside.

Drain the soaked lentils. Bring the stock to the boil with the dried thyme, add the lentils and cover. Lower the heat and simmer slowly for 10-20 minutes. Check the lentils now and then, to make sure they don't overcook.

In the meantime, prepare the celery, onions and flat-leaf parsley.

Drain the lentils in a sieve. Tip them back into the saucepan and season the warm lentils with salt, pepper, lemon juice and olive oil. Gently fold in the capsicum, celery, onions and parsley. Taste, and adjust the seasoning a little if necessary. Arrange the salad in a serving dish and allow to cool.

A green potato salad

This summer salad, full of fresh green herbs and new potatoes tossed in a creamy dressing, is excellent with gravlax, smoked trout and cold roast lamb.

SERVES 6-8:
1.25 kg new potatoes, freshly boiled
   and still a bit warm
2 medium eggs
1 tablespoon white wine vinegar
1 tablespoon Dijon mustard
1 teaspoon sea salt flakes
freshly ground black pepper
a good handful each of chopped fresh dill,
   flat-leaf parsley and chives
about 150 ml sunflower oil
50 ml water (optional)
1 garlic clove, crushed
a few rocket leaves

· Peel and cut the potatoes in half or into large chunks, leaving any tiny potatoes whole. Set aside in a bowl.

To make the dressing, bring water to the boil in a saucepan. Lower the eggs into the water with a spoon and cook for exactly 3 minutes. Remove and immediately rinse the eggs in cold water. Halve and scoop the very soft eggs directly into a food processor using a teaspoon. Add the vinegar, mustard, salt, pepper and the chopped herbs and then mix. Slowly pour the oil in a thin stream into the machine while on. You can also mix everything with a hand-held blender. Lastly, add the water if needed.

Season with the garlic and quickly whiz again (adding garlic from the start can make the dressing bitter). Season to taste, pour the dressing over the potatoes and gently toss to combine. Top with a few rocket leaves.

Herb-roasted vegetables

When making these vegetables, we always fill a large roasting tin because they usually go like hot cakes. We often serve the vegetables with chicken, roast lamb or chops, or simply topped with crumbled feta or soft goat's cheese.

FOR A LARGE BATCH:

2 tablespoons olive oil + 2 tablespoons extra
4 medium carrots
1-2 parsnips
6 medium potatoes
3-4 medium red onions
1 yellow + 2 red capsicums (peppers)
1 whole bulb of garlic
a handful of fresh thyme or
  1-2 tablespoons dried thyme
small sprigs of fresh rosemary
sea salt flakes
freshly ground black pepper

· Grease a large roasting tin with the olive oil. Preheat the oven to 200°C/400°F.

Peel and cut the carrots, parsnips and potatoes into large chunks or slice them lengthwise. Add the peeled red onions in large wedges and fairly large pieces of the red and yellow capsicum. Break the garlic into cloves, crush them lightly (skin and all) with the side of a knife and spread them out among the vegetables. Sprinkle the thyme and rosemary on top, and drizzle with the extra olive oil. Season with salt and pepper.

Bake for 40-45 minutes. Adding some extra fresh thyme and rosemary just before serving is a nice touch.

Right: Feta and bean salad

Feta and bean salad

The key to this bean salad is to first oven-roast the tomatoes, red onions and eggplant before adding the beans, feta cheese and the leafy greens. Best served when the vegetables are still a bit warm.

SERVES 4-5:

20-25 cherry tomatoes
1 small eggplant (aubergine)
2 medium red onions
2 tablespoons olive oil
sea salt flakes
600 g home-cooked white and small black beans (about
  250 g dried beans) or 400 g tin large white beans +
  400 g tin small black beans
a large handful of baby English spinach leaves
200 g feta cheese, in pieces
vinaigrette (page 60)
freshly ground black pepper
fresh sprigs of thyme
a handful of fresh basil leaves

· Preheat the oven to 200°C/400°F. Arrange the tomatoes in an ovenproof dish. Cut the eggplant into large pieces, and peel and cut the red onions into wedges, then add to the dish. Drizzle with the olive oil and sprinkle with sea salt. Roast for 25-30 minutes, then remove from the oven and allow to cool down a bit.

Meanwhile, pour the beans into a colander, rinse with cold water and drain well. Rinse the spinach and gently pat dry.

Arrange the beans, spinach and still-warm vegetables on individual plates. Crumble feta cheese on top and drizzle with the vinaigrette. Season with a good grinding of black pepper and top with the thyme and torn basil leaves.

Eggplant pasta della casa

A rustic pasta sauce with eggplant, tomatoes and fresh herbs. It may not look all that appealing, but it's a comforting vegetarian dish with lots of lovely flavour.

SERVES 4-5:

2 medium eggplants (aubergines)
2 teaspoons salt for the eggplants
1 large onion, chopped
2 tablespoons olive oil
2 x 400 g tins chopped tomatoes
sea salt flakes
freshly ground black pepper
1 teaspoon caster sugar
1 tablespoon dried oregano
1 small sprig of fresh rosemary, chopped
1 large garlic clove, crushed
300 g penne or other pasta
200 g mozzarella cheese, torn into large pieces
fresh basil leaves
grated parmesan cheese, to serve

· Top and tail the eggplants, and cut them into long, thick slices lengthwise. Place them in a colander and sprinkle with the salt. Let stand for 20-30 minutes.

Gently sauté the chopped onion in olive oil for a few minutes in a large frying pan.

Rinse the eggplant, dry with paper towels and then dice. Add the eggplant to the pan, stir, then add the tomatoes. Season with salt, pepper, sugar, oregano and rosemary. Bring to the boil, then cover the pan and simmer for 15-20 minutes over low heat. Remove the lid and add the garlic when only 5 minutes remain. Taste, and adjust the seasoning.

Pour the sauce over the freshly boiled pasta. Scatter the pieces of mozzarella over the top and gently combine, before finishing off with plenty of basil and parmesan cheese.

Pasta puttanesca

Classic Italian pasta — quick and easy to prepare, with simple ingredients. If you chop everything ahead of time, the sauce won't take long to cook. Boil the spaghetti while the sauce is cooking, so that it's ready just in time to toss through the flavourful sauce.

SERVES 4:

4 tablespoons mild olive oil
3 garlic cloves, finely chopped
1 fresh red chilli, deseeded and finely chopped
8 anchovies, very thinly sliced + 1 tablespoon of the oil
  from the anchovies
6-8 medium, ripe tomatoes, cubed
freshly ground black pepper
400 g spaghetti or other pasta
125 g good-quality black olives, pitted
  and chopped
1 tablespoon capers
10 fresh sage leaves, shredded (optional)
a handful of fresh flat-leaf parsley, chopped

· Prepare and chop all the ingredients. Heat the olive oil in a heavy-based casserole dish and sauté the garlic and chilli over medium heat.

Add the anchovies and mash them around a bit with a wooden spoon, then add the tomatoes and the oil from the anchovies. Season with pepper and let everything simmer for about 15 minutes, stirring every so often.

Meanwhile, cook the spaghetti until barely al dente.

Add the olives, capers and sage (if using) to the tomato sauce, and let simmer, uncovered, for 2-3 minutes. Towards the very end, add the chopped parsley and the cooked and drained pasta. Toss, and cook for just a minute more for the flavours to blend. Season to taste with black pepper and perhaps a touch of salt, and serve at once.

Asparagus and herb risotto

Risotto is such a fabulous invention. The rice should be creamy while the grains should remain slightly springy. To get that perfect consistency, use Italian risotto rice such as carnaroli or arborio.

The secret to a great risotto is to only add small amounts of (warm) liquid at a time. Once the risotto is ready, stir in a few knobs of butter and freshly grated parmesan cheese and enjoy straight away.

ASPARAGUS RISOTTO FOR 4:
400 g tender green asparagus
1.2 litres chicken or vegetable stock
2 tablespoons butter + 2 tablespoons at the end
2 tablespoons good-quality olive oil
1 medium onion, finely chopped
325 g carnaroli rice or other risotto rice
200 ml dry white wine
½ teaspoon sea salt
75 g parmesan cheese, grated + extra to serve
3 tablespoons chopped fresh basil
3 tablespoons chopped fresh flat-leaf parsley
2 tablespoons chopped fresh thyme
1 tablespoon finely grated lemon zest

· Rinse the asparagus. Cut or break off the lower end of each spear, then cut the asparagus into 4-5 cm pieces. Set aside.

Bring the stock to the boil, remove from the heat and set aside. Heat the butter and oil in a heavy-based pot and sweat the onion over low heat until slightly translucent.

Increase the heat, then add the rice and sauté quickly while stirring. Pour in the white wine and let the rice absorb the wine as you stir.

Gradually add about 200 ml of the warm stock and bring the rice to the boil, stirring well. When the stock has absorbed, add another 200 ml. Slowly simmer the rice for a total of 18-20 minutes, adding the stock a little at a time. Taste the rice towards the end of the cooking time: it should be cooked but still have a firm core (al dente).

When the risotto is nearly done, cook the asparagus in a pan of lightly salted boiling water for 2-3 minutes, or until just tender, and then quickly rinse in cold water.

Season the risotto with sea salt, a few knobs of butter and the freshly grated parmesan cheese. Gently fold in the chopped herbs and the lemon zest. Give the risotto a good stir, and then gently fold in the asparagus. Cover and let sit for 2-3 minutes.

Bring the risotto to the table with some extra parmesan and black pepper on the side.

MUSHROOM RISOTTO is another appetising option, particularly with dried porcini mushrooms (ceps). You need 15 g dried mushrooms for the risotto recipe above, leaving out the asparagus and using only half the quantity of herbs.

· Soak the mushrooms in 200 ml tepid water for at least 1 hour. Remove the mushrooms but reserve the liquid. Finely chop the mushrooms.

In a heavy-based pot or saucepan, start by slowly sautéing the mushrooms in butter and oil. After a few minutes, add the onions and continue to sauté. Then proceed with the rice, stock and wine as in the previous recipe. Serve the risotto with grated parmesan.

Parsley potatoes provençale

These potatoes are just the thing with a good steak and a fresh green salad. For best results, you need both oil and butter when frying.

• Preheat the oven to 225°C/435°F. Peel and slice 3-4 medium potatoes per person into 1 cm slices. Heat a frying pan with a little olive oil and butter, and pan-fry the raw potato slices in batches until just nicely browned but not yet cooked through.

Arrange the slices in an ovenproof dish, crush 1-2 large garlic cloves on top and add a few knobs of butter. Season with sea salt and freshly ground black pepper. You can prepare the recipe up to this point ahead of time.

Cook the potatoes for 20-25 minutes, or until soft. Sprinkle generously with finely chopped fresh flat-leaf parsley and enjoy!

Rosemary and carrot potatoes

Preheat the oven to 200°C/400°F. Wash whole organic baby potatoes carefully, peeling them only if necessary. Pat dry and place in a greased roasting tin. Add a few peeled carrots in thick slices. Lightly season with sea salt and freshly ground black pepper. Sprinkle with roughly chopped fresh rosemary and drizzle with a little olive oil.

Roast the potatoes in the middle of the oven for about 35 minutes. Sprinkle with an extra pinch of sea salt before serving.

Left: Rosemary and carrot potatoes

Jerusalem artichoke soup

Jerusalem artichokes are such marvellous root vegetables, and well worth the effort it takes to peel them. Here they are used in a soup with porcini mushrooms and thyme. You can exclude the mushrooms if you wish; the soup will be delicious either way.

MAIN COURSE FOR 4 OR STARTER FOR 8:
15 g dried porcini mushrooms (ceps) (optional)
200 ml water for soaking the mushrooms
800 g Jerusalem artichokes
2 medium potatoes
1 medium onion
800 ml mild chicken or vegetable stock
100 ml dry white wine
200 ml pure (whipping) cream
sea salt
freshly ground black pepper
2-3 teaspoons truffle oil (optional)
tender fresh thyme leaves

• Soak the dried porcini for 30 minutes, if using. Peel and cut the Jerusalem artichokes and potatoes into large pieces. Peel and roughly chop the onion.

Put three-quarters of the stock into a pan and cook the vegetables and porcini for about 20-25 minutes. Use a hand-held blender directly in the pan to mix the soup until more or less smooth. Dilute with the rest of the stock, white wine and cream. Season with salt and pepper and cook for another 5-10 minutes. Season to taste, then divide among serving bowls. Drizzle with a little truffle oil if you like, and sprinkle with fresh thyme leaves.

A hearty fish soup

In a fish soup like this one, it's nice to use different kinds of fish: we often choose salmon and a firm white fish such as cod. And the fennel is a must, as it gives such a pleasant flavour to the soup.

SERVES 4–5:

500 g raw prawns, unpeeled
about 15 mussels (optional)
800 g in total of salmon fillet and any firm
  white fish fillet
2 medium onions, chopped
3–4 garlic cloves, finely chopped
1 bulb of fennel, trimmed and thinly sliced
1 large carrot, peeled and sliced
5 medium potatoes, peeled and diced
5 medium tomatoes, cored and cut into large pieces
2–3 tablespoons olive oil
1 tablespoon butter
about 20 saffron threads
½–1 tablespoon ají (chilli in oil, page 124)
  or ¼ teaspoon cayenne pepper
1–2 teaspoons dried thyme
2 sprigs of fresh rosemary, chopped
250 ml dry white wine
1.2 litres fish stock
200 ml pure (whipping) cream
juice of ½ lemon, or to taste
a good pinch of sea salt
freshly ground black pepper
fresh flat-leaf parsley or thyme leaves

PREPARE IN ADVANCE: To prepare the seafood, peel the prawns and wash the mussels carefully, if using (see text on the right). Cut the fish into 3 cm cubes. Cover the seafood and set aside in the fridge. Peel and chop all the vegetables and set aside.

THE SOUP: In a large saucepan or casserole dish, gently sauté the onion and garlic in the olive oil and butter. Flavour with the saffron, ají or cayenne pepper, thyme and rosemary. Stir to combine, then add the fennel, carrot, potatoes and tomatoes. Pour in the wine and stock and cook for about 30 minutes. You can prepare the recipe up to this point ahead of time if you like.

To finish, add the cream and bring the soup to the boil again. Season with lemon juice, salt and pepper. Add the fish and let simmer in the soup for 2–3 minutes. Carefully add the peeled prawns (do not allow to boil) and season to taste. Add the freshly cooked mussels, if using. Top with roughly chopped flat-leaf parsley or thyme leaves. Serve with bread, lemon wedges and ideally some extra ají, our chilli in oil.

COOKING MUSSELS: To prepare the mussels, first make sure they are alive by gently tapping the shells. If they close, the mussels can be used. If not, throw them away. Scrub the shells and pull out the hairy beards.

In a large saucepan, sauté 1 chopped shallot in 2 tablespoons olive oil. Pour in 200 ml water and 200 ml white wine, and bring to the boil. Add the mussels and cover tightly. Cook over high heat for about 4 minutes, or until the mussels open (making sure to discard any closed mussels). Remove the mussels with a slotted spoon and serve them in the soup.

Fish stew from Mariestad

This dish incorporates mild Swedish flavours in a fish stew with tender vegetables, fresh herbs and new potatoes.

SERVES 3-4:
600 g firm white fish or skinless salmon fillet
about 1 teaspoon salt for the fish
8-10 baby potatoes (250 g)
2 small onions
2 small carrots
10 radishes
20 snow peas (mangetout), topped and tailed
40 g butter
100 ml dry white wine
100 ml water
fresh flat-leaf parsley leaves + a few sprigs of fresh dill
salt + white pepper
lemon wedges

· Cut the fish fillets into 4-5 cm pieces, place them in a dish and sprinkle lightly with salt. Cover and refrigerate for now.

Peel and cut the potatoes in half. Peel and cut the onions in half and then into thin wedges. Peel and cut the carrots into julienne sticks. Slice the radishes and roughly shred the snow peas on the diagonal.

Melt the butter in a sauté pan, then add the potatoes, onions and carrots and sauté until glossy. Pour in the wine and water and bring to the boil. Cover and simmer for 5-8 minutes, or until the potatoes are almost soft. Add the radishes, snow peas, parsley leaves, a few sprigs of dill and then the fish.

Cover and simmer for another 3 minutes. Set aside (without removing the lid) and wait about 2 minutes more before lifting the lid and enjoying the wonderful aroma! Season with sea salt and pepper, if needed.

Serve immediately in deep bowls, with lemon wedges, crusty bread, sea salt flakes and a pepper mill on the table.

Herb-crusted salmon

This salmon is lightly cured before being covered with plenty of fresh herbs and baked in the oven. Simple and fresh, this dish is perfect for a summer buffet.

SERVES 6-7:
1.5 kg whole salmon fillet with skin
1 tablespoon caster sugar
2 teaspoons salt
about ½ teaspoon coarsely ground white
   or black pepper
2 tablespoons mild olive oil
25 g fresh mixed herbs (see below)

· Remove any bones from the salmon fillet, leaving the skin on. Rub the flesh side with a mixture of sugar, salt and coarsely ground pepper. Place the salmon on a large chopping board or platter. Cover with plastic wrap and place in the fridge for 2 hours.

Preheat the oven to 200°C/400°F. Scrape off some of the salt mixture, and place the salmon skin-side down on a greased baking tray.

Brush the salmon flesh with a bit of olive oil. Sprinkle generously with finely chopped herbs: lots of flat-leaf parsley and a bit less thyme, marjoram, oregano and/or dill. Pat the herbs onto the flesh with your hand. Bake in the oven for 20-25 minutes.

Serve with boiled new potatoes, snow peas (mangetout) tossed in butter and perhaps the delectable summer sauce on page 85.

Saltimbocca

This is an easy-to-prepare Italian classic, made with veal, sage and a Marsala sauce.

SERVES 4:
4 x 150 g veal escalopes
8 wafer-thin slices of prosciutto
8 large sage leaves
wooden toothpicks
sea salt flakes + freshly ground black pepper
2 tablespoons olive oil
2 tablespoons butter

SAUCE:
150 ml Marsala
1 tablespoon butter
1 tablespoon fresh lemon juice

· Flatten the veal slices with a rolling pin between two layers of plastic wrap, then remove the plastic. Place 2 slices of prosciutto and 2 sage leaves on top of each veal slice. Use toothpicks to secure the sage leaves into the two layers of meat. Season with a bit of sea salt and some freshly ground black pepper.

Fry the veal in the oil and butter in a hot frying pan for a few minutes on each side, until nicely browned. Remove the veal from the pan, cover and keep warm.

Pour the Marsala into the pan, scraping the base of the pan with a wooden spoon to loosen any flavourful bits. Simmer uncovered for just a few minutes. Add the butter and lemon juice, and stir. Season with salt and pepper, if needed. Put the meat back into the sauce and let it reheat for a minute or so.

Serve the saltimbocca sage-side up, with roasted potatoes or pappardelle pasta, or just with snow peas (mangetout) or green beans tossed in butter.

Herb-marinated roast beef

A simple and flavourful way to smarten up some leftover cold roast beef.

SERVES 4:
300 g cold roast beef, thinly sliced
fresh chives and flat-leaf parsley, finely chopped

MARINADE:
100 ml red wine + 100 ml beef stock
2 teaspoons Japanese soy sauce
1 teaspoon Dijon mustard
3 tablespoons chopped fresh thyme
1 garlic clove, crushed

· Spread out the roast beef slices in a wide glass or porcelain dish. Combine the marinade ingredients and spoon over the meat. Cover and chill for 1-2 hours. Discard any excess marinade. Roll the roast beef into rolls, arrange on a platter and sprinkle generously with finely chopped chives and parsley.

Chicken and thyme pâté

This rustic chicken liver pâté is a real treat on toasted sourdough bread.

· Barely thaw 400 g frozen chicken livers.

In a large frying pan, sauté 2 finely chopped shallots in 3 tablespoons butter. Add the liver and fry for 10-12 minutes. Add 200 ml pure (whipping) cream, about ½ teaspoon sea salt, freshly ground black pepper, 1 teaspoon dried thyme and just a touch of cayenne pepper. Simmer for 5 minutes. Allow to cool slightly, then mash with a fork or a hand-held blender. Taste to see if you need more salt, pepper or thyme. Transfer to a small bowl.

Fanny's 'all-in-one' chicken

Cooking this just couldn't be easier, and the outcome is delicious. A colourful chicken dish with lots of vegetables and olives, conveniently using frozen chicken.

SERVES 4–5:
2 tablespoons olive oil for the roasting tin
4–5 frozen whole chicken legs (thigh and drumstick)
1 small zucchini (courgette), in large pieces
2 medium red onions, in wedges
2 red capsicums (peppers), in large pieces
2 medium carrots, in large pieces
6 medium potatoes, in wedges
15 black olives
7–8 garlic cloves, peeled and lightly bruised
1–2 teaspoons sea salt
freshly ground black pepper
1–2 teaspoons dried thyme
1–2 teaspoons dried rosemary
a good drizzle of olive oil
200–300 ml dry white wine
tender sprigs of fresh rosemary or thyme

• Preheat the oven to 200°C/400°F. Lightly grease a large roasting tin with the olive oil. Put the still-frozen chicken legs in the tin, together with all the prepared vegetables. Place the olives and lightly bruised garlic cloves in between. Season the chicken pieces with sea salt and quite a bit of pepper. Sprinkle with the dried thyme and rosemary, and drizzle a little olive oil over everything.

Bake for about 1 hour, pouring over the wine after 15 minutes, and then continuing to cook until the chicken is completely cooked through. Baste a few times with the pan juices. Garnish with the sprigs of fresh herbs.

Serve with a green salad topped with crumbled goat's cheese and toasted pine nuts.

One-pot Parma chicken

Another delightful 'all-in-one' recipe with chicken, this time with Parma ham or other prosciutto, leek and celery. (Photo, page 78)

SERVES 4:
2 tablespoons soft butter
  or olive oil for the dish
6 large potatoes
1 large leek
3 celery stalks
4 chicken breast fillets
about 1 teaspoon sea salt
freshly ground black pepper
4–8 thin slices of prosciutto
200 ml pure (whipping) cream

• Preheat the oven to 225°C/435°F. Grease a large ovenproof dish or roasting tin with the butter or olive oil.

Peel the potatoes and cut into large wedges. Place them in a saucepan of lightly salted boiling water and boil for exactly 3 minutes (no more, no less). Drain and then place the potatoes in the dish.

Carefully clean, slit and rinse the leek to remove any traces of soil. Slice it and spread it out among the potato wedges.

Cut the celery into thin pieces and add them as well. Season the chicken with salt and freshly ground pepper, then wrap each piece in the slices of prosciutto, and place on top of the potatoes. You can prepare the recipe up to this point ahead of time.

Pour the cream around the chicken in the dish. Bake for 25–30 minutes, or until the chicken is completely cooked through. Serve with bread and a green salad.

Left: Fanny's 'all-in-one' chicken

A warming winter soup

This is a full-flavoured and substantial soup with infinite variations. Sometimes we include potatoes or pasta, and sometimes we add only beans, vegetables and good-quality chorizo.

SERVES 4-5:
2 chorizos or other spicy sausages
1 medium onion, chopped
2 large carrots, sliced
1 medium parsnip, sliced
1 small zucchini (courgette), in pieces
6 large tomatoes, in chunks
2 tablespoons olive oil
1.5 litres chicken or vegetable stock
400 g tin white beans, rinsed and drained
50 g spaghetti (optional)
3 celery stalks, finely chopped
1 large garlic clove, crushed
a large handful of English spinach leaves
about 3 tablespoons pesto (page 84)
sea salt + freshly ground black pepper
fresh flat-leaf parsley for garnish

· Cut the chorizo into 2 cm thick slices. Prepare all the vegetables.

Heat the olive oil in a pot or saucepan over medium heat and sauté the onion and chorizo. Add the carrots, parsnip, zucchini and tomatoes. Pour in the stock, bring to the boil, cover and simmer gently for about 15 minutes. Add the white beans, spaghetti (if using), celery and garlic. Cook for another 6-7 minutes, or until the pasta is done. Stir in the pesto and add the spinach (it should only just wilt).

Season to taste with salt and pepper, and serve the soup sprinkled with flat-leaf parsley.

Left: A warming winter soup

Pitinga's cazuela

A genuine, country-style broth with tender lamb, pasta and a few vegetables. Our tía Pitinga makes her Chilean cazuela with large pieces of meat and vegetables according to season, often using colourful ones such as red capsicum, carrots, pumpkin and corn — true comfort food in a bowl. (Photo, page 115)

SERVES 4-6:
1.4 kg lamb meat with bone
1 large onion, finely chopped
3-4 garlic cloves, chopped
1 large red capsicum (pepper), in pieces
1 medium carrot, sliced
2 litres water
2 teaspoons salt + some freshly ground black pepper
1 bay leaf

AFTER ONE HOUR:
3 celery stalks, finely chopped
500 g pumpkin, peeled and in chunks
5 medium potatoes, halved
2 corn cobs, in pieces
100 g pasta, 10 minutes before serving
fresh coriander leaves, chopped

· Trim the meat and place it in a large pot with the onion, garlic, capsicum and carrot. Pour in the water, add the salt, pepper and bay leaf. Bring to the boil, lower the heat, cover and simmer for 1 hour or so, until the meat is very tender. Skim off the foam with a slotted spoon.

Add the celery, pumpkin, potatoes and corn and cook for 10 minutes more. Add some pasta and boil until the pasta is almost done (it will continue cooking in the broth). Set the pot aside. Remove the meat, cut it into pieces (discard the bones) and return to the pot. Serve the cazuela in deep bowls, with fresh coriander, ají (chilli in oil, page 124) and crusty bread.

Roast lamb in a lovely herb jus

Roasting lamb in a heavy-based casserole dish may be a bit unusual these days, but we think it turns out absolutely delectable. The meat does reduce somewhat in size, but it tastes great, and the jus at the bottom of the pot is exquisite. You only need a tablespoon or two of the jus per serving.

SERVES 6:
3 tender sprigs of fresh rosemary
4 tender sprigs of fresh thyme
a large handful of fresh flat-leaf parsley
2 garlic cloves
½–1 fresh red chilli
deboned leg of lamb (about 1.5 kg)
2 teaspoons sea salt
about ½ teaspoon freshly ground black pepper
kitchen string
2 tablespoons olive oil
  + 1 tablespoon butter
200 ml dry white wine
about 200 ml water
2 tablespoons butter for the jus

· Remove any coarse stalks from the herbs. Peel and finely chop the garlic. Deseed and finely slice the chilli. Combine the rosemary leaves, thyme and parsley with the garlic and chilli, and place the herb mixture inside the meat (where the bone was).

Season with about half the salt and pepper. Roll up the meat and tie it with kitchen string. Rub the rest of the salt and pepper onto the meat.

Brown the lamb in the oil and butter in a large casserole dish or heavy-based pot. It should be nicely browned all over, which will take at least 10 minutes.

Place a meat thermometer in the centre of the lamb. Add the white wine (wait with the water) and cover. Bring to the boil and then lower the heat. Simmer the roast over very low heat for 1 hour and 15 minutes, or until the thermometer reaches 62°C/145°F for pink meat or 70°C/160°F for well done.

Remove the roast from the dish and keep it warm under a piece of foil. Return the dish to the heat and add the water, little by little, scraping the base of the dish with a wooden spoon to loosen any flavourful bits. Simmer the jus, uncovered, for about 3 minutes and then stir in 2 tablespoons of butter.

Cut the roast into fairly thick slices, removing the string as you go. Serve on individual plates and spoon some of the marvellous jus over the meat. Serve ideally with a large green salad and some bread to soak up the jus. You could also serve the lamb with oven-roasted potato wedges, potato gratin or maybe even a plain risotto.

Lamb kebab with labneh

Making your own kebab is an excellent way of using leftover roast lamb.

· Cut gently reheated roast lamb into very thin slices. Place inside warm pita bread together with tomato slices, wafer-thin slices of red onion, crumbled feta cheese and crisp lettuce leaves. Add a good dollop of labneh (the delicious spiced yoghurt on page 86) and serve at once.

Herb-crusted leg of lamb with anchovies

Roast lamb encrusted with herbs is wonderfully succulent. In this recipe we also stud the roast with anchovies and garlic. Put potatoes and vegetables around the meat and everything is conveniently cooked in the same roasting tin. (Photo, page 115)

SERVES 6-8:

1 leg of lamb on the bone (about 2.5 kg)
50 g tin anchovies
4 large garlic cloves, halved
1 teaspoon sea salt + some freshly ground black pepper
3 tablespoons fresh thyme
    or 1½ tablespoons dried thyme
4-5 sprigs of fresh rosemary
kitchen string
potatoes, carrots, red onions (optional)

· Preheat the oven to 175°C/345°F. Using a small sharp knife, make 8 small incisions in the lamb. Put ½-1 anchovy and half a garlic clove into each hole. Season the meat with salt and pepper. Pat thyme all over the lamb, arrange the rosemary on top and attach them with kitchen string. Place a meat thermometer in the lamb, making sure the tip of the thermometer is not near the bone.

Put the meat in a roasting tin and roast it in the oven for 1 hour. At this point, you can place potato halves or quarters, carrot pieces and wedges of red onion around the roast. Continue roasting, raising the temperature to 200°C/400°F for the last 15 minutes. The roast lamb will be pink inside when the thermometer reaches 62°C/145°F, and well done at 70°C/160°F. Let the meat rest under foil for 15 minutes before serving.

Lamb skewers with rosemary

Alternate pieces of lamb, vegetables and sausage onto wooden or metal skewers – or use sturdy rosemary sprigs if you are lucky enough to have some to spare. (Photo, page 114)

SERVES 6-8:

about 700 g boneless lamb meat
400 g sausage, such as chorizo or merguez
12-16 small skewers or rosemary sprigs
2 medium onions, in wedges
2 green capsicums (peppers), in large pieces
4 tablespoons olive oil
2 garlic cloves, crushed
1 fresh red chilli, deseeded and finely chopped
2 tablespoons fresh thyme, chopped
2 sprigs of fresh rosemary, chopped
sea salt flakes + freshly ground black pepper

· Cut the lamb into large cubes and cut the sausages into 3-4 cm thick pieces. Use metal skewers, wooden skewers (soaked in water for at least 1 hour) or woody rosemary sprigs with the lower leaves removed, and skewer the lamb cubes, alternating with the onion, sausage and green capsicum.

Brush with a mixture of olive oil, crushed garlic and chopped chilli. Let the skewers sit for about 30 minutes while you get the barbecue coals going (or preheat the barbecue grill).

Sprinkle the skewers with the chopped thyme and rosemary, then barbecue the skewers for about 10 minutes, turning them a few times. When almost done, season with salt and a bit of freshly ground black pepper.

Lamb skewers with rosemary, page 113

Freshly picked herbs

Pitinga's cazuela, page 111   *Herb-crusted leg of lamb with anchovies, page 113*

chillies

mild, medium or hot...

Which chilli to choose? Chillies are a fascinating and exciting subject, after you get past the beginner's level. Chillies are not just hot and spicy, they also bring out and accentuate other flavours in food. Once you get used to the heat, you start to discover a whole new set of nuances. You may detect a certain sweetness (especially in ripe, red chillies) or even fruity, flowery or earthy tones, and sometimes a sultry, pleasant smokiness as well. For us personally, the use of chilli has grown over the years, starting out with the occasional Southeast Asian dish and turning into a daily 'must-have', inspired by the Chilean side of the family. One example is the homemade chilli mix in the jar shown on the left, which we call 'indispensable ají' (ají is a Spanish word for chilli), because that's simply what it's become to us...

Every year, chilli sales increase all around the globe, and chilli is now the world's most frequently used condiment. Chillies are also used for medicinal purposes, as their spiciness is considered beneficial to your health. Chillies are believed to release endorphins (the body's own pain relievers), increase your metabolism and provide a general feeling of well-being.

Above: Dried chillies at a market in India; Pad Thai, page 134. Left: Roberto's indispensable ají in the glass jar, page 124; Dried chilli flakes (at front), and Smoky merquen powder (page 125) in the Sainsbury's pot; Indonesian sambal oelek and small dried piri piri chillies (at back)

chillies and red capsicums are cousins

Fruits from the genus *capsicum* come in a variety of colours, shapes and sizes: red, orange, yellow, brown or purple, and round, pointy or oval. There are approximately 150 different varieties and thousands of hybrids, and the number increases every year. All chillies contain the strong substance capsaicin in greater or smaller amounts. Capsaicin can be found throughout the entire fruit, but is more concentrated near the stem, in the seeds and – particularly – in the membranes holding the seeds. Sometimes the same type of chilli varies significantly in heat, and the heat can even vary individually among fruits harvested from the same plant. As a general rule, the smaller and pointier the chilli, the hotter it is. But there are exceptions, like the puffy habanero, which is one of the hottest chillies. The heat of chillies is measured in Scoville heat units. Regular capsicums (peppers) only measure 1 unit while jalapeños can reach 3000-6000, and one of the hottest varieties, savina habaneros, measures up to 577,000. The hottest of them all is said to be the naga jolokia from northern India, which can reach up to 1,000,000 Scoville units.

a brief history of chilli

A large part of the global population eats chilli on a daily basis, and countless varieties of chilli blends, oils and sauces are used in traditional cuisines all over the world. Some examples include harissa in northern Africa, smoky merquen in Chile, berbere in Ethiopia, curry paste in Thailand and sambals in Indonesia. However, chillies originally come from Peru and Mexico, where traces of chilli have been found in graves dating back to thousands of years BC. In 1493, when Christopher Columbus and his explorers arrived in the New World on his second voyage, they encountered chillies for the first time. They called them *pimientos* (Spanish for capsicum/pepper), because of their hot, peppery taste, and subsequently took the fruit back to Spain. Chillies soon spread to Asia via Spanish and Portuguese colonists, and became immensely popular in the Philippines, Korea, China and the small Portuguese territory of Goa in India. The hottest cuisines are currently found in Thailand, India and the Chinese province of Sichuan.

poblano, jalapeño, chipotle and piri piri…

THE MOST COMMON FRESH CHILLIES are often long, narrow and either green or red. They range anywhere from mild to fairly hot, and measure 2500–5000 Scoville units.

JALAPEÑO is a rather small, chubby, green Mexican chilli that is medium to hot and turns red when fully ripe. Jalapeños are used in all kinds of salsas, and are often sold pickled in vinegar and oil. Jalapeños are smoked instead of dried, and are then called chipotle. They are a very good variety for marinades and sauces.

SERRANO is a Mexican green or red chilli, ranging from hot to very hot. Wonderful in a guacamole, ceviche or fresh salsa.

POBLANO is mild when green and unripe, and mildly hot when mature. It is usually a deep red, almost brownish-black, with subtle flavour notes of cocoa. Widely used in Mexican dishes, such as in *chiles rellenos* (stuffed chillies). A dried poblano is called *chile ancho*.

HABANERO, with its characteristic puffy pods, is a superhot chilli (it's about 100 times hotter than the jalapeño) with floral, citrusy notes. It is a popular ingredient in really spicy dishes, but should always be used with caution. There is also a black habanero, and another variety called Scotch bonnet, which resembles a hat.

CAYENNE is yet another very hot chilli that is often dried and ground into powder. Use cayenne with care: the heat only emerges after a while, so it's best to add just a little at a time and allow the flavours to develop.

PIRI PIRI is a tiny, superhot chilli that most people associate with African cooking, but which the Portuguese allegedly took from South America to their African colonies. Just two crumbled dried piri piri chillies may be enough to flavour an entire stew.

BIRD'S EYE is a small green or red, extremely spicy chilli, measuring 50,000–100,000 Scoville heat units. It is often used in Southeast Asian cuisines, such as those of Indonesia and Thailand. There is also an even hotter African variety known as African bird's eye.

TABASCO is a small and very hot chilli used in the famous Tabasco sauce. It is about as hot as bird's eye chilli, and the two are closely related.

PEPERONCINI, also known as golden greek, is a mild to medium hot variety, often pickled in vinegar and salt, and a given accompaniment to kebabs.

CASCABEL is a tiny, round chilli that is brownish-red and quite mild when dried. Great for flavouring savoury sauces and soups.

CHILLI POWDER is sometimes pure, finely ground chilli, but more often a blend of chilli, garlic, cumin and oregano. Chilli flakes, on the other hand, are plain dried chillies that have been coarsely ground or crushed into flakes, often including the seeds.

tips and tricks

STORING CHILLIES: When buying fresh chillies, the skin should be even and taut. If you're not using them straight away, store the chillies in the vegetable drawer of the fridge. If sold tightly wrapped in plastic, make some air holes to prevent the chilli from softening.

BEWARE OF THE HEAT: Remember *never* to touch your eyes after cutting chillies – it will sting. One idea is to use thin latex gloves when chopping really hot chillies, another to rub a few drops of oil on your hands first, and then wash them properly when done. The oil prevents the heat from sticking to your skin as much. This is a useful trick, since water won't dissolve capsaicin but oil or grease will. So, if you've eaten something too spicy, it's much better to drink a glass of milk or eat some yoghurt (which contains a bit of fat) than to drink water.

DESEEDING AND CHOPPING CHILLIES: Start by cutting off the stems plus a few millimetres of the chilli. Cut it in half lengthwise, use the point of a small sharp knife to remove the seeds and membrane, and then cut each half in two. Once the membrane and seeds are gone, it's easy to chop or finely slice the chilli. Wash the knife and chopping board when you're done. *Note!* The more seeds you add, the hotter the dish.

Right: The beautiful, slightly puffed up habanero chilli is one of the hottest varieties

Roberto's indispensable ají

In our house, we use this flavourful 'chilli mash in oil' for practically everything: to spice up and deepen the flavour of soups, stews, sauces, lentils, beans, sandwiches, marinades and barbecued meats. It has become quite indispensable in our everyday cooking, and we simply can't be without a jar of ají in the fridge. The bottom of the jar has a thick layer of fairly hot, mashed chillies, covered by a second layer of milder, chilli-infused oil. Both can liven up pretty much anything, and a little ají goes a long way...

YOU WILL NEED:
10 large dried chillies,
   ideally lightly smoked
3 garlic cloves, roughly chopped
½ teaspoon salt, or to taste
vegetable oil to cover the chilli in the jar

· Put the chillies in a saucepan with water and quickly bring to the boil, then reduce the heat to low and simmer for 2-3 minutes. Remove the pan from the heat and let the chillies soften in the water for 15 minutes.
   Drain the chillies, discard any stems or seeds (the more seeds, the hotter the chilli mash), and then roughly chop the chillies. Use thin rubber gloves to protect your hands, or wash them well when done.
   Pound the chillies and garlic by hand using a large mortar and pestle for a few minutes (best), or pulse in a food processor until the chilli is ground into fairly small pieces. Add the salt and stir to combine. Transfer to a perfectly clean glass jar and cover with oil. Close the lid tightly and store in the fridge for up to a month, as long as the oil *always* covers the chilli. *Note!* Fill up with oil as soon as needed.

Mojo rojo

This spicy red sauce from the Canary Islands is traditionally served with *papas arrugadas*, wrinkled potatoes boiled in heavily salted water, but we often use it as a dip for roasted potato wedges or at barbecues.

FOR 1 BATCH:
2 fresh red chillies
½-1 teaspoon sea salt
3 garlic cloves, lightly crushed
½-1 teaspoon ground cumin
1 teaspoon sweet paprika
1 teaspoon dried oregano
1 tablespoon sherry vinegar
   or 1-2 tablespoons fresh lemon juice
100 ml good-quality olive oil

· Deseed and chop the chilli and put it in a mortar. Add the sea salt and garlic and use the pestle to pound to a fairly smooth paste, then add the cumin, paprika and oregano. Pour in the vinegar or lemon juice and combine. Lastly stir in the oil, little by little. Taste and adjust the seasoning if necessary.

Ají verde – green chilli mix

A fresh chilli mix that enhances anything from a tomato salad with fresh coriander to a small cracker with soft goat's cheese and a sprig of parsley... Simply addictive!

· Deseed and chop a few mild green chillies (we use large, light-green ají blancos that we grow in big pots). Add as many (or few) seeds as you like: the more seeds, the hotter the mix. Place in a small bowl, add finely chopped garlic, sea salt and cover with vegetable oil. Lasts up to 1 week in the fridge.

Cinnamon chipotle salsa

A savoury Mexican salsa with tomatoes, dried smoked chipotle (the best option) and a touch of cinnamon.

YOU WILL NEED:
½–1 chipotle or other smoked chilli
400 g tin crushed or chopped tomatoes
  or 6 medium fresh tomatoes, chopped
1 teaspoon tomato paste (concentrated purée)
¼ teaspoon ground cinnamon, or to taste
1 tablespoon caster sugar
½ teaspoon salt

• Begin by slowly roasting the chilli in a dry frying pan over low heat just until it softens. If necessary, add a few drops of water.

Transfer to a chopping board and roughly chop the chilli. Return to the pan, and add all the other ingredients. Bring to the boil and gently simmer for 4–5 minutes, then cool slightly. Next, mix in a food processor until more or less smooth. Season to taste. Serve with fajitas (page 139), barbecued chicken, tacos, burritos or other Mexican food.

Smoky merquen

The indigenous inhabitants of southern Chile, the Mapuches, make a traditional blend of dried smoked chillies and coriander seeds. A sprinkle of merquen adds a delightful, smoky flavour to beans, lentils, soups or stews, and it's easy to make at home.

• In an electric spice grinder, put equal amounts of coriander seeds and roughly chopped dried (and ideally, smoked) chillies. Add a touch of sea salt, grind into a fine powder and store in an airtight jar.

Berbere

This fragrant Ethiopian spice mix is lovingly used in Doro wat (page 139). Here is our own humble version.

YOU WILL NEED:
2 teaspoons cayenne pepper
2 teaspoons chilli powder
2 teaspoons sweet paprika
2 teaspoons ground ginger
½ teaspoon ground cardamom
½ teaspoon ground fenugreek seeds
¼ teaspoon ground cinnamon
¼ teaspoon finely grated nutmeg
¼ teaspoon ground allspice
2 teaspoons salt

• Combine everything into a reddish-brown powder, and store the berbere in an airtight jar.

Harissa paste

YOU WILL NEED:
25 g dried red chillies
1 teaspoon ground cumin
2 teaspoons caraway seeds, ground
2 teaspoons ground coriander seeds
2 garlic cloves, finely chopped
a pinch of salt
5 tablespoons olive oil

• Pour hot water over the dried chillies and soak for 2 hours, then drain and finely chop the chillies. Place the spices in a mortar and add the chilli, garlic and salt. Pound to a fairly smooth paste, then combine with about half of the oil. Place in a jar and pour over the rest of the oil. Keep in the fridge for up to 1 month.

Harissa is used in many North African dishes and is also sold ready-made.

Nuoc cham dipping sauce

This dipping sauce is a Vietnamese classic, and goes beautifully with fish cakes, spring rolls or other Asian-inspired finger food.

YOU WILL NEED:
1 garlic clove, minced or chopped
¼ fresh red chilli, finely sliced
  or 1 small bird's eye chilli
2 teaspoons rice vinegar
2 tablespoons fish sauce
3 tablespoons fresh lime juice
1 tablespoon caster sugar
  or 2 teaspoons grated palm sugar
2 tablespoons water
a few fresh mint leaves, finely chopped
finely julienned carrot
  or finely diced cucumber

• Combine the garlic, chilli, vinegar, fish sauce, lime juice and sugar in a bowl, making sure the sugar dissolves properly. Add the water, finely chopped mint and the julienned carrot or a little diced cucumber.

Green chilli and lime salsa

A hot, lime-flavoured salsa to go with barbecued meat, chicken or fish, or with any number of Mexican dishes.

• Deseed and chop 2 fresh green chillies, ideally jalapeño or serrano. Place the pieces in a mortar or a small blender, along with 3 thinly sliced spring onions and 2 large handfuls of chopped fresh coriander leaves.
  Pound thoroughly by hand or pulse until fairly smooth. Add 1-2 tablespoons of vegetable oil, season with the juice of 1 lime and a little sea salt. Transfer to a small bowl and serve.

A Balinese sambal

A fragrant Balinese-style sambal made with fresh chillies, shallots, lemongrass, kaffir lime leaves, ginger and more. Its aromatic heat goes well with seafood, chicken skewers or grilled fish. Sometimes we add a bit of freshly grated coconut as well. *Note!* Roast the shrimp paste before adding it (see below).

YOU WILL NEED:
5 Asian shallots
2 garlic cloves, minced
3 mild red chillies + 3 bird's eye chillies,
  deseeded and finely chopped
5 kaffir lime leaves, washed and finely shredded
2 teaspoons grated fresh ginger
1 tablespoon grated fresh galangal
2 lemongrass stalks, white part only, finely chopped

MIX AND POUR OVER:
3 tablespoons fresh lime juice
1-2 teaspoons grated palm sugar
½ teaspoon shrimp paste (terasi)
3-4 tablespoons oil,
  ideally coconut oil or peanut oil
sea salt, to taste

• Finely chop the shallots and soak them in cold water in a small bowl: this makes them especially mild and tasty. In the meantime, prepare the rest of the ingredients and place them in a bowl. Strain the shallots and add them as well.
  Pour the lime juice into a jug, add the palm sugar and stir to dissolve. Quickly roast the shrimp paste until fragrant in a small frying pan, add it to the lime mixture, then add the oil. Pour the liquid over the sambal and fold through to combine. Season to taste with salt.

Right: Nuoc cham; Chilli powder from India

Thai fish cakes

These deep-fried little fish patties are lovely as a small starter or as finger food, along with lime wedges and dipping sauces. Always use fresh fish here; frozen fish makes the mixture too loose.

FOR 20-25 SMALL CAKES:

500 g boneless, skinless firm white fresh fish fillets
75 g snake beans or green beans
4–5 kaffir lime leaves
2 bird's eye chillies
  or 1–2 fresh red or green chillies
3 tablespoons fresh coriander leaves
2 garlic cloves
1½–2 tablespoons fish sauce
1 medium egg
2 tablespoons plain flour
peanut or vegetable oil for deep-frying
Thai sweet chilli sauce and/or Nuoc cham
  dipping sauce on page 126

· Remove any bones from the fish and then cut the fish into small pieces and set aside. Thinly slice the beans. Rinse the lime leaves well, discard the centre veins and then finely shred the leaves. Deseed and thinly slice the chillies, chop the coriander and mince the garlic, then set everything aside.

Place the fish pieces in a food processor along with the fish sauce, egg and flour. Quickly pulse into a fairly smooth mixture. Add the prepared ingredients and combine. Shape into small round patties with lightly oiled hands.

Heat the oil in a deep heavy-based saucepan. Deep-fry the fish cakes for a few minutes until golden brown and cooked through. Remove with a slotted spoon and drain on paper towels. Serve with the dipping sauces.

Left, clockwise from top: Bird's eye chillies; Hot chicken salad; Thai fish cakes; Fiery steak skewers

Fiery steak skewers

These delicious beef skewers are prepared with a hot peanut marinade. Soak the wooden skewers in water while the meat is marinating.

FOR 20-25 SKEWERS:

4–5 minute steaks (about 500 g in total)
3 garlic cloves, finely chopped
2 teaspoons chilli flakes, or to taste
2 tablespoons soy sauce
2 tablespoons peanut butter
1 tablespoon honey
2 tablespoons vegetable oil
1 tablespoon water

· Cut the meat into 5 cm strips and place snugly in a bowl as you go. Combine everything else for the marinade, and pour it over the meat. Gently fold to coat all the pieces with marinade. Cover and chill for about 2 hours. Next, skewer the meat and quickly grill over hot coals or in a chargrill pan, and then season with a pinch of salt once done.

Hot chicken salad on greens

A spicy little chicken salad, served on decorative green leaves. Use half a barbecued chicken or two poached chicken breasts.

· Combine 1 minced garlic clove, 1 teaspoon grated fresh ginger, 1½ tablespoons fish sauce, the zest and juice of 1 lime, 2 tablespoons hot water, 1 deseeded and finely chopped red chilli and 2–3 small bird's eye chillies.

Finely shred the cold chicken, place it in a bowl, fold in 4–5 tablespoons chopped fresh coriander and toss with the dressing. Pile the chicken onto well-rinsed betel leaves or crisp lettuce leaves. Makes 10-12 servings

Chilli and garlic prawns

These Spanish-style prawns, *gambas*, are full of flavour. Serve them with lots of crusty bread. (Photo, page 132)

• Peel 1 kg raw prawns, leaving the tips of the tails, or use cooked prawns (thawed if frozen). Finely chop 3 garlic cloves and a large handful of fresh flat-leaf parsley.

Gently heat 2-3 tablespoons of olive oil in a large frying pan. Put the chopped garlic and ½-1 tablespoon chilli flakes in the pan. Stir and add the prawns, then stir-fry for a few minutes, or until the prawns turn pink and are cooked through (or quickly stir-fry if using cooked prawns). Season to taste with a little sea salt, and scatter plenty of parsley on top. Stir to coat the prawns, and then tip them into a dish and serve at once.

Tuna tapas from Seville

This small tuna salad is infused with finely chopped chilli. It's very good on top of toasted day-old baguette rubbed with a cut clove of garlic, or just with bread and olives.

• Combine 1 tin (100 g) of drained tuna in oil with 1 large, finely chopped tomato, 1 finely chopped shallot, ¼ finely chopped red capsicum (pepper), ½-1 deseeded and finely chopped fresh red chilli and 1-2 tablespoons olive oil. Season with salt and freshly ground black pepper and top with finely chopped fresh flat-leaf parsley before serving.

Manchego with rosemary

An effortless and slightly unexpected appetiser. Place toothpicks or small forks on the side of the platter. (Photo, page 132)

• Cut Manchego cheese into strips or cubes and arrange them on a platter. Drizzle with fruity olive oil and crumble with fresh or dried rosemary (or you could use thyme). Scatter very thin slices of mild red chilli on top and, lastly, add a few tasty green and black olives. Serve with bread and a glass of wine.

Pimientos de Padrón

Sautéed small green chillies, *pimientos de Padrón*, are simply divine as little tapas. It's a bit of a gamble though; most of the Padrón chillies are mildly hot, but once in a while a really hot one comes along... (Photo, page 132)

• Gently heat a thin layer of olive oil in a frying pan over medium heat. Add the whole Padrón chillies (or other mildly hot chillies) and sauté while stirring for 6-7 minutes, or until they are soft and start to blister. Sprinkle generously with sea salt flakes and serve while still warm.

Chilli mussels in white wine

These mussels are prepared *à la moules marinières* with an added touch of red chilli. The mussels should be closed, or shut when you tap them lightly on the shell. Debeard and scrub the mussels to remove any traces of sand or seaweed.

SERVES 4–5:

1–1.5 kg fresh mussels, cleaned
3 shallots, finely chopped
1 large garlic clove, finely chopped
1 fresh red chilli, deseeded and thinly sliced
2–3 tablespoons olive oil
400 ml dry white wine
200 ml water
2 tablespoons soft butter
1 tablespoon plain flour
2 tablespoons chopped fresh flat-leaf parsley

· In a 6–8 litre saucepan (large enough to fit the mussels), gently sauté the shallot, garlic and chilli in the olive oil over low heat for a few minutes, until the shallot is soft and translucent.

Add the wine and water and bring to the boil. Add the cleaned mussels, cover tightly and cook over the highest possible heat for 6–8 minutes, or until the mussels have opened.

Remove the mussels with a slotted spoon, discarding any unopened mussels. Place them in a preheated soup tureen or large bowl, and cover with foil.

Combine the butter and flour in a cup, pop it into the cooking liquid and let the paste melt. Bring rapidly to the boil, then fold in the parsley, reserving some for garnish. Carefully pour the hot liquid over the mussels, leaving any sandy remnants in the bottom of the pan. Serve immediately in deep bowls sprinkled with the remaining parsley, and with a little extra chilli if you like.

Lentil and chilli soup

There is nothing better than a comforting lentil soup — perfect for weekdays. Add a dollop of yoghurt and some chopped flat-leaf parsley when serving.

SERVES 4:

200 g green lentils
2 tablespoons olive oil
1 large onion, chopped
1 fresh red chilli, deseeded and thinly sliced
* or 1–2 teaspoons ají (page 124)*
1 red capsicum (pepper),
* deseeded and thinly sliced*
½–1 teaspoon ground cumin
* or sweet paprika*
3 medium potatoes, cubed
1 litre chicken or vegetable stock
400 g tin whole tomatoes
sea salt, to taste
1 garlic clove, crushed
2 teaspoons honey
chopped fresh flat-leaf parsley, to serve

· Soak the lentils in cold water for 1–2 hours. Drain and rinse the lentils in a colander and then set aside.

Gently heat the olive oil in a saucepan and sauté the onion, chilli and capsicum for a few minutes over medium heat. Add the cumin, potatoes, stock, tomatoes and drained lentils. Cover and cook for about 30 minutes, seasoning with salt towards the end. Flavour with the garlic and honey, then scatter with the parsley and serve.

A tapas table with Pimientos de Padrón, Manchego with rosemary, and Chilli and garlic prawns, page 130

Everyday pasta with tuna, page 134

Chilli mussels in white wine, page 131

Everyday pasta with tuna

Piping-hot pasta with tuna, chilli, garlic, anchovies and parsley – delightful to eat and easy to make. (Photo, page 133)

SERVES 4:
350 g pasta of your choice
200 g tin tuna in oil
1 large garlic clove
50 g tin anchovies + oil
1 fresh red chilli
1 large bunch fresh flat-leaf parsley
1 tablespoon olive oil
sea salt + freshly ground black pepper
freshly grated parmesan cheese (optional)

· Boil the pasta in plenty of salted water. In the meantime, lightly mash the tuna (discard the excess oil) in a small bowl.

Peel and finely chop the garlic, and chop the anchovies. Split the chilli in half lengthwise, carefully remove the seeds and finely chop the chilli. Chop the parsley and set aside.

Heat a frying pan over low heat, then add the olive oil and gently sauté the anchovies, garlic and chilli for 2–3 minutes. Put in the mashed tuna and some of the oil from the anchovies. Season sparingly with salt and cook until thoroughly warm. Combine with the parsley and the freshly boiled, drained pasta.

Serve immediately with (or without) grated parmesan cheese and black pepper.

Right: Pad Thai. Overleaf: Ethiopian doro wat, page 139; Chilli-baked sweet potatoes, page 138

Pad Thai

A beloved dish from Thailand, where street vendors stir-fry noodles with all kinds of delicacies, and the most enticing scent spreads through the streets...

SERVES 4:
300 g flat, wide dried rice noodles
200 g pork fillet
150 g peeled raw prawns
150 g bean sprouts
4 spring onions
3 garlic cloves
3–4 tablespoons vegetable oil
2–3 tablespoons fish sauce
1–2 teaspoons grated palm sugar
1 teaspoon chilli flakes
  or 2–3 bird's eye chillies, deseeded and sliced
2 tablespoons fresh lime juice, or to taste
2 eggs
100 g toasted peanuts, chopped
chopped fresh coriander leaves, to serve
Thai sweet chilli sauce (optional)

· Soak the noodles according to the packet instructions. Drain and set aside. Cut the pork into very thin slices, peel the prawns, trim the bean sprouts, slice the spring onions on the diagonal and finely chop the garlic.

Gently heat the oil in a wok. Quickly stir-fry the garlic, then add the pork and stir-fry for a few more minutes until the meat is nicely browned. Add the prawns, spring onions, fish sauce, sugar, chilli and lime juice, and stir-fry for another 1 minute. Crack the eggs into the wok and stir until they start to cook. Then add the bean sprouts and noodles and stir-fry a bit more.

Serve right away, scattered with the chopped peanuts and coriander, and perhaps some Thai sweet chilli sauce on the side.

Chilli-baked sweet potatoes

You can serve these sweet potatoes with feta cheese, the Chèvre and thyme dip on page 87, grilled chicken or just on their own. We sometimes bake pumpkin in the same way, which is just as delicious. (Photo, page 137)

SERVES 4-5:
1 kg sweet potatoes
5-6 shallots
6 garlic cloves
2 fresh chillies or 2-3 teaspoons ají (page 124)
4-5 tablespoons olive oil
1 teaspoon dried thyme
1 teaspoon dried rosemary
sea salt flakes

· Preheat the oven to 200°C/400°F. Peel and cut the sweet potatoes into wedges. Peel the shallots and cut them lengthwise into wedges. Peel and halve the garlic cloves. Deseed and thinly slice the chilli, if using fresh chillies.

Pour half of the olive oil into the base of a large roasting tin. Arrange the sweet potato wedges, shallots and garlic in the tin. Scatter the thyme, rosemary and chilli over it all (or drizzle with ají). Lastly, trickle the rest of the olive oil on top and sprinkle generously with sea salt flakes.

Bake for 35 minutes, or until the vegetables are nicely coloured. Check them from time to time; if they look dry, spoon over some of the liquid from the bottom of the tin.

Ratatouille Provençale

A popular vegetable dish from Provence, here made with an additional touch of chilli. Serve the ratatouille as a side dish, or with French baguette, black olives and plain boiled eggs as a main meal.

YOU WILL NEED:
2 medium onions, chopped
3 medium red onions, chopped
4 garlic cloves, chopped
6 large tomatoes, in chunks
1 fresh red chilli, deseeded and sliced
  or ½-1 teaspoon chilli flakes
2 small zucchini (courgettes)
1 yellow + 3 red capsicums (peppers)
1 small eggplant (aubergine)
3-4 tablespoons olive oil
sea salt + freshly ground black pepper
2-3 teaspoons dried thyme

· Prepare the onions, garlic, tomatoes and chilli as above. Cut the zucchini in half lengthwise and then slice. Deseed and cut the capsicums into 2 cm pieces. Rinse the eggplant, then remove the stem and cut into large cubes.

In a heavy-based casserole dish, sauté the onions in the olive oil for 3-4 minutes. Add all the vegetables and garlic. Sprinkle with the salt, pepper, thyme and the sliced chilli or chilli flakes. Stir to coat the vegetables with the oil, garlic and herbs, and then sauté for a few minutes. Cover the dish and simmer over low heat for 50-60 minutes, stirring occasionally. Remove the lid towards the end, and season to taste with salt, pepper and perhaps a touch more garlic.

Ethiopian doro wat

This is our simplified version of the delicious, traditional Ethiopian chicken stew, doro wat. Onions, ginger, tomato paste and the fragrant spice blend berbere all fuse into a rich sauce that you slowly simmer the chicken in. (Photo, page 136)

SERVES 4:
5 large red onions, chopped
2 tablespoons butter or olive oil
1 tablespoon grated fresh ginger
300-400 ml water
1 chicken (about 1.2 kg)
1-2 teaspoons berbere
  (page 125)
100 ml tomato paste (concentrated purée)
1½ teaspoons salt
4 hard-boiled eggs

• Sauté the onion in butter or oil in a heavy-based casserole dish. After a few minutes, add the ginger, pour in some of the water, then cover and slowly cook the onion over low heat for 20 minutes, or until soft.

Cut the chicken into smaller pieces and remove the skin (this recipe is better without it). Stir the berbere and tomato paste into the dish, add the rest of the water and stir again. Add the chicken pieces and season with the salt. Bring to the boil and then lower the heat. Put the lid on and slowly cook the stew for about 35 minutes, or until the chicken easily falls off the bone. You can prepare the recipe ahead of time up to this point, then reheat it.

Peel the eggs and add them to the dish just before serving. Serve with Ethiopian teff bread or other flatbread.

Rob's chicken fajitas

These appetising chicken-filled tortillas are served with chopped tomatoes, guacamole and preferably a savoury chipotle salsa.

SERVES 4:
1 large onion
1 large green or red capsicum (pepper)
2 chicken breast fillets
2 tablespoons olive oil
sea salt + freshly ground black pepper
½ teaspoon chilli powder or
  1-2 teaspoons ají (page 124)
100 ml dry white wine or water
8 tortillas
a handful of fresh coriander leaves

ACCOMPANIMENTS:
4-5 tomatoes, finely chopped
guacamole (page 20)
cinnamon chipotle salsa (page 125)

• Peel and slice the onion. Deseed and finely slice the capsicum.

Cut the chicken fillets into strips. Heat a frying pan, add a little olive oil and lightly brown the chicken in batches. Season with salt and pepper. Add the onion and, after a minute or so, add the capsicum as well. Sauté for a few minutes more. Season with the chilli powder or ají, pour in the wine or water, cover and let simmer for 5 minutes, or until the chicken is cooked through. Scatter with the roughly chopped coriander.

Heat an ungreased frying pan. Fry the tortillas briefly on each side, and then fill with the warm chicken. Serve at once with the accompaniments, and a nice, cold beer too, if you like.

Roast chicken with chorizo

A one-pot roast chicken with a bit of a punch, thanks to the chorizo and the ají, our favourite chilli mix. (Photo, on the left)

SERVES 4:
1 chicken, jointed into 8 pieces
sea salt + freshly ground black pepper
2 tablespoons olive oil for the roasting tin
  + a bit more for drizzling
8 medium potatoes
6 garlic cloves
10 shallots
sprigs of fresh rosemary and thyme
1-2 teaspoons ají (page 124)
  or 2 dried piri piri chillies
250 g chorizo or other spicy sausage, thickly sliced
200 ml dry white wine or chicken stock

• Preheat the oven to 200°C/400°F. Season the chicken pieces with sea salt and freshly ground black pepper. Grease a roasting tin with the olive oil. Peel and cut the potatoes into halves or large wedges, and place them in the tray with the chicken pieces on top.

Peel and lightly crush the garlic cloves with the side of a knife, and place them among the potatoes. Add the peeled and halved shallots. Season with rosemary, thyme and a bit more salt and pepper, especially on the potatoes. Drizzle the chicken and vegetables with a little olive oil mixed with ají or crumbled piri piris. Roast in the oven for 30 minutes, then remove the tin and add the sliced chorizo. Gently pour in the wine or stock and return to the oven for a further 15-20 minutes, or until the chicken is cooked through.

Scatter a few sprigs of rosemary and thyme on top of the nicely browned chicken and potatoes, and serve with a green salad.

Chilli con carne

Beans and minced meat in a simplified yet delicious chilli con carne.

SERVES 6-8:
400 g dried brown beans
  or 3 x 400 g tins kidney beans
600 g minced beef
2 tablespoons corn oil or olive oil
3 large onions, chopped
2 red capsicums (peppers), chopped
2 fresh red chillies, deseeded and sliced
  or 1-2 teaspoons chilli powder
2 x 400 g tins crushed tomatoes
200 ml beef stock or perhaps a bit more
2 teaspoons cocoa powder
1 large bay leaf
1 teaspoon ground cumin
sea salt + freshly ground black pepper
2 garlic cloves, crushed

• Soak the dried beans for at least 8 hours in lots of unsalted water, then drain. Gently boil the beans in fresh unsalted water for 30 minutes. Add a little salt and boil for another 15 minutes, or until the beans are tender yet firm. If using tinned beans, rinse them well in cold water using a colander, then drain and set aside.

Fry the minced beef in the oil in batches and transfer to a heavy-based casserole dish as you go. Then sauté the onion, capsicum and chilli, and combine with the beef.

Add the tomatoes, stock, cocoa, bay leaf and cumin. Cover and cook for 45-60 minutes, diluting with a bit of water if needed. Towards the end of the cooking time, season with salt, pepper, garlic and perhaps a bit more chilli. Add the beans and heat gently until warmed through. Season to taste, and serve with bread and a large green salad.

horseradish

the nice thing about horseradish...

... is its invigorating and pleasantly fiery heat. Horseradish seems to have fallen into neglect in modern cooking, but is well worth a revival. A horseradish vinaigrette on a winter beetroot salad, or a piece of turbot served with chopped egg, brown butter and freshly grated horseradish are real delicacies. Horseradish is a traditional condiment that is deeply rooted in Scandinavian cuisine. Just a generation or so ago, having a sturdy piece of horseradish in the pantry was a matter of course; its extraordinary piquancy was commonly used to enhance slow-cooked beef casseroles and Baltic herring dishes. But horseradish still has a given place in various cuisines. In Poland, a hearty horseradish and sausage soup is a traditional Easter dish; in England, horseradish sauce is a classic with roast beef; and in Russia, the root is frequently used as a condiment. Long before the arrival of chillies, horseradish and mustard provided the 'sting' in many European dishes.

Horseradish is believed to have originated in western Asia. The root has long been used medicinally to cure headaches, gout and rheumatic pains, and as a cough medicine mixed with honey. It has been used as a condiment since medieval times, and grated horseradish in a bottle was one of the first industrial preserves back in the 1860s. The French word for horseradish is *raifort*, meaning strong root, and in Swedish, horseradish is called *pepparrot*, or peppery root. Unbroken, the horseradish root is practically odourless, but once grated, its piercing, pungent aroma can really make your eyes water. Luckily, this enzymic reaction is fleeting, and the irritation passes almost immediately. As delicious as it is, freshly grated horseradish can quickly turn bitter when exposed to air. Therefore, always add the horseradish *just* before serving. And as the intensity can vary greatly from one root to another, it's best to add just a little, then taste it before adding more.

Hopefully, you'll find something on the following pages to spark a renewed interest in this good old-fashioned condiment. Perhaps the creamy potato salad with smoked trout that is so simple to make, or the fresh-tasting green pea soup served with horseradish cream. Or why not the Danish smørrebrød pictured on the left, with roast beef, curry remoulade sauce and lots of freshly grated horseradish on top. Such a delicious, classic treat!

Left: A Danish smørrebrød with roast beef, curry remoulade sauce and grated horseradish, page 148

Horseradish, *Armoracia rusticana*, is a fast-growing perennial, which can spread like wildfire if left untended. Commercial horseradish cultivation is still a manual craft, and horseradish is largely grown as a biennial plant. Pieces of the previous year's plants are dug up and replanted in the spring, in order to harvest thick roots in the autumn. However, our personal experience of growing horseradish in the garden only resulted in thin, rather dry roots. We definitely need to give it another go...

When using fresh horseradish, try not to let it dry out. Wrap the horseradish in plastic wrap and store it in the vegetable drawer in the fridge. Peel and grate small amounts of horseradish using a grater; larger quantities can be grated in a food processor just before serving.

japanese wasabi

Fiery, green wasabi — the classic accompaniment to sushi and sashimi — is often called Japanese horseradish, and also belongs to the *Brassicaceae* family (which includes horseradish, mustard and rocket, among others). Wasabi and regular horseradish do resemble each other, both in their flavour and the manner in which they are used. In fact, you will often find that the green substance sold in tubes as wasabi is actually dyed horseradish mixed with oil and mustard powder. Real wasabi, *Eutrema wasabi* (previously called *Wasabia japonica*), is expensive and difficult to cultivate. It is grown in running water on hillside terraces in the Japanese mountain areas, but it also grows wild in cool streams, where the water must maintain a temperature of 11-14°C /52-57°F for the wasabi to thrive. In general, only the rhizome is used, but the leaves and stalks can also be cooked or pickled. There are special graters just for wasabi, and one way of grating the precious root is to use dried shark skin. In Japan, wasabi is sold fresh and is used to accompany raw fish, but also to spice up noodles and other dishes. The rest of us can usually only find wasabi in tubes or powder form in our local supermarkets.

Right: Horseradish with its large leaves; Japanese wasabi is also sold as a powder

Swedish renklämma wrap

Horseradish butter is traditionally used in this Swedish wrap with smoked reindeer meat. You can also use mayonnaise with grated horseradish, and replace the reindeer meat with smoked leg of lamb or bresaola.

WRAPS FOR 4:
3-4 teaspoons freshly grated horseradish
50 g butter, at room temperature
4 pieces of soft unleavened flatbread
8-10 thin slices of smoked reindeer meat
a handful of tender rocket leaves

• Blend the horseradish into the butter. Spread it on the bread, cover with the meat and a few rocket leaves. Fold the bread into a roll, wrap it in foil and chill. Cut the wraps in half on the diagonal when serving.

Salmon hors d'oeuvres

Canapés with smoked salmon, cream cheese and horseradish or wasabi.

FOR 32 CANAPÉS:
200 g Philadelphia cream cheese, at room temperature
1 tablespoon fresh lemon juice
2 tablespoons grated horseradish
  or 1-2 teaspoons wasabi paste
8 slices of toast or Danish rye + butter
200 g smoked salmon, in thin slices
sprigs of fresh dill + lemon wedges for garnish

• Combine cream cheese with the lemon juice and horseradish. Butter the toast and place the salmon on top. Trim the edges, then cut each slice into 4 pieces. Top with the horseradish cheese (easiest if piped) and garnish with dill sprigs and lemon wedges.

Danish smørrebrød

Smørrebrød is a Danish open-faced sandwich, prepared here with cold slices of roast beef, curry-flavoured remoulade sauce, fried onion and grated horseradish. (Photo, page 144)

• Lightly butter a thin slice of Danish rye bread and cover with a couple of small lettuce leaves. Place a few thin slices of cold roast beef on top (folding the slices so that they fit nicely on the bread). Garnish with a dollop of curry remoulade sauce (see below), some fried onion flakes (store-bought), pickled gherkins and half a radish, then top with some freshly grated horseradish. Serve with a glass of cold beer.

CURRY REMOULADE SAUCE: Combine 150 ml whole egg mayonnaise, 1 teaspoon Dijon mustard and 1 tablespoon each of finely chopped gherkins, capers and sweet pickled onions. Season with about 1 teaspoon curry powder and a few drops of lemon juice. (This makes enough sauce for 4-5 smørrebrød.)

Quick horseradish pinwheels

Serve these nice little nibbles, either as finger food at a party or as part of a picnic basket.

• Spread a soft mixture of room temperature Philadelphia cream cheese and some freshly grated horseradish (or store-bought prepared horseradish) on soft unleavened flatbread. Cover with a layer of wafer-thin slices of cold smoked salmon or smoked turkey. Roll tightly into thin rolls, wrap them in plastic wrap and chill for at least 1 hour.
  Slice the rolls into 3 cm thick pinwheels and arrange on a serving platter garnished with a bit of watercress or fresh parsley.

Apple and carrot slaw

A fresh-tasting salad for a barbecue, or serve with cold cuts for a light meal.

SERVES 4–5:
3 medium carrots
1 firm apple
200 g crème fraîche
finely grated zest of ½ lemon
2–3 tablespoons freshly grated horseradish
2–3 tablespoons snipped chives
sea salt + freshly ground black pepper

• Peel and coarsely grate the carrots and place them in a serving bowl. Finely chop the apple, then fold it into the carrot.

In another bowl, mix the crème fraîche with the lemon zest, horseradish and chives. Season with salt and pepper.

Finally, toss the carrot and apple with the sauce to combine. Sprinkle with some more snipped chives and pepper.

Horseradish sauce

SERVES 4–5:
200 g crème frâiche
3–4 tablespoons freshly grated horseradish
finely grated zest of 1 small lemon
2 tablespoons fresh lemon juice
1 tablespoon mild olive oil
sea salt + freshly ground black pepper

• Combine all the ingredients in a small bowl, then season to taste with salt and pepper. Horseradish sauce is a classic side to roast beef, ideally with some roasted onions or other vegetables as well.

Coleslaw with a zing

This salad gives a pleasant crunch alongside lamb or turkey, roast beef or barbecued meats.

SERVES 4:
about 350 g shredded white cabbage,
  as tender as possible (remove the core)
1 tablespoon apple cider vinegar
  or white wine vinegar
2 tablespoons mild olive oil
at least ½ teaspoon sea salt flakes
freshly ground white or black pepper
200 g crème fraîche
2 tablespoons freshly grated horseradish
1 red apple, in small pieces
5 tablespoons finely snipped chives

• Place the shredded cabbage in a colander and pour boiling water over the cabbage to soften it. Rinse with cold water and set aside to drain.

Combine the vinegar, oil, salt and pepper in a bowl, then stir in the crème fraîche and horseradish. Fold in the cabbage, apple pieces and chives. Season to taste with more sea salt and freshly ground pepper.

Kim's wasabi dressing

SERVES 4:
½ teaspoon wasabi paste
2 teaspoons Japanese soy sauce
1 tablespoon caster sugar
3 tablespoons rice vinegar
1 teaspoon sesame oil

• Dissolve the wasabi in the soy sauce, and add the sugar, vinegar and sesame oil. An excellent dressing for crudités or perfectly ripe avocado.

Creamy mustard potato salad with smoked trout

A summery potato salad with hot smoked trout and a creamy mustard dressing – perfect for an outdoor meal.

SERVES 4:

750 g baby new potatoes
about 100 ml mayonnaise
1–2 tablespoons red wine vinegar
2–3 teaspoons wholegrain mustard
  (or a bit more)
a pinch of sea salt
freshly ground white or black pepper
2–3 tablespoons freshly grated horseradish
400 g hot smoked fish, such as
  rainbow trout or salmon
a few sliced radishes (optional)
dill, chives and lemon wedges for serving
a handful of baby English spinach
  or mixed baby greens

· Wash and rinse the potatoes, and boil them in lightly salted water.

While the potatoes are boiling, prepare the dressing. Put the mayonnaise in a bowl and stir in the vinegar, mustard, salt, pepper and about half of the grated horseradish. Set aside.

Carefully clean the fish, remove any small bones and flake the fish into chunks.

Let the potatoes cool just a little bit. Cut them into large pieces and transfer to a bowl. Gently fold in the dressing and then the fish pieces. Garnish with the radishes (if using), a bit more horseradish and perhaps some dill or chives.

Give the salad a good grinding of black pepper and top with a small pile of baby greens. Serve with lemon wedges.

Green pea soup with horseradish and chives

This bright-green pea soup can be made with either frozen or fresh green peas. If serving the soup as a starter in small bowls, the recipe will serve about eight people.

SERVES 4:

700 ml mild chicken stock
600 g shelled fresh or frozen green peas
100 ml pure (whipping) cream
a pinch of sea salt
freshly ground white or black pepper
200 g crème fraîche
2–4 tablespoons freshly grated horseradish
lemon juice and finely grated zest, to taste

· Bring the chicken stock to the boil in a large saucepan. Add the peas, then cover the pan and cook for 5–7 minutes.

Next, purée the peas and stock with a hand-held blender in the saucepan (or pulse everything in a food processor). Whip the cream.

Season the soup with sea salt and freshly ground pepper. Finally – and a bit sloppily – stir in the whipped cream, leaving visible white streaks of cream throughout the soup.

Combine the crème fraîche with the grated horseradish and a touch of lemon juice and grated zest. Serve the soup topped with a dollop of the horseradish crème fraîche, and with crusty bread. Fresh and simple.

Left: Creamy mustard potato salad with smoked trout

Pernilla's smoked herring

This is one of the nicest smoked herring dishes we know. We usually serve it with crispbread and a bit of cheese.

SERVES 4–5:
8 smoked Baltic herrings, in fillets
1 medium onion
4 medium pickled beetroots
4 tablespoons finely snipped fresh dill or chives
2 tablespoons white wine vinegar
¼ teaspoon salt
a pinch of freshly ground white pepper
3 tablespoons canola or corn oil
2 tablespoons water
2–3 tablespoons freshly grated horseradish

· Pull the skin off the herrings and remove any small bones. Line up a single layer of fillets on a platter, nice and snugly. Peel and finely chop the onion. Finely chop the beetroots.

Place individual rows of onion, beetroot and snipped dill or chives on top of the herring fillets, creating colourful stripes.

Prepare a dressing by blending the vinegar, salt, pepper, oil and – last of all – the water, and pour over. Just before serving, sprinkle with the grated horseradish.

Smoked herring mousse

Clean and fillet 1 large smoked Baltic herring, carefully removing all the small bones. Use a hand-held blender to mix the herring with 150 g crème fraîche and about 2 tablespoons grated horseradish. Season with salt and freshly ground white pepper. Serve on dark rye bread or crispbread. Serves 3–4

Salmon and wasabi rolls

Serve these great smoked salmon, cream cheese and wasabi appetisers on thin slices of lightly salted cucumber.

SERVES 4–5:
2 tablespoons sesame seeds
200 g smoked salmon, in thin slices
1–2 teaspoons sesame oil
100 g Philadelphia cream cheese,
  at room temperature
1–2 teaspoons wasabi paste
  from a tube
8–10 long chives
½ cucumber
sea salt flakes
freshly ground white or black pepper

· Toast the sesame seeds in a dry frying pan, then remove from the pan and cool on a plate.

Place the salmon slices on a large piece of plastic wrap, overlapping the slices to create a 30 x 20 cm rectangle.

Stir the sesame oil into the cream cheese and gently spread it over the salmon. Squeeze a very thin line of wasabi all the way down the centre of the rectangle, and place whole chives on top (saving 2–3 for the cucumber). Sprinkle with the sesame seeds, saving some for garnish.

Carefully roll the salmon into a long and narrow roll. Wrap it in the plastic wrap and chill for at least 3 hours.

When about to serve, remove the plastic and cut the roll into thick slices and arrange on individual plates on a bed of peeled and thinly sliced cucumber. If you wish, sprinkle a pinch of sea salt and pepper over the cucumber. Finish off with the reserved whole chives and the toasted sesame seeds.

Horseradish brisket

An old-fashioned Swedish classic with tender, slowly cooked beef in a sauce made from the flavourful stock. Serve with boiled new potatoes and snow peas (mangetout).

SERVES 4:
800 g boneless prime rib or brisket
water + 2 teaspoons salt per litre of water
1 bay leaf
8 whole white peppercorns

FOR THE SAUCE:
2 tablespoons butter
2 tablespoons plain flour
400 ml of the cooking liquid, strained
salt + freshly ground white or black pepper
250 ml pouring (single) cream
1 tablespoon butter
2–3 tablespoons freshly grated horseradish
a handful of fresh flat-leaf parsley, chopped

· Place the meat snugly in a saucepan and cover with water. Add the salt, bay leaf and the peppercorns. Bring to the boil, cover and simmer slowly for 1½–2 hours, or until the meat is very tender. Leave to cool in the liquid.

To make the sauce, gently melt the butter in a saucepan. Stir in the flour, then add the cooking liquid little by little, stirring continuously. Season with salt and pepper, then add the cream and cook for a few minutes. You can prepare the recipe up to this point ahead of time.

Thinly slice the meat and reheat it in a saucepan (lid on) in some of the remaining cooking liquid. Season the warm sauce with the butter, horseradish and chopped parsley. Serve the meat with the sauce.

Warm beetroot salad

Beetroot and horseradish complement each other beautifully. This is a simple salad with warm or just-cooled baby beets dressed in a creamy horseradish vinaigrette.

SERVES 4:
750 g small beetroots,
  ideally both red and yellow
1 litre water + 1 teaspoon salt
a few small rocket leaves (optional)
sea salt flakes
lemon wedges, to serve

HORSERADISH VINAIGRETTE:
2 tablespoons apple cider vinegar
4 tablespoons olive oil
4 tablespoons sour cream
  or crème fraîche
½ teaspoon sugar, or to taste
a pinch of salt + freshly ground black pepper
freshly grated horseradish, to taste
chives or fresh flat-leaf parsley, chopped

· Rinse and trim the beetroots, cutting off all but 3 cm of the stems and leaving the root tips intact. Cook the beetroots in lightly salted water for 20–35 minutes, or until just soft.

Meanwhile combine the ingredients for the vinaigrette and season to taste.

Drain and allow the boiled beetroots to cool slightly before peeling. Leave the small ones whole and cut the larger ones in half.

Arrange the beetroots on a platter, scatter with a few rocket leaves, season sparingly with sea salt flakes and spoon over the horseradish vinaigrette. Garnish with lemon wedges.

Salmon and potato hash

Fried potatoes, red onions, zucchini and salmon in a hash with a Scandinavian twist.

SERVES 4:
800 g baby new potatoes
500-600 g salmon fillet,
  skinless and boneless
about 1 teaspoon salt
freshly ground white or black pepper
2 medium red onions, chopped
2 small zucchini (courgettes)
oil and butter for frying
1-2 tablespoons finely grated lemon zest

SAUCE:
200 g crème fraîche
2-3 tablespoons freshly grated horseradish
sea salt + pepper, to taste
a good handful of fresh dill, snipped + extra to serve

· Wash the potatoes and cut them in half. Boil until nearly soft, then drain and allow to cool. Combine the sauce ingredients and set aside.

Cut the salmon into large cubes and transfer to a plate. Season with salt and pepper and set aside for a while. Peel, halve and thinly slice the onions. Halve the zucchini lengthwise, scoop out the core and then cut the zucchini into fairly small cubes.

Gently sauté the onion in a little oil and butter in a large frying pan, adding the zucchini after a few minutes. Throw in the potatoes as well, and fry until heated through. Only then add the salmon cubes, and cook for a few minutes until the fish is done. Garnish with extra dill and grate the lemon zest straight over the hash. Serve at once with the sauce.

Right: Boiled cod with egg, melted butter and horseradish

Turbot in beurre noisette

Tender pieces of boiled turbot or cod are a real delicacy, served with brown butter (or use just melted butter if you like), chopped egg, grated horseradish and boiled new potatoes with dill.

SERVES 4:
2 eggs
1 litre mild fish stock
4 servings of turbot or cod loin, 175 g each,
  or other white fish
150 g butter
freshly grated horseradish

· Boil the eggs for 8 minutes, remove from the saucepan and leave to cool. Peel the eggs, chop them, then cover and set aside.

Bring the fish stock to the boil in a sauté pan. Place the fish in the pan, bring to a simmer and cook gently for 2-3 minutes. Transfer the pan, lid on, to a wooden board and leave the fish to cook in the liquid for another 4-8 minutes, depending on the thickness of the fish.

Meanwhile, prepare the brown butter (beurre noisette). Melt the butter in a small saucepan over low heat and cook until light brown. Or simply melt the butter and pour it into a jug.

Use a spatula to transfer the fish onto serving plates, drizzle with the brown butter and scatter with the chopped egg and a generous amount of grated horseradish. Serve with boiled new potatoes garnished with small sprigs of dill.

Horseradish butter

Blend 150 g soft butter with 2 teaspoons lemon juice, 2-3 tablespoons grated horseradish, a pinch of salt and 3 tablespoons finely chopped fresh flat-leaf parsley. Delicious with fried fish or warm boiled beetroots or carrots. Serves 3-4

Lamb with spring vegetables

Slow-cooked lamb with colourful vegetables in a parsley and horseradish-flavoured jus.

SERVES 4–5:
2 litres water + 1 tablespoon salt
8 black peppercorns
1.5 kg lamb brisket
  or other lamb meat
700 g mixed spring vegetables such as baby carrots,
  potatoes, turnips, parsnips, button or baby onions,
  a few radishes and some snow peas (mangetout)
a large handful of fresh flat-leaf parsley
salt + freshly ground black pepper
freshly grated horseradish + crème fraîche, to serve

· Bring the water, salt and peppercorns to the boil in a pot, and add the meat. Lower the heat, then cover and simmer the meat, skimming the broth occasionally (using a large spoon to remove any foam that floats to the surface). Slowly cook the meat for 1–1¼ hours, or until cooked through and really tender. Once the meat is cooked, strain the broth through a sieve and reserve. Let the meat cool, remove any bones and cut the meat into fairly small pieces.

Peel the vegetables of your choice, and cut into the desired size. Pour some of the broth into a saucepan and first boil the carrots, whole onions, parsnips and potatoes, as they take the longest. Add the meat and reheat it in the broth. In the last few minutes of cooking, add the snow peas, parsley, baby turnips and radishes. Season with salt and pepper, and stir in a bit of grated horseradish. Serve with crème fraîche and extra horseradish.

Swedish Lindström patties

These juicy minced meat patties are typically Swedish in flavour and a genuine example of traditional home cooking.

SERVES 4–5:
500 g minced beef
1 teaspoon salt
about ¼ teaspoon ground white pepper
100 ml water
2 egg yolks
3 tablespoons finely chopped onion
3 tablespoons finely chopped pickled gherkins
2 tablespoons chopped capers
5 tablespoons finely chopped pickled beetroots
butter for frying
freshly grated horseradish + snipped chives for serving

· First combine the mince with the salt and pepper, then add the water, egg yolks and all the chopped ingredients. Immediately shape the mixture into small round patties.

Heat a frying pan, add a generous knob of butter and fry the patties in batches over medium heat. Turn them once, frying for a few minutes on each side, or until just cooked through.

Serve the patties straight away, with the cooking juices from the pan poured over. Top with grated horseradish and some snipped chives. Lovely with pan-fried or boiled potatoes and steamed snow peas (mangetout).

Left: Lamb with spring vegetables

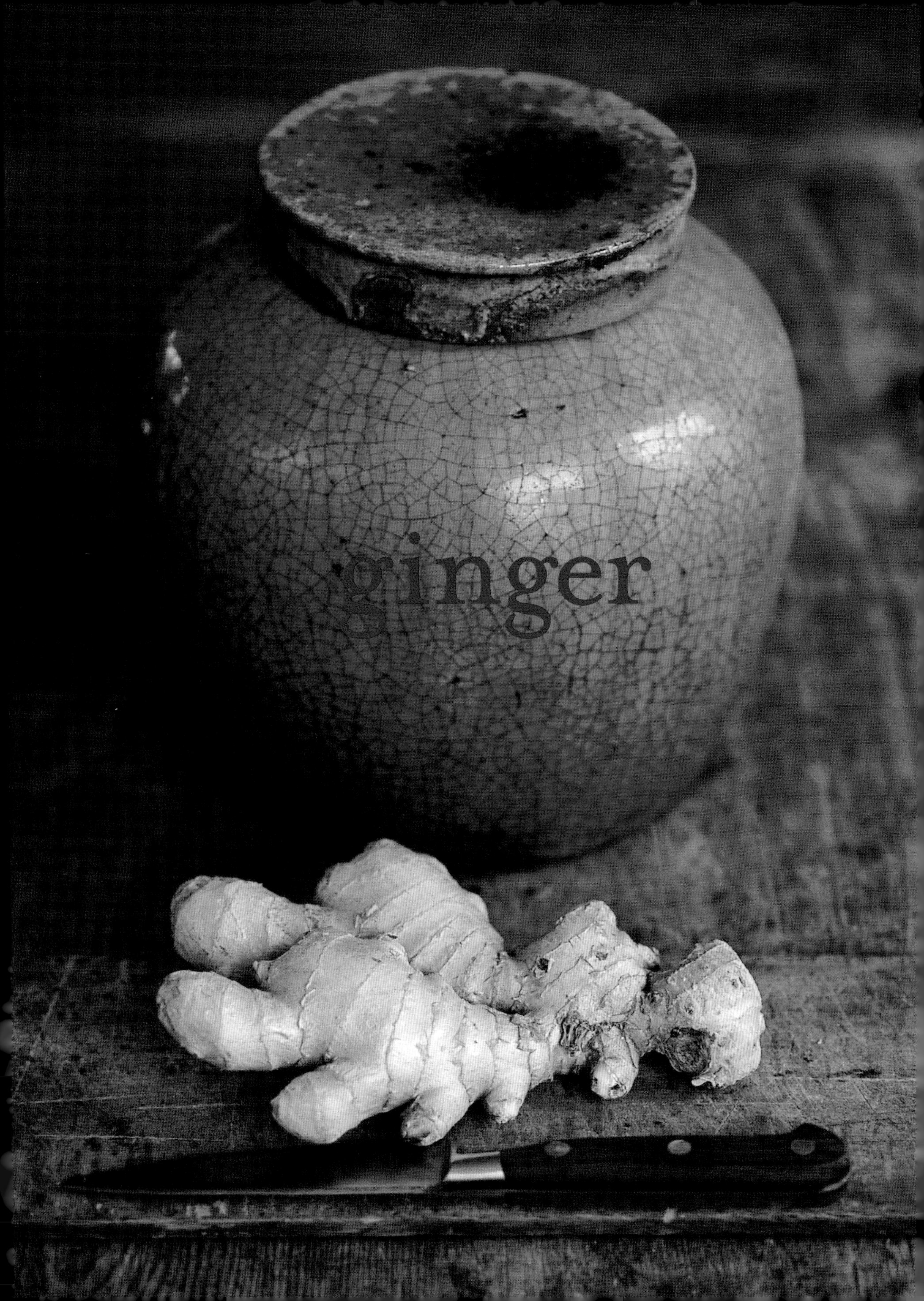
ginger

ginger – a good friend in the kitchen

When choosing our favourite ingredients for this book, ginger was an obvious choice. It has so much character, with its odd appearance, intense aroma and pungent flavour. And it simply feels so fresh, whether it is used in sparkling ginger ale, an aromatic broth with noodles or in a luscious fruit salad…

Ginger is the knobbly rhizome of a metre-high herb, *Zingiber officinale*. The word zingiber is derived from Sanskrit and apparently means 'horn-shaped', referring, of course, to its peculiar shape. Ginger has been cultivated in India and China for thousands of years, but its origins are still uncertain. One theory is that it originally grew wild in the rainforests of Southeast Asia, another that it stems from northern India or East Asia. What we do know for sure is that ginger was an important commodity, and that Arabian merchants brought it to the Middle East and Europe; Portuguese travellers then took it to Africa, where it's still an essential cooking ingredient. In Europe, ginger has been used since the Middle Ages, mainly as a dried spice in pickles, puddings and baked goods such as gingerbread.

These days ginger is commercially grown in tropical countries all over the world, with China and India topping the list. It has been cultivated in the central and mountainous parts of Jamaica since the 16th century, and Jamaican ginger is renowned worldwide for its high quality.

Ginger has an extensive medicinal history. Biblical scriptures describe the plant's healing properties and, as such, it also plays an important part in Chinese medicine. For example, ginger is traditionally used to prevent nausea, and chewing on a little piece of ginger can actually alleviate motion sickness. Ginger also has anti-inflammatory properties, and is used as a pain reliever. In addition, brewing a simple tea with ginger and honey is both delicious and effective against colds and coughs.

Left: Young ginger; Fresh ginger tea with cinnamon and honey

young, old, preserved or candied…

Ginger can vary in flavour and appearance, depending on where it is grown and when it is harvested. It pops up in all shapes and sizes on supermarket shelves. When buying fresh ginger, look for pieces that are nice and firm, and not wrinkled. Always store ginger in the vegetable drawer in the fridge.

YOUNG GINGER is harvested after 5-6 months, and is quite supple with very few fibres. Its skin is pale and thin, and the pulp is juicy. Young ginger is perfect for mixing in juices and drinks, and excellent for brewing tea or livening up a fruit salad. Young ginger is often pickled, preserved or crystallised.

OLD (MATURE) GINGER is harvested after 8-10 months, and is more fibrous than young ginger, and has a much thicker and greyish-brown skin. Old ginger is the most common type found in stores, and is suitable for stews, stir-fries, curries and other Asian dishes. Ground ginger is usually made from old ginger.

PRESERVED GINGER is ginger pieces preserved in sweet syrup, usually sold in glass or ceramic jars. This is a very popular dessert in China, and one that goes well with ice cream on the side. Preserved ginger also gives an excellent flavour to sponge cakes, ice cream and other desserts.

PICKLED GINGER can be found in a number of different varieties, such as grated ginger pickled in vinegar, Japanese *gari* preserved in sugar and rice vinegar and served with sushi, or spicy ginger pickle to accompany Indian food.

DRIED GINGER comes in whole pieces or as ginger powder. In Eastern cuisines, ground ginger is used in fragrant spice mixes and curry powders, and in Western cooking primarily in baked goods. Dried ginger, however, is seldom a good substitute for fresh ginger, as dried ginger has a rather savoury and spicy flavour.

CRYSTALLISED (CANDIED) GINGER consists of young ginger pieces or slices that have been cooked in sugar syrup, dipped in sugar and then dried. It is sometimes used in desserts.

Left, clockwise from top: Preserved ginger; Asian ginger candy; Japanese pickled ginger; Crystallised ginger

galangal, krachai and other relatives

GALANGAL, greater galangal, *Alpinia galanga*, and lesser galangal, *Alpinia officinarum*, also belong to the ginger family, *Zingiberaceae*. As with ginger, you use the actual rhizomes. Galangal is wonderfully fragrant, reminiscent of ginger but smaller, whiter (or rather pinkish-white) and with a more perfumed flavour. Galangal grows in Southeast Asia, China and India. Greater galangal is frequently used in Malaysian, Thai and Indonesian cuisines. The lesser type, which is redder in colour and stronger in flavour, is sometimes called Siamese ginger. There is also a third kind, *Kaempferia galanga*, which is very popular in Indonesia, where it is called *kencur*.

KRACHAI, *Boesenbergia rotunda*, also known as fingerroot or Chinese ginger, grows in the tropical rainforests of Asia, but is now cultivated in Africa as well. It has long, supple 'fingers' and is much tangier than ginger. Krachai is quite soft in texture, which is why it's best to use it whole and then discard it before serving. Krachai is commonly used in Southeast Asia, and is excellent for seasoning pork or chicken stews or curries.

TURMERIC, *Curcuma longa*, is native to Southeast Asia and India, and is also a member of the ginger family. The rhizomes are quite hard, and bright yellow or orange on the inside. Fresh turmeric is frequently used in Southeast Asian and Indian cooking. Turmeric is used to colour curry dishes a deep yellow, or adding a bit of turmeric to boiling water before adding the rice will turn it a lovely yellow. The primary producer of turmeric is India, where it's mainly used in powder form. The French sometimes call it *safran d'Inde*, Indian saffron.

JAPANESE GINGER, *Zingiber mioga*, is a mild ginger used both fresh and pickled, often with sashimi. In this case, you eat the buds and not the rhizomes. Sushi is served with pink-coloured *gari*, which is actually regular ginger pickled in rice vinegar, sugar and salt.

Right: Aromatic galangal enhances many Southeast Asian dishes

Ginger ale

A glass of ginger ale is cool, refreshing and incredibly pleasant. It's a perfect non-alcoholic party alternative or thirst quencher on a hot summer day.

FOR ABOUT 2 LITRES:
10 cm piece fresh ginger
150 ml fresh lemon juice
1 litre water
140 g caster sugar
1 litre sparkling mineral water
crushed ice or ice cubes
small fresh mint leaves

· Peel and slice the ginger. Squeeze the lemons and measure out the quantity. Bring the water to the boil.

Put the sugar in a large, heat-resistant jug. Pour over the boiling water, then add the lemon juice and sliced ginger and stir until the sugar dissolves. Let stand for at least 2 hours and then strain.

Pour in the mineral water and add plenty of crushed ice or ice cubes just before serving. Decorate with a few shredded mint leaves or small whole sprigs of mint. Serve at once.

TIP: Make an extra batch and keep it in a jug in the fridge, but don't add the mineral water until you are ready to serve.

Fresh ginger tea

Ginger tea is both beneficial and invigorating, particularly when coughs and colds abound. Here are a few ways to brew ginger tea directly in your tea cup.

ONLY GINGER: Peel and then slice a small piece of ginger. Pour over boiling water, let it steep for 5-10 minutes and then sweeten with honey to taste.

WITH LIME OR LEMON: A couple of slices of ginger, a couple of slices of lemon or lime and boiling water. Honey to taste.

WITH LEMONGRASS: Sliced ginger, a couple of large pieces of lemongrass (gently bruised to release the flavour) and boiling water. Sweeten with honey or sugar if you like.

WITH MINT: Sliced ginger, a few small fresh mint sprigs or leaves, boiling water and a little sugar or honey, to taste.

WITH SPICES: Sliced ginger, a few whole cardamom pods, a small piece of cinnamon stick, boiling water and a little milk. Honey or sugar, to taste.

AS ICED TEA: Make a batch of the lemon iced tea on page 381, but add 10 cm ginger, peeled and sliced. Let draw for 1 hour before adding the ice. Serve at once.

CHAI WITH GINGER: Bring 500 ml water to the boil in a saucepan. Add 2 tablespoons black tea leaves, 500 ml full-fat milk, 40 g sugar (or to taste) plus a thumb-sized piece of peeled ginger. Simmer for 5-6 minutes. Strain, then serve piping hot in small cups or glasses. See also the Chai masala recipe on page 380.

Pickled ginger

This sweet-and-sour pickled ginger can be an invigorating complement to Asian dishes.

MAKES ONE SMALL JAR:
½ fresh red chilli
100 g fresh ginger
1 litre water
2 tablespoons Chinese rice vinegar
2 teaspoons salt
100 g caster sugar

· Deseed and finely chop the chilli, and then peel and cut the ginger into wafer-thin slices, ideally using a mandoline.

Bring the water to the boil, add the ginger and boil for 1 minute. Rinse with cold water in a sieve and drain well. Place the ginger and the chilli pretty snugly in a small jar. Pour in the vinegar, then add the salt and sugar. Stir gently and let the ginger steep in the fridge for a few days. Will last up to 1 week.

Deep-fried ginger

These thin, crispy ginger strips can be scattered on top of various Asian dishes, such as noodles, chicken, soups or stir-fries.

· Peel a knob of nice, supple ginger with a small knife, then cut it into very thin julienne strips.

Carefully heat a bit of peanut or vegetable oil in a wok or a small heavy-based frying pan. Quickly deep-fry the ginger strips until golden. As soon as they are done, remove them with a slotted spoon and place on double sheets of paper towel to drain.

Ginger sambal dip

YOU WILL NEED:
200 g crème fraîche
1 tablespoon finely grated fresh ginger
1 teaspoon sambal oelek
1 garlic clove, crushed
10–12 fresh mint leaves, chopped
a pinch of sea salt
freshly ground black pepper

· Mix all the ingredients in a bowl and season with salt and black pepper. Let the flavours develop for about 10 minutes.

Serve the dip with barbecued meat or chicken, or with crudités.

Ginger and lime dressing

YOU WILL NEED:
1½ teaspoons finely grated fresh ginger
2 tablespoons fresh lime juice
1 teaspoon fish sauce
1 teaspoon grated palm sugar
2 tablespoons sunflower oil

· Combine everything in a bowl, and let stand for 5–10 minutes to infuse. Trickle the ginger and lime dressing over crispy salad greens.

Ginger-glazed pork in lettuce

A spicy and sweet marinade that is excellent for pork or chicken. The photo shows pieces of pork that have been marinated for an hour, and then quickly stir-fried and served in lettuce leaves with crunchy peanuts and wedges of lime. Truly delicious!

SERVES 4:

2 tablespoons grated fresh ginger

3 garlic cloves, grated

1 teaspoon chilli flakes
  or 1 fresh red chilli

3–4 tablespoons honey

2 tablespoons soy sauce

3 tablespoons vegetable oil or olive oil
  + a little oil for stir-frying

500 g lean pork
  or 3 chicken breast fillets

crisp green lettuce leaves

chopped peanuts

lime wedges

· Prepare the ginger and garlic. Deseed and finely chop the fresh chilli, if using. Put the ginger, garlic and chilli in a bowl and stir in the honey, soy sauce and oil.

Cut the meat into pieces or strips, transfer to a small bowl and then pour the marinade over the meat. Stir to cover the pieces and marinate for at least 1 hour in the fridge.

Heat the oil in a wok or a large frying pan, and stir-fry the meat in batches over medium heat for 3–4 minutes, or until cooked through.

Arrange the lettuce leaves on a large platter, add the ginger-glazed meat and serve with plenty of chopped peanuts and with the lime wedges, to squeeze over.

Chickpea and ginger salad

This exotic chickpea salad with ginger, cumin, parsley and orange zest can be enjoyed on its own or as a side dish on a buffet.

SERVES 4:

250 g dried chickpeas (to give about 600 g cooked beans)
  or 2 x 400 g tins chickpeas

4–5 cm piece fresh ginger

½–1 orange

1 bunch fresh flat-leaf parsley, leaves picked

½–1 teaspoon ground cumin

2–3 tablespoons good-quality olive oil

fresh orange juice, to taste (optional)

sea salt flakes

freshly ground black pepper

· Soak the dried chickpeas for 12 hours in water without salt, then tip them into a colander and rinse well. Cook the chickpeas in fresh unsalted water for about 1 hour or until soft, adding a good pinch of salt when 15 minutes remain, and then drain. If using tinned chickpeas, rinse well in cold water and drain well.

Peel and grate the ginger (you need about 1 tablespoon grated ginger). Wash and dry the orange. Grate the orange skin, making sure to leave out the bitter white pith. Chop the parsley quite roughly.

Transfer the chickpeas to a bowl and stir in the ginger, orange zest, parsley and cumin. Drizzle with the olive oil and season to taste with a little freshly squeezed orange juice (if using), sea salt and freshly ground pepper. Toss well to combine.

Right: Ginger-glazed pork with greens, peanuts and lime

An aromatic broth with noodles and whatnot

This is a very pleasant way to enjoy a meal: a pot of piping-hot broth is placed in the centre of the table, surrounded by various accompaniments. Let each guest take a soup bowl and fill it with cooked noodles, a few julienned vegetables, toasted cashew nuts and tofu, or thin slices of cooked chicken or beef; and then scoop some of the warm, flavourful broth over it all...

BROTH FOR 4-5:

5 Asian shallots

3 garlic cloves

5 cm piece fresh ginger

5 cm piece fresh galangal (optional)

5 kaffir lime leaves

  + 5 extra leaves for serving

3 lemongrass stalks

3 tablespoons peanut or vegetable oil

1-1½ teaspoons Thai green curry paste

2.5 litres mild chicken or vegetable stock

2-3 tablespoons fish sauce

juice of 2 limes

salt, to taste

lime wedges, to serve

THE BROTH: Start by preparing all the ingredients. Peel and finely chop the shallots and garlic. Peel and thinly slice the ginger and the galangal, if using. Rinse the kaffir lime leaves and roughly shred them. Trim and lightly bruise the lemongrass, and then cut it into large pieces.

Heat the oil in a large saucepan over medium heat. Sweat the shallots and garlic for a few minutes without colouring. Add the curry paste and 'mash' it around, then add the ginger and galangal and sauté for another minute or so while stirring.

Pour in the stock, adding the shredded kaffir lime leaves and large pieces of lemongrass. Cover and let everything simmer slowly for about 30 minutes, to release all the flavours. Towards the end, pour in the fish sauce and lime juice and simmer for another 1-2 minutes. Taste, and adjust the seasoning if necessary.

Strain the broth, wipe the saucepan clean and pour the broth back in. You can serve the broth either as soon as it's done, or gently reheat it later on. As you are about to serve, garnish with the last kaffir lime leaves torn in half, and place a bowl of lime wedges on the table. Use a portable hotplate, if you have one, to keep the broth in the saucepan warm.

TO SERVE WITH THE BROTH:

boiled rice noodles or glass noodles

carrots in thin (julienned) strips

red capsicum (pepper), in thin strips

Asian shallots, in wafer-thin slices

baby spinach or torn, crisp lettuce leaves

mung bean sprouts

fresh shiitake or other mushrooms,
  thinly sliced

cashew nuts or peanuts, chopped

fresh mint, coriander or Thai sweet basil

cooked chicken or beef,
  or firm tofu, in cubes

Our friends' carrot soup with a hint of orange

A warming soup for cold winter days. Our friends often serve it with a dollop of yoghurt or crème fraîche, and freshly baked bread.

SERVES 4:
2 medium onions
4–6 large carrots (500 g)
3 cm piece fresh ginger
200 ml fresh orange juice
   (from 2 large oranges)
2 tablespoons butter or olive oil
½ teaspoon salt, or to taste
700 ml vegetable stock
salt + freshly ground black pepper
200 g crème fraîche or thick yoghurt

· Peel and chop the onions, peel and coarsely grate the carrots, and peel and finely grate the ginger. Wash one of the oranges, finely grate the peel and cover to keep from drying. Squeeze both oranges, then set everything aside.

Gently heat the butter or olive oil in a pot or large saucepan. Sweat the onion over low heat until soft, and season with salt. Add the ginger and carrots and sauté for a couple of minutes. Pour in the stock and orange juice, bring to the boil and then simmer for 10-15 minutes.

Take a hand-held blender and mix everything right in the pot. Season with salt and freshly ground black pepper. Serve the soup topped with a dollop of crème fraîche or thick yoghurt. Sprinkle with the grated orange zest.

Ginger and honey-glazed root vegetables

Parsnips, carrots and swede glazed with honey, thyme and finely chopped ginger go beautifully with smoked leg of lamb, or roast beef or lamb.

SERVES 5-6:
4 medium carrots
200 g swede
   or 1 large sweet potato
3 medium parsnips
2–3 tablespoons chopped fresh ginger
100 ml water
50 g butter
3 tablespoons honey
roughly ½ teaspoon sea salt flakes
a pinch of freshly ground black pepper
1–2 teaspoons dried thyme

· Peel and cut the carrots, swede or sweet potato and parsnips lengthwise into thick strips. Prepare the ginger.

Bring the water and butter to the boil in a sauté pan. Tip the root vegetables and ginger into the pan and bring to the boil. Cover and simmer for 5 minutes, stirring every now and then. At the very end, trickle in the honey and stir carefully to blend. You can prepare the recipe up to this point ahead of time.

Preheat the oven to 200°C/400°F. Transfer the vegetables to a lightly greased ovenproof dish and season with salt, pepper and thyme. Cook for 20 minutes or so until the vegetables are soft and nicely browned. Serve while warm.

Polly's sesame salmon patties

In this recipe, the salmon is cooked in the easiest way imaginable, and then mashed with a fork and seasoned with ginger, lime and sesame seeds. You can cook the patties ahead of time then reheat them at a low oven temperature.

SERVES 4-5:
400 g salmon fillet, skinless and boneless
1 litre mild fish stock
2 medium potatoes, boiled and riced (or mashed well)
1 fresh red chilli, deseeded and finely chopped
1 spring onion, finely chopped
1 medium egg
2 teaspoons finely chopped fresh ginger
2 teaspoons fish sauce
3 tablespoons chopped fresh coriander leaves
4 tablespoons fresh lime juice
5 tablespoons sesame seeds
vegetable oil for frying

· Cut the salmon into 3 pieces. Bring the fish stock to the boil in a sauté pan. Add the salmon and bring to the boil again, then place the pan onto a wooden chopping board. Let stand for 5-7 minutes (with the lid on), then take the lid off and let the salmon cool slightly.

Put the salmon in a bowl and mash the flesh with a fork. Add the riced potatoes and all the other ingredients except the sesame seeds. Work into an even mince, then shape into about 20 small patties.

Pour the sesame seeds onto a plate and gently press both sides of the patties into the seeds.

Fry the patties in the oil in a non-stick frying pan until golden. Serve with lime wedges and a green salad.

Oven-baked ginger salmon

A simple dish with an Asian touch, perfect with steamed rice and stir-fried vegetables.

SERVES 4:
700 g skinless salmon fillet
butter or oil for greasing the dish
2 tablespoons sesame seeds

MARINADE:
2 tablespoons light soy sauce
2 tablespoons grated fresh ginger
2 teaspoons brown sugar
1 large garlic clove, crushed

· Preheat the oven to 225°C/435°F. Place the salmon in a greased ovenproof dish. Combine the ingredients for the marinade and pour it over the fish. Scatter sesame seeds on top, and bake in the oven for 15-20 minutes. Serve while warm.

Glazed barbecued salmon

SERVES 4:
4 pieces of skinless salmon (150 g each)

GLAZE:
1 tablespoon grated fresh ginger
2-3 tablespoons golden syrup
1 tablespoon Japanese soy sauce
2-3 teaspoons fresh lemon or orange juice

· First, combine all the ingredients for the glaze and let the flavours develop for at least 1 hour.

Brush the salmon with the glaze both before and after barbecuing. Estimate 5-6 minutes on the barbecue. Serve with rice and a green salad.

Indian curry from Stockholm

This Indian-inspired curry is just as good with chicken as it is with lamb – or simply vegetables. First you prepare the curry base, and then add whatever you want to include in your stew.

Serve the curry with fresh coriander, basmati rice, thick natural yoghurt or Indian raita with mint (page 86). Ideally, serve also with mango chutney and a fresh green salad.

CURRY BASE FOR 4:

4–5 tablespoons vegetable oil
2 medium onions, finely chopped
4 garlic cloves, finely chopped
3 tablespoons grated fresh ginger
½ teaspoon ground turmeric
½ teaspoon ground cumin
1 teaspoon garam masala (optional)
¼ teaspoon cayenne pepper
  or chilli powder, or to taste
600 ml mild stock or water
5 medium tomatoes, finely chopped
1 tablespoon honey
salt
300 ml pouring (single) cream
  towards the end

CURRY BASE: Gently heat the oil in a large pot. Add the finely chopped onion and slowly sweat for about 10 minutes without colouring. Add the finely chopped garlic and grated ginger and sauté for a couple of minutes more.

Add all the ground spices and sauté for another minute while stirring, then pour in the stock or water.

Finally, add the chopped tomatoes and honey, cover and simmer for 25 minutes. Season to taste with salt. The recipe can be prepared up to this point ahead of time.

VEGETABLE CURRY: Cut 1 zucchini (courgette), 1 piece of broccoli, 4 potatoes, 2 carrots and a bit of cauliflower into small pieces, or use the vegetables of your choice. We sometimes add green beans, peas or snow peas (mangetout) as well. In a wok, sauté the vegetables in a bit of oil for a couple of minutes over medium heat. Transfer the greens to the curry pot, cover and simmer until tender. When only a few minutes remain, stir in the cream, heat once more and season with salt and pepper.

CHICKEN CURRY: Cut 8 chicken thigh fillets (600 g) into 3 cm pieces. Heat some oil in a frying pan, and brown the chicken pieces lightly all over. Season with salt and pepper and transfer the chicken to the warm curry base. Cover and simmer for 6–8 minutes, or until the chicken is cooked through. When only a few minutes of cooking time remains, stir in the cream, heat and season to taste.

LAMB CURRY: Cut 600 g boneless lamb meat into cubes. Brown them all over in a bit of oil in a frying pan, and season with salt and pepper. Place the lamb cubes in the curry base, cover and cook for 30–40 minutes, or until tender (you may need to add a splash more water). Stir in the cream towards the end, heat and season to taste.

Overleaf: Easy ginger ice cream, page 180; Pineapple with ginger and mint, page 178

Luscious fruit salad with ginger and mint

Make sure to choose perfectly ripe and fresh fruit for this beautiful fruit salad, as it really does make all the difference.

SERVES 4-6:
1 mango
1 pomelo
1 small green melon
½ pineapple (not too big)
½ papaya
1-2 tablespoons finely chopped ginger
  (ideally young ginger)
a small handful of fresh mint leaves
juice of 1-2 limes
sugar, to taste

· Cut the fruit into neat pieces and arrange them in a bowl or on a platter. Sprinkle with finely chopped ginger, finely chopped fresh mint (preferably spearmint, which is rather mild but full of flavour) and squeeze the lime juice over the salad. Sprinkle with sugar, to taste; the amount of sugar needed will depend on the sweetness of the fruit. Toss gently and serve as is, or with ice cream.

WITH PINEAPPLE: Instead of making an entire fruit salad, simply sprinkle finely chopped ginger and mint over sweet, juicy pineapple pieces. Arrange on a large leaf or in the actual pineapple shell. (Photo, page 177)

Sweet ginger and mascarpone delight

This dessert is easy to make yet rather refined – a fusion of pungent, sweet preserved ginger and smooth mascarpone.

FOR 6 SMALL SERVINGS:
4 knobs of preserved ginger
200 g mascarpone, at room temperature
100 g thick Greek yoghurt
4 tablespoons sifted icing sugar,
  or to taste
1 tablespoon ginger syrup,
  from the preserved ginger jar
a pinch of freshly ground black pepper
Italian biscotti or amaretti biscuits

· Use a sharp knife to cut the ginger into very thin slices and set aside.

In a bowl, blend the mascarpone, yoghurt and icing sugar until smooth. Season with the ginger syrup and chill for at least 30 minutes.

Serve the ginger slices with a dollop of the mascarpone yoghurt, topped with a touch of freshly ground black pepper, which, strangely enough, complements the flavours very nicely. Serve a few Italian almond biscotti or amaretti biscuits on the side.

Right: Luscious fruit salad with ginger and mint; Sweet ginger and mascarpone delight

Tiramisu with ginger

This tiramisu is somewhat unusual, marrying the tanginess of preserved ginger with chocolate and mascarpone.

SERVES 8:
250 ml full-fat milk
60 g dark chocolate (70%)
a small splash of really strong coffee (optional)
24 savoiardi biscuits (ladyfingers or sponge fingers)
3 knobs of preserved ginger
3 eggs, separated
5 tablespoons caster sugar
2 tablespoons ginger syrup, from the preserved ginger jar
250 g mascarpone, at room temperature
2–2½ tablespoons sifted good-quality cocoa

· Put the milk and chocolate in a saucepan over low heat, and stir until the chocolate melts. Add the coffee (if using) and leave the mixture to cool a little. Dip the underside of 12 savoiardi biscuits in the lukewarm chocolate milk. As you go, line up the biscuits, dipped-side down, in a shallow dish or square platter with edges.

Slice and finely chop the ginger. Beat the egg whites until really stiff and set aside.

Whisk the egg yolks and sugar until fluffy, then fold in the ginger and syrup. Add the mascarpone and give it a good stir. Last of all, gently fold in about half the beaten egg whites, and then gradually fold in the rest.

Spread half of the mascarpone mixture over the biscuits. Add another layer of chocolate milk-dipped savoiardi, and distribute the rest of the mascarpone on top. Refrigerate for at least 3 hours, to allow the flavours to mingle nicely. Dust the tiramisu with sifted cocoa just before serving.

Easy ginger ice cream

We once had this charming and completely effortless ice cream at a party, where it was served with a fruit salad. Since then, it has become one of our favourites, with or without fruit on the side. (Photo, page 176)

· Quickly pulse partly thawed, good-quality vanilla ice cream with some roughly chopped preserved ginger for just a few seconds in a food processor (or mix in finely diced ginger by hand). Place in a freeze-proof container and freeze for about 2 hours, then voilà: glorious ginger ice cream!

Use approximately 3-4 knobs of preserved ginger per litre of ice cream.

Ginger swiss

First of all, prepare a flavourful chocolate sauce, such as the one on page 395. You can make it ahead of time and then carefully reheat it.

Thinly slice a few knobs of preserved ginger and then shred them very finely. Or cut the ginger knobs into very small cubes.

Whip some cream. Place a few scoops of good-quality vanilla ice cream in a large bowl or in small individual bowls. Add the whipped cream and sprinkle sparingly with ginger pieces (preserved ginger can be quite sharp). Trickle either warm or cold chocolate sauce on top and serve at once.

Ginger's tangy cinnamon carrot cake

This delectable carrot cake has an invigorating hint of preserved ginger, which is also daintily echoed in the icing.

YOU WILL NEED:
2 tablespoons soft butter for the tin
3 knobs of preserved ginger
2 medium carrots (200 g)
200 ml sunflower oil or corn oil
225 g caster sugar
3 medium eggs
175 g plain flour + extra for dusting
2 teaspoons baking powder
1 heaped teaspoon ground cinnamon
icing (optional)

· Fasten a piece of non-stick baking paper to the base of a 22 cm springform tin by clasping it shut over the paper. Grease the inside of the tin with the butter, then dust with flour. Shake off any excess flour and set the tin aside for now.

Preheat the oven to 175°C/345°F. Slice, then finely chop the ginger. Peel and grate the carrots.

Mix the oil and sugar in a bowl and then add one egg at a time, stirring thoroughly after each egg. Add the grated carrot and chopped ginger. Combine the flour, baking powder and cinnamon and add that as well.

Pour the mixture into the greased tin and bake for 50-60 minutes, or until a skewer inserted into the centre of the cake comes out clean.

ICING: Combine 300 g room temperature Philadelphia cream cheese with 75 g sifted icing sugar and 2-3 tablespoons syrup from the ginger jar. Use a spatula to spread the glaze evenly on the cold cake. Grate a bit of orange zest on top.

Our family recipe for ginger thins

Serve these thin, crisp ginger biscuits with a cup of tea, or with a bit of blue cheese — a surprisingly good combination. *Note!* Let the dough rest for 24 hours before baking.

FOR ABOUT 60 BISCUITS:
100 g butter
100 g sugar
½ teaspoon pure vanilla extract
4 tablespoons golden syrup
50 ml water
260 g plain flour + extra for dusting
a scant teaspoon bicarbonate of soda
3 teaspoons ground ginger
1 teaspoon ground cinnamon

· Melt the butter in a small saucepan over low heat. Stir in the sugar, vanilla, golden syrup and water until combined. Set aside.

Measure out the flour, bicarbonate of soda, ground ginger and cinnamon in a large bowl and combine. Pour in the butter mixture and work into a dough with a wooden spoon.

Sprinkle a bit of flour on the work surface and tip the crumbly dough on top. Lightly knead the dough, then divide it in half. Shape into two logs about 6 cm thick. Flatten each log slightly and square the edges with your hands. Wrap in non-stick baking paper or plastic wrap and refrigerate for about 24 hours.

Preheat the oven to 180°C/350°F. Line two baking trays with non-stick baking paper.

Use a sharp knife to cut the dough into very thin slices. Spread out the slices on the baking trays and bake (one tray at a time) for about 6-8 minutes. Leave the ginger thins on the tray to cool.

citrus

newly picked oranges can be...

... almost addictive, and a glass of freshly squeezed orange juice can be pure bliss. Our favourite oranges are the ones we enjoy on the island of Mallorca. In the green valleys surrounding the small town of Sóller they grow the most wonderful navel oranges, so exceptionally sweet and juicy. Luckily we find navels at home as well. When in season, we always look for them specifically and end up buying 3-4 kilos at a time. And they run out in the twinkling of an eye...

And lemons, of course, are practically a necessity. A large bowl of lemons on the kitchen table is just as decorative as a bunch of flowers, and this vibrant yellow fruit can brighten your spirits as well as almost any dish. But there are many ways to add fresh notes of citrus to your cooking. Aside from lemons and limes, fragrant kaffir limes and their shiny leaves give a unique flavour to Asian-inspired curries and soups, and tangy, pink grapefruits or pomelos can be splendid additions to green salads. And then there's lemongrass, which doesn't belong to the citrus family at all, but its sweet lemony scent made us want to include it in this chapter anyway.

Above: Kaffir limes and lemongrass; Oranges in Sóller, Mallorca. Left: Stunning saffron oranges, page 220

citrus provides that little extra something

… adding a mild tartness to a stew, or balancing the sweetness and acidity of a sauce. Sometimes a little splash of lemon is all that it takes to give a dish that special finishing touch. It's hard to imagine cooking without citrus in some shape or form.

In the Mediterranean region, dried orange peel is commonly used as seasoning, and the tiniest hint gives a nice tinge of citrus to various dishes, such as a fish soup from southern France or a bean salad from Tunisia. We also like to add a small ribbon of dried peel when cooking a boeuf bourguignon or other slow-cooked casseroles. Once dried, the orange peel has a more refined and well-rounded flavour than a ribbon of fresh peel. Citrus can also enhance the flavour of berries: for instance, by adding a bit of grated lime or lemon zest when marinating strawberries or blueberries. A few drops of orange juice squeezed over a bowl of strawberries is also a simple dessert. And slices of elegant blood oranges – with their spectacular crimson flesh – make a striking contrast in a green leaf salad. Many North African and Provençal desserts and pastries are flavoured with orange-blossom water, *eau de fleur d'oranger*, and just a few fragrant drops can add a whole new dimension to sliced oranges dusted with cinnamon and icing sugar, or a pastry with almonds…

organic lemons just taste better

If possible, choose certified organically grown citrus fruits whenever you can. The sensation of holding an organic lemon in your hand completely outshines the feel of waxy, conventionally grown fruit. Organic lemons, oranges and limes all have beautifully fragrant, soft, dull skins that are perfect for grating and zesting. These fruits are so much more flavourful, and we often find them juicier and easier to squeeze as well. And it's simply more gratifying to use fruit that has been sustainably grown.

grating, squeezing, segmenting, storing

STORING CITRUS FRUITS: All citrus fruits taste better at room temperature, but will keep longer if stored in a cool pantry, or in the least cold part of the fridge. A good idea, though, is to bring the fruit to room temperature before squeezing: cold fruit is harder both to squeeze and to zest.

PEELING AND SEGMENTING: Cutting out completely membrane-free orange or grapefruit wedges is easy enough, once you get the hang of it. First, cut off a thin slice at the top and bottom of each fruit. This allows you to place the fruit steadily on a chopping board, and makes it easier to peel the entire fruit with a sharp knife. Cut or carve off a bit of peel at a time, removing all the bitter white pith as well. Then it will be easy to finely slice the orange, or cut out the wedges into segments. To segment a citrus fruit: hold the peeled fruit in one hand and very carefully cut out the wedges, one by one, cutting them loose from the membrane.

TIPS FOR SQUEEZING: A simple trick before squeezing a citrus fruit is to first soften it a bit against the kitchen counter. Place the flat of your hand over the fruit, and press lightly while rolling it back and forth. This will help release the juice, particularly with limes and lemons.

GRATING CITRUS PEEL: Wash the fruit in warm water and scrub it with a brush. Rinse and dry well. Grate the outermost peel using the fine edge of a regular grater or a rasp grater. Another practical kitchen tool is a citrus or lemon zester, which makes it easy to cut thin, elegant ribbons of citrus peel for decorating drinks and desserts.

DRYING ORANGE PEEL: Wash the oranges very thoroughly, rinse and dry them well. Use a regular potato peeler to cut wafer-thin slices of the very outermost orange-yellow peel. Place the orange ribbons on paper towels in a loose basket, and leave it in a dry and airy place. The ribbons will dry within a couple of days. Once dried, store in an airtight glass jar for up to 6 months.

A freshly picked lemon

Lemon tree, Mallorca

Passionate oranges, page 217

Freshly squeezed orange juice is a simple luxury

red grapefruit, kaffir lime, bitter orange and lemon

ORANGES, *Citrus sinensis*, originated in China, like so many other citrus fruits. The first orange arrived in Europe in the 15th century, and Columbus took orange seeds with him on his second journey to America in 1493. Thanks to Columbus and his followers, fruits, berries and plants went back and forth between the continents. Today, oranges are cultivated in many areas, such as Brazil, the United States and around the Mediterranean. Succulent and graceful blood oranges, with their crimson pulp, are frequently grown in Italy. In Europe, most of the large and sweet navel oranges come from Spain. Just like all the other citrus fruit, oranges are full of vitamin C, which is very beneficial to our immune system and can help stave off the occasional cold.

BITTER ORANGES, *Citrus aurantium*, are sometimes called Seville oranges, because they are primarily grown in the regions surrounding the city of Seville in Spain. They are usually only available during a few short winter months. Bitter oranges are sour and aren't usually eaten raw, but they are unrivalled for use in marmalades. Bitter orange peel is often dried, and its mild and delicate aroma is used to flavour bread or to season Swedish aquavit. The flowers have a heavenly scent, and are used in the perfume industry, and to make orange-blossom water, which is a common seasoning in Provençal and North African cuisines. Bergamot, *Citrus bergamia*, is a spicy citrus fruit related to bitter oranges, used to flavour Earl Grey tea. Bergamot is grown in Italy, among other places.

LEMONS, *Citrus limon*, are so uplifting with their bright yellow colour and superbly fresh and tangy flavour. A few splashes of lemon may be all you need to enhance a dish, and we tend to use lots of lemons in our cooking. There are about 100 different types of lemons, but certain varieties are cultivated more often than others. Primofiori, Limoni and Vernas are some usual types available in Europe.

LIME, *Citrus aurantifolia*, is also marvellous, but the flavour can sometimes become a bit too dominant, and doesn't always match as many different kinds of food as lemon does. In the Middle East, particularly in Iran, dried lime is used to season stews and casseroles. Fresh lime is also a key ingredient in many Asian and South American cuisines, where it's often used together with chillies and coriander – a splendid combination. The smaller, lighter variety called key lime provides the dainty flavour of a classic key lime pie.

KAFFIR LIME or makrut lime, *Citrus hystrix*, is a green, knobbly citrus fruit with beautifully fragrant leaves commonly used in Southeast Asian cooking. You seldom need more than three or four lime leaves to season an entire dish. Kaffir lime has a unique and distinctive flavour that is hard to substitute with any other ingredient. Carefully wash the leaves before using, and then tear or roughly shred them to release the flavour. Fresh leaves will keep for about a week in the fridge, but you can also freeze them or buy dried leaves. The flavoursome kaffir lime peel is also grated and used in cooking, but the juice is generally considered too acidic. In Thailand, the kaffir lime is called bai makrut and is a primary ingredient in curry paste.

CLEMENTINES and satsumas, *Citrus reticulata*, are small and sweet orange-like citrus fruits that are usually only eaten fresh. Their season extends from late autumn to the end of winter. Clementines are almost seedless and easy to peel. Buy nice, heavy fruits; a loose skin often signifies that the fruit is overripe. Clementines and satsumas are hybrids created from mandarins, and are traditionally enjoyed around Christmas in Northern Europe. Mandarins are especially tasty and are easy to peel, but usually have quite a few seeds.

GRAPEFRUITS, *Citrus paradisi*, are believed to have originated in the West Indies, and didn't reach Europe until 1910. Grapefruits grow in large bunches, and the pulp contains small amounts of quinine, which gives the grapefruit its characteristic, somewhat bitter taste. The pink grapefruit variety is a bit sweeter than the white one, and can bring a delightfully sweet yet tangy touch to salads and desserts.

pomelo, kumquats, baby limes and fragrant lemongrass

POMELO, *Citrus grandis*, is the largest citrus fruit of all. It has a very thick, yellowish-green skin, and the flesh is wonderfully tasty but often quite dry. Pomelo has unusually tough membranes between the wedges, but fortunately the flesh is easy to release from the bitter pith. Pomelo is delicious in salads with Asian flavours, ideally scattered with toasted peanuts for a nice contrast in texture.

UGLI FRUIT is a citrus variety that was discovered in Jamaica in 1914. It is slightly smaller than a grapefruit, and is most likely a spontaneous hybrid between a grapefruit and a tangerine. It has a rough, wrinkled and quite ugly skin, but the flesh is succulent and full of flavour.

KUMQUAT, *Fortunella margarita*, is a tiny oval citrus fruit (although some kumquats are round) that comes from China. The fruit is barely the size of a walnut, and it is eaten as a snack, skin and all. Kumquats are great to preserve and pickle with aromatic spices.

TANGERINE, *Citrus tangerina*, is an orange or reddish-orange citrus fruit. It is very tasty and easy to peel, but with quite a few seeds.

TANGELO, *Citrus x tangelo*, is a hybrid between a tangerine and a pomelo. The fruits are juicy and perfect to squeeze or to enjoy in fruit salads.

LEMONGRASS, *Cymbopogon citratus*, is obviously not a citrus fruit, but a type of tall grass from Southeast Asia, where it is an essential ingredient in many traditional dishes. Lemongrass is fresh-tasting and has a lovely lemony scent. To fully release its flavours, lightly bruise the thick lower end of each stalk. Then simply shred the lemongrass (if using it in a broth that will be strained), or place long pieces straight in the pot and remove them before serving.

Left, clockwise from top: Lemongrass; Small key limes and regular limes; A pomelo sliced in half; Citrus platter with red grapefruit, a large yellowish-green pomelo, tiny kumquats, kaffir limes, regular limes, mandarins, bitter oranges, lemons and oranges. Overleaf: Grapefruit; Grapefruit tonic label; Green oranges in Brazil

Lemonade or limeade

YOU WILL NEED:
200 ml water
90 g caster sugar
1 litre sparkling mineral water
2–3 small lemons or 4–5 limes
1 well-washed lemon or 2 limes,
  thinly sliced, to serve
crushed ice or ice cubes

• Bring the water to the boil. Put the sugar in a large, heat-resistant jug. Carefully pour in the hot water and stir until the sugar dissolves. Let cool. Squeeze the lemons or limes and pour in the juice. Taste and add extra sugar if needed. To serve, add the citrus slices, then pour in the mineral water and add plenty of ice.

Warm or cold sangria

YOU WILL NEED:
1 bottle (750 ml) red wine
5 tablespoons sugar, or to taste
1 well-washed lemon, sliced
1 well-washed orange, sliced
2 tablespoons cognac (optional)

WARM SANGRIA: Gently heat the wine (without boiling) and stir in the sugar. Add the sliced citrus fruits and cognac, if using. Set aside for 3–4 minutes and then ladle into glasses.

We often make sangria as an alternative to glühwein, and just add a piece of cinnamon stick.

COLD SANGRIA: Pour the sugar into a jug, pour in the wine and stir until the sugar dissolves. Add the lemon and orange slices.

The sangria can be laced with a touch of cognac, if you like, before serving it with plenty of ice.

Javanese limeade

YOU WILL NEED:
1 medium cucumber
juice of 5 limes (about 100 ml)
75 g sugar, or to taste
plenty of ice
1 litre sparkling mineral water

• Peel, halve and seed the cucumber. Squeeze the limes. Mix the cucumber, lime juice, sugar and ice in a blender. Pour in the mineral water and serve right away.

Barley water

This is an enduring favourite of ours, refreshing as both a table beverage and a thirst-quencher on a hot day.

YOU WILL NEED:
4 tablespoons pearl barley + 1 litre water
3 organic lemons
90 g caster sugar
2 litres water

• Boil the pearl barley in 1 litre of water for 30–40 minutes.

Meanwhile, scrub the lemons in hot water and dry them well. Peel off the yellow lemon peel using a potato peeler. Place the strips of lemon peel and the sugar in a stainless steel bowl. Set the lemons aside for now.

Bring 2 litres of water to the boil and pour it over the lemon peel. Pour in the cooked pearl barley, cooking water and all, and let cool. Squeeze the lemons and stir the juice into the mixture in the bowl. Strain and store in the fridge for no more than 5 days. Serve the barley water chilled, preferably without ice.

Creamy lemon and dill sauce

YOU WILL NEED:

1 organic lemon
300 g thick Greek yoghurt
1 tablespoon sweet mustard or honey mustard
1 small garlic clove, crushed
salt + a pinch of freshly ground black pepper
½ teaspoon herb salt
a large handful of fresh dill, chopped
2 tablespoons finely snipped chives

· Scrub the lemon in warm water and dry well. Grate the yellow lemon peel, avoiding the bitter white pith. Squeeze half the lemon. Combine the yoghurt with the mustard, garlic, salt, pepper, lemon juice and zest and the herb salt. Stir in the dill and chives at the end. A fresh-tasting all-round sauce with many uses, ideal with salmon or grilled fish.

Citrus and herb dressing

YOU WILL NEED:

1 tablespoon chopped fresh thyme leaves
2 tablespoons finely chopped fresh basil leaves
300 g thick Greek yoghurt
3 tablespoons olive oil
finely grated zest of 1 lime + ½ lemon
1 tablespoon fresh lime or lemon juice
salt + freshly ground black pepper
1-2 pinches of cayenne pepper
1 teaspoon honey, or to taste

· Finely chop the herbs (no stems) with a sharp knife. Combine with the yoghurt and all the other ingredients. Taste, season and let the flavours mingle for about 1 hour. This dressing goes beautifully with prawns, fish or barbecued meat.

Lemon mayonnaise

This lemon mayonnaise is simply terrific on freshly boiled asparagus, with seafood and much more. The trick to making great mayonnaise is to have all the ingredients at room temperature, and to pour the oil in very slowly at first. If you add garlic, the mayonnaise turns into aioli, a French classic to go with fish soup, or lamb with baked vegetables.

YOU WILL NEED:

2 egg yolks
1 teaspoon Dijon mustard
a touch of salt
a pinch of freshly ground white or black pepper
200-250 ml vegetable oil such as
  corn oil, or half vegetable oil
  and half mild olive oil
1 tablespoon fresh lemon juice, or to taste
½-1 tablespoon finely grated lemon zest (optional)

· Put the egg yolks, mustard, salt and pepper in a bowl. Slowly and carefully pour in the oil in a thin stream. Stir or whisk vigorously to let the yolks absorb all the oil before pouring in more. You will end up with a lovely thick mayonnaise. Season with lemon juice to taste, and stir in the lemon zest as well, if using. Taste, and adjust the seasoning if necessary.

LEMON AIOLI: This recipe is pretty much the same as for mayonnaise (above), except that you leave out the Dijon mustard and start by placing 2-3 peeled and sliced garlic cloves in a mortar. Sprinkle with a pinch of salt and pound the garlic well with the pestle. Add the egg yolks and slowly trickle in the oil, drop by drop. Stir or whisk vigorously. Season with freshly squeezed lemon juice, pepper and perhaps a bit more salt.

Lovely lemony beans

Large white beans, fresh citrus, lots of chopped dill and a little mint...

SERVES 4:
600 g home-cooked white beans (about 250 g
  dried beans) or 2 x 400 g tins large white beans
3 shallots, finely chopped
finely grated zest and juice of 1 organic lemon
2 teaspoons honey
a pinch of sea salt
freshly ground black pepper
3 tablespoons mild olive oil
a large handful of fresh dill, chopped
a small handful of fresh mint leaves, chopped

· Cook the white beans in a pan of boiling water until soft, or rinse the tinned beans well and let them drain. Put the beans in a bowl and add the chopped shallots.

Combine the lemon juice with the honey, salt, pepper and olive oil. Pour the dressing over the beans and gently fold in the dill, mint and lemon zest. Let the flavours develop for 30 minutes or so before serving.

Citrus-marinated olives

MARINATED OLIVES: Combine 300 g olives with the grated zest of 1 organic orange or lemon (or ideally a bit of both), 2 teaspoons dried thyme, 1 teaspoon dried chopped rosemary and 4-5 tablespoons good-quality olive oil. Stir and set aside to infuse for at least a couple of hours. First-rate finger food.

QUICK OLIVES: Add thin lemon slices or pieces to a bowl of olives and combine. Eye-catching and fresh-tasting at the same time!

A great hummus

If you have a food processor, this versatile chickpea dip is very easy to make. It will be tastier if you cook the chickpeas yourself: although you need to soak them overnight, it really isn't all that complicated. If time is of the essence, just use (well-rinsed) tinned chickpeas instead, and it will be delicious just the same.

HUMMUS FOR 4-5:
600 g home-cooked chickpeas (about 250 g
  dried chickpeas) or 2 x 400 g tins chickpeas
100-150 ml cooking liquid or water
about 1 teaspoon salt
3-4 tablespoons fresh lemon juice
3-4 tablespoons tahini (sesame paste)
a scant teaspoon ground cumin
3-4 tablespoons olive oil
1-2 garlic cloves, crushed
½ teaspoon sweet paprika + a drizzle
  of olive oil, to serve

· Soak the chickpeas for at least 12 hours in plenty of unsalted water. Discard the soaking water and boil the chickpeas in new water, lid on, until really soft. Don't use any salt in the cooking water. The cooking time is usually around 1½-2 hours. If using tinned chickpeas, simply rinse well in a colander, then drain.

Blend the chickpeas in a food processor until smooth, adding a *little bit* of the cooking liquid or water at a time. Season with the salt, lemon juice, tahini, cumin and olive oil. Last of all, add the crushed garlic to taste, and pulse for a few seconds more. Season to taste.

Hummus is excellent on various kinds of buffets, as a starter or as part of a meal with small meze dishes. Serve the hummus sprinkled with the paprika and drizzled with olive oil.

Sunny citrus salad

In the wintertime, this colourful and sunny salad lifts your spirits. Choose nice, juicy citrus fruits, and simply top with fresh mint leaves, rocket, baby spinach or a little fresh coriander.

FOR A LARGE PLATTER:
2 sweet oranges
1 pink grapefruit
2 tangerines
  or 1 blood orange
½ red onion, thinly sliced
sea salt flakes
freshly ground black pepper

DRESSING:
1 tablespoon red wine vinegar
1 teaspoon honey
3 tablespoons mild olive oil

· Combine the ingredients for the dressing. Peel the citrus fruits with a sharp knife, removing all the bitter white pith. Cut the fruit into slices and arrange them on a platter. Top with the thinly sliced onion and sprinkle with sea salt. Spoon over the dressing, grind a bit of black pepper on top and scatter with a few mint leaves or other leaves of your choice.

Lemony chickpea salad

This recipe is for a zesty chickpea salad with a hint of India. It's a nice accompaniment to chicken, grilled fish or as part of a vegetarian meal. (Photo, page 203)

SERVES 5-6:
600 g home-cooked chickpeas (about 250 g
  dried chickpeas) or 2 x 400 g tins chickpeas
5 boiled potatoes (about 400 g)
1 fresh red chilli
1 large red onion
1 organic lemon
½-1 teaspoon garam masala
a good pinch of sea salt
mild olive oil, to taste
a large handful of fresh flat-leaf parsley, chopped

· Cook the dried chickpeas until tender (see the method on page 199). Tip the chickpeas into a colander, rinse with cold water and drain well. If using tinned chickpeas, rinse them well.

Peel and dice the boiled potatoes. Deseed and finely chop the chilli, and peel and finely chop the red onion.

Scrub the lemon in warm water and dry well. Grate the yellow lemon peel, avoiding the bitter white pith. Squeeze the lemon juice.

In a salad bowl, combine the chickpeas and potatoes with the red onion, lemon zest, lemon juice (add half the lemon juice to start, then taste and add more if needed) and chilli. Sprinkle with the garam masala and a pinch of salt. Drizzle with olive oil and sprinkle with the chopped parsley, then gently toss to combine.

Pomelo and prawn salad

Pomelo is such a gorgeous fruit; it is used here in a Thai-inspired salad.

YOU WILL NEED:

1 large pomelo
250 g peeled and deveined prawns,
* raw or cooked*
30 g desiccated coconut
60 g unsalted peanuts
4 Asian shallots, thinly sliced
1 fresh red chilli, deseeded and sliced
crisp lettuce leaves
a handful of fresh mint leaves
a handful of fresh coriander leaves

DRESSING:

1 tablespoon fish sauce
1 small garlic clove, minced
2 tablespoons lime juice
1 teaspoon grated palm sugar

· Peel the pomelo by cutting off the coarse peel and removing all the bitter white pith. Break the membrane-free flesh into small pieces and set aside. Bring a bit of water to the boil in a large saucepan and cook the raw prawns (if using) for 2-3 minutes until cooked through. Drain and let cool.

In a dry frying pan, toast the coconut, stirring constantly, until lightly golden. Tip onto a plate to cool. Similarly, toast the peanuts in the frying pan. Set aside, then chop when cool.

Combine the dressing ingredients and season to taste. Prepare the shallots and chilli.

Assemble the pomelo, prawns, shallots and chilli on top of the lettuce leaves on a platter. Pour over the dressing and scatter with the toasted nuts and coconut, the torn mint and fresh coriander.

Fish on rosemary skewers

Citrus-scented fish skewers with fresh herbs for a summer meal. (Photo, page 203)

SERVES 4:

800 g firm white fish or salmon fillets,
* or a mix of both*
8 sturdy sprigs of rosemary, bottom leaves removed,
* or use small wooden skewers*
sea salt + freshly ground black pepper

FOR THE MARINADE:

1 tablespoon finely grated lemon zest
1 tablespoon finely grated orange zest
1 tablespoon finely chopped fresh lemon thyme
1 tablespoon finely chopped fresh rosemary
1 teaspoon honey
5 tablespoons olive oil

· Carefully remove any bones from the fish and then cut the fillets into large pieces.

Grate the lemon and orange zest and finely chop the herbs for the marinade. Combine all the ingredients for the marinade in a bowl, add the fish and cover with plastic wrap. Let the fish marinate for 1 hour or so in the fridge.

Meanwhile, prepare the rosemary sprigs, if you are fortunate enough to have some to spare, or soak the wooden skewers in water to prevent them burning.

Preheat a barbecue grill or chargrill pan. Gently push the skewers through the fish pieces, then barbecue or grill for about 3 minutes on each side, or until the fish is cooked through. Season with salt and pepper while cooking.

Ginger and lime ceviche, page 205

Easy summer tonnato, page 206

Lemony chickpea salad, page 200

Fish on rosemary skewers, page 201

Minced fish on lemongrass

Try these tasty fish skewers with a hint of lime, chilli and kaffir lime. The recipe may seem complicated but it's not, once you get started. If you prefer, you can shape the mince into patties and either barbecue or fry them in a bit of oil. (Photo, on the left)

FOR 6 SKEWERS:
400 g firm white fresh fish fillets
2 shallots, finely chopped
1 fresh red chilli, finely chopped
2–3 tablespoons chopped fresh coriander leaves
2 kaffir lime leaves, finely chopped
1 tablespoon fish sauce
juice of ½ lime
1 tablespoon caster sugar
2 tablespoons plain flour
a scant ½ teaspoon salt
1 egg white
6 lemongrass stalks

· Cut the fish into very small pieces, or pulse very briefly (or it will become tough) in a food processor. Place the minced fish in a bowl and add the shallots, chilli, coriander, lime leaves, fish sauce, lime juice, sugar, flour and salt. Stir gently until combined.

In another bowl, lightly beat the egg white and carefully fold it into the minced fish. Shape the mince into 6 balls (or flat patties), transfer them to a plate, then cover and refrigerate for a couple of hours.

Take the fish balls out just before grilling, then press the balls around the lemongrass stalks, reshaping the fish mince into oblong patties. Barbecue the skewers for a few minutes on each side and serve them straight away.

Ginger and lime ceviche

In this ceviche with an Asian twist, the fish and prawns are marinated in freshly squeezed lime juice and seasoned with chilli, kaffir lime leaves and ginger. A nice little appetiser. (Photo, page 202)

AS A STARTER FOR 4-6:
250 g salmon fillet, skinless and boneless
250 g firm white fresh fish fillets, skinless and boneless
juice of 10 limes
1 tablespoon vegetable oil
2 teaspoons fish sauce
3 lemongrass stalks
2–3 shallots
5 kaffir lime leaves + 5 extra for garnish
5–6 cm piece fresh ginger
1 fresh red chilli
300 g cooked prawns, unpeeled

· Cut the fish into small pieces and place the pieces snugly in a glass or ceramic bowl. Squeeze over the lime juice, making sure you cover all of the fish. Add the oil and fish sauce.

Trim and lightly bruise the lemongrass stalks and then cut them into 3-4 cm lengths. Peel and finely chop the shallots.

Carefully rinse the lime leaves and tear them in half. Peel and thinly slice the ginger, ideally with a mandoline slicer. Halve and deseed the chilli and then shred or cut it into thin slivers. Add everything (reserve a few lime leaves for later) to the bowl with the fish and lime juice.

Peel and devein the prawns and put them in the bowl. Cover and marinate in the fridge for at least 2-3 hours. Garnish with the reserved lime leaves before serving.

Easy summer tonnato

In this version of vitello tonnato – the Italian dish of roast veal slices covered in a tuna sauce with lemon and capers – we use pork or turkey fillets instead of veal. Fabulous buffet food, or as a main course for a summer dinner. (Photo, page 202)

SERVES 6-8:

800-900 g trimmed pork fillet
  or 2 turkey fillets (750 g)
a scant teaspoon salt
white or black pepper
1 tablespoon olive oil
1 tablespoon butter

TUNA SAUCE:

320 g tinned tuna in oil
4-5 tablespoons whole egg mayonnaise
3 anchovies
2 tablespoons capers + extra to garnish
2 tablespoons fresh lemon juice + extra to season
50 ml cooking juices + 50-100 ml water
lemon slices + fresh thyme for garnish (optional)

• If necessary, trim the pork fillet by cutting off the stringy white membrane. Cut the pork fillet into 15-20 cm lengths. If using turkey, the fillets can be fried whole.

Season the meat well with salt and pepper, and fry it in the oil and butter until nicely browned. Pour in a bit of hot water, perhaps 50 ml, then cover and continue to cook over low heat for 15-20 minutes. Reserve 50 ml of the cooking juices, wrap the meat in foil and allow to cool.

Thinly slice the meat on the diagonal, and arrange in a single layer (like roofing tiles) on a large serving platter.

Mix the drained tuna, mayonnaise, anchovies, capers and lemon juice to an almost smooth mixture or sauce in a food processor or with a stick blender. Dilute the sauce with the cooking juices from the meat and a little water. Season with a little more lemon juice if needed, then spoon the sauce over the meat.

Garnish with capers, and with some lemon slices and thyme if you like. Serve with boiled new potatoes and snow peas (mangetout).

Classic vitello tonnato

For a classic vitello tonnato, the veal can either be slowly simmered in a casserole dish or roasted in the oven like this. Estimate about 1.5 kg boneless joint of veal for 6-8 people.

• Preheat the oven to 225°C/435°F. Season the veal with salt and pepper. Place the meat snugly in a small ovenproof dish. Drizzle with about 2 tablespoons melted butter or olive oil. Place a meat thermometer in the veal, put it in the oven and let the meat brown nicely all over. Take the dish out a couple of times and turn the veal, so that it gets browned on all sides. This will take roughly 20 minutes.

Carefully pour about 200 ml dry white wine into the dish with the veal. Lower the heat to 175°C/345°F, and cook until the thermometer shows 68°C/155°F. Check occasionally; you may need to add a splash of water or wine towards the end of the cooking time.

Remove from the oven, cover with foil and allow to cool. Cut the roast into very thin slices, and then make the tuna sauce and proceed according to the previous recipe.

Osso buco

Another flavourful Italian classic: braised veal shanks in a savoury sauce, perfectly accentuated with gremolata, a fresh mixture of lemon, garlic and flat-leaf parsley.

SERVES 4-5:
4-6 thick slices of veal shank (1.6 kg)
a good pinch of sea salt
freshly ground black pepper
2 tablespoons butter or olive oil for frying
2 medium onions
1 medium carrot
150 g celeriac
3 tablespoons plain flour
400 g tin whole tomatoes
  or 6 medium fresh tomatoes, peeled
300 ml white wine
300 ml chicken or beef stock
2-3 tablespoons tomato paste (concentrated purée)
½ teaspoon caster sugar
2 teaspoons chopped fresh basil
1 bay leaf
gremolata (see following recipe)

· Season the meat with salt and pepper. Add half the butter or oil to a large cast-iron casserole dish, and slowly brown the veal a few slices at a time. Set the meat pieces aside.

Peel and finely chop the onions. Peel the carrot and celeriac and cut into neat cubes.

Sauté the vegetables in the remaining butter or oil in the dish. Return the meat to the dish and dust with flour. Stir to combine the flour, then add the tomatoes. Pour in the wine and stock, then add the tomato paste, sugar, basil and bay leaf. Bring to the boil and, if the dish has ovenproof handles and lid, place it in the oven at 190°C/375°F for about 1½ hours.

Otherwise you can continue cooking it on the stovetop with the lid on, over very low heat. Check the dish from time to time, and cook for about 1½ hours.

When the osso buco is cooked, gently stir in the gremolata and cook for 2-3 minutes more. Season with salt and pepper. This is lovely served the classic way, with saffron-scented risotto, or simply with fresh pasta and some grated parmesan.

Gremolata

This remarkably simple Italian mixture is usually stirred in at the last minute to flavour osso buco or other stews. But it can just as easily be used on freshly cooked cannellini or other beans, or to season a tomato sauce served with piping-hot pasta or grilled fish.

GREMOLATA FOR 4-6:
2 tablespoons finely grated lemon zest
1 bunch fresh flat-leaf parsley
  (about 20 g leaves)
1-2 garlic cloves

· Scrub the lemon in warm water and dry well. Finely grate the yellow lemon peel, avoiding the bitter pith. You will need 2 tablespoons of grated zest.

Combine the lemon zest with the finely chopped parsley and finely chopped or crushed garlic. Stir to combine. Add the gremolata as a last-minute seasoning to the dish of your choice.

Tarragon chicken with lemon and artichoke

We usually prepare this chicken with potatoes and a side salad, but sometimes we leave out the potatoes and serve it with pappardelle instead.

SERVES 4:

2 tablespoons olive oil
2 tablespoons butter
1 whole chicken (about 1.3 kg),
  jointed into 8 pieces
2 medium onions, chopped
4 garlic cloves, finely chopped
2 teaspoons salt
freshly ground black pepper
1 bay leaf
1 thin strip lemon peel
a scant teaspoon dried tarragon
400 g tin artichoke hearts
300 ml dry white wine
150 ml water
6 medium potatoes,
  peeled and quartered
300 ml pouring (single) cream
1 tablespoon chopped fresh flat-leaf parsley
1 tablespoon finely grated lemon zest
1 small bunch rocket, roughly chopped

• Heat half the olive oil and half the butter in a pot and brown the chicken pieces in batches until nicely coloured. Remove and set aside.

In the same pot, gently sauté the onion and garlic in the remaining oil and butter, then return all the chicken to the pot. Sprinkle with salt and pepper. Add the bay leaf and lemon peel. Sprinkle sparingly with tarragon.

Next, cut the artichoke hearts in half and add them to the pot. Pour in the wine and water. Bring to the boil, then lower the heat, cover and simmer for around 10 minutes.

Add the potatoes and then pour in the cream. Cover and simmer slowly for 20-30 minutes. Add the parsley and lemon zest, and cook for a few minutes more. Finish off by gently folding the roughly chopped rocket leaves into the stew. Serve with salad and crusty bread, or with pappardelle or other pasta.

Chicken limone

This is an easy recipe for lemon chicken in a pot, inspired by a trip to northern Italy. (Photo, on the right)

• Brown chicken pieces in some olive oil and butter until nicely coloured. Season with salt and pepper. Transfer the pieces to an ovenproof dish. Add some leek sliced on the diagonal, tender zucchini (courgettes) in pieces, a few lemon wedges (the lemon must be really ripe and yellow, or it may taste bitter) and a handful of whole, lightly bruised garlic cloves. Drizzle with a little olive oil, pour in 200 ml chicken stock and 4-5 tablespoons white wine mixed with a trickle of honey. Put a few sprigs of fresh lemon thyme or regular thyme in between the vegetables. Bake at 200°C/400°F for about 30 minutes, or until cooked through. Serve with a green salad, potatoes or a plain risotto.

Lamb and apricot tagine

We serve this hearty Moroccan lamb dish with couscous, a dollop of yoghurt and a large green salad.

SERVES 4-6:

2 tablespoons olive oil
2 tablespoons butter
1.5 kg lamb with bone, in pieces
3 medium onions, chopped
8 garlic cloves, finely chopped
1 medium carrot, sliced
1-2 teaspoons salt
½ teaspoon freshly ground black pepper
¼-½ teaspoon cayenne pepper
2 bay leaves
1 teaspoon ground cumin
1 teaspoon dried ginger
1 small cinnamon stick
500 ml chicken stock
60 g sultanas
10 dried apricots, halved
400 g tin chickpeas, rinsed and drained
2 tablespoons honey
2 tablespoons tomato paste (concentrated purée)
½ Moroccan preserved lemon or
   ¼ ripe lemon, in thin slices

· Heat half the olive oil and butter in a pot and brown the meat in batches. Set aside on a plate. Gently sauté the onion and garlic in the remaining oil and butter in the pot, then return the meat to the pot and add the carrot. Season with salt and pepper. Add all the other spices, pour in the stock and stir in the sultanas, apricots, chickpeas, honey and tomato paste.

Cover and cook gently for about 1½ hours, adding the lemon slices after 1 hour. Towards the end of cooking time, check if the meat is tender; the stew may need another 30 minutes or so until done. Serve with couscous.

Casserole from Gotland

A lovely aroma fills the kitchen when we make this lamb casserole. It's quite easy to prepare, full of flavour and has a nice touch of lemon.

SERVES 4-5:

1 kg boneless lamb, in cubes
3 tablespoons plain flour mixed with 1½ teaspoons salt
   + ½ teaspoon freshly ground black pepper
2 medium onions
3 medium carrots
about 2 tablespoons olive oil
400 ml lamb or beef stock
300 ml white or red wine
2-3 tablespoons tomato paste (concentrated purée)
15-20 small potatoes (400 g)
1 small rosemary sprig
5 garlic cloves, chopped
grated zest of ½ lemon
½ teaspoon caster sugar (optional)
a large handful of fresh flat-leaf parsley, chopped

· Coat the meat pieces with a mixture of flour, salt and pepper. Set aside.

Peel and roughly chop the onions and cut the carrots into pieces. Pour the olive oil into a large pot and gently sauté the onion for around 5 minutes, then add the carrot. Add the meat to the vegetables and stir. Pour in the stock and wine and add the tomato paste. Bring to the boil, then lower the heat, cover and simmer over low heat for 1-1¼ hours.

Add the potatoes towards the end of cooking time, together with the rosemary and garlic. Cook until the potatoes are fork-tender. Season with a touch more salt and pepper, lemon zest and perhaps a hint of sugar. Sprinkle generously with chopped parsley and bring to the table.

Greek lamb in lemon sauce

A nice and mild lamb stew, with a refreshing taste of lemon and dill.

SERVES 4-6:
1.5 kg boneless lamb
2-3 medium carrots, in pieces
1 large onion, in wedges
2 tablespoons olive oil
200-400 ml water (start with 200 ml)
sea salt + freshly ground black pepper
300 ml dry white wine
2 small bay leaves
1 small sprig of rosemary
3 eggs
juice of 1-1½ ripe lemons (6 tablespoons)
a handful of fresh dill, chopped

• Start by cutting the meat into 3 x 4 cm pieces. Prepare the vegetables.

Heat a frying pan with the olive oil and fry the meat in batches until nicely browned. Transfer the meat to a heavy-based casserole dish or pot. Deglaze the frying pan by adding about 200 ml water, and stir well. Pour the juices into the dish, and add the carrots and onion. Season the stew with salt and freshly ground black pepper.

Add the white wine, followed by the bay leaves and rosemary. Bring to the boil and then lower the heat. Cover and allow the meat to slowly simmer for 45-60 minutes, or until the meat is really tender. Dilute with a bit more water towards the end of the cooking time.

Remove the meat and vegetables using a slotted spoon, and keep warm under foil. Strain and reserve the cooking liquid.

Lightly beat the eggs in a bowl, and while whisking, pour in the hot cooking liquid, a little at a time. Pour the mixture back into the dish and simmer very gently over low heat so that the sauce doesn't separate (which it will if you let it boil). Stir continuously.

Season the sauce with the lemon juice, salt and possibly a bit more black pepper, and then put the warm meat back in.

Garnish with a sprinkling of chopped dill (or use parsley if you prefer), and serve with boiled rice or plain potatoes and a leafy green salad.

Lemon potatoes from Patmos

Simple and delicious potato wedges with lemon and oregano, flat-leaf parsley and garlic. Lovely with fish or meat, or with feta cheese, sun-ripened tomatoes, tzatziki and crusty bread.

• Preheat the oven to 200°C/400°F. Peel 8-9 large waxy potatoes. Cut them in half lengthwise, then cut each half into three long wedges. Arrange them in a single layer in a roasting tin or other ovenproof dish. Season with sea salt flakes and freshly ground black pepper, and sprinkle with a good pinch of dried oregano. Add 2-3 sliced garlic cloves.

Combine 3 tablespoons lemon juice with 3 tablespoons olive oil, and pour half of the liquid over the potato wedges, saving the rest.

Bake the potato wedges for about 30 minutes, or until golden (increase the heat a bit towards the end if the potatoes are too pale). Drizzle with the reserved lemon oil and scatter with chopped fresh flat-leaf parsley. Serve while hot. Serves 4

Overleaf: Old-style lemon mousse, page 220; Torta della Nonna, page 214

Torta della Nonna

Torta della Nonna, or Grandma's cake, is a fabulous Italian creation with raspberry jam and grated lemon zest. (Photo, page 213)

PIE CRUST DOUGH:
1 organic lemon
150 g butter, at room temperature
2 egg yolks
70 g caster sugar
180 g plain flour

FILLING:
200 g raspberry jam
350 g ricotta cheese or thick Greek yoghurt
80 g caster sugar
2 medium eggs
50 g pine nuts

· Scrub the lemon in warm water and dry well. Finely grate the yellow lemon peel.

For the dough, stir together the soft butter with the egg yolks, then add the sugar, flour and half of the lemon zest (reserve the rest for the filling). Use a floured thumb to press the dough into 6-8 individual pie tins, or one large fluted 22-24 cm pie tin. Prick the dough with a fork and chill for at least 30 minutes.

Meanwhile, preheat the oven to 175°C/345°F. After refrigerating, prebake the pie shell or shells for 12-15 minutes. Allow to cool.

Gently spread out a fairly thin layer of jam in the pie shell(s).

In a bowl, combine the ricotta or yoghurt with the sugar, eggs and the rest of the lemon zest. Distribute the mixture on top of the jam and sprinkle with the pine nuts. Bake the small pies for about 25 minutes, and the one large pie for 35 minutes, or until lightly golden. Serve completely cooled.

Creamy lime pie

Lime provides a mild yet well-rounded citrus flavour to this tasty pie, which is wonderful as a dessert or just with a cup of tea. Top the pie with fresh strawberries or blueberries and dust with sifted icing sugar for a more festive look.

DOUGH FOR A PIE SERVING 6:
180 g plain flour
3 tablespoons caster sugar
175 g cold butter, in cubes

FOR THE CREAM:
juice of 5 limes (100 ml)
3 medium eggs
180 g caster sugar
200 ml pure (whipping) cream

· To make the dough, measure out the flour and sugar in a food processor. Add the butter and quickly work into a dough. Tip the dough straight into a non-stick 22-24 cm springform tin, and use floured fingers to press the pastry well into the tin. Prick the base with a fork. Put the tin in the freezer while you prepare the rest of the pie.

Cut the limes in half, squeeze the juice and measure out the right amount. Preheat the oven to 175°C/345°F and prebake the cold pie shell for 10-15 minutes, or until very lightly golden.

Meanwhile, whisk together the eggs, sugar and lime juice in a bowl (the mixture may look a bit odd, but it will work itself out in the oven). Pour the lime mixture into the prebaked pie shell and bake for another 30 minutes. *Note!* Lower the heat to 160°C/320°F when about 10 minutes cooking time remains.

Lemon delicious

This is our version of the sweet and tart lemon pudding, which we serve with cream and sometimes garnished with a little caramelised lemon peel on top. (Photo, page 219)

SERVES 6:

2 tablespoons butter for the dish(es)
2 organic lemons
50 g butter
3 medium eggs
200 g sugar
4 tablespoons plain flour
100 ml full-fat milk
pouring (single) cream, to serve

· Preheat the oven to 180°C/350°F. Grease 1 large or 6 individual ovenproof dishes with soft butter. Finely grate the peel of 1 lemon and juice 2 lemons. Melt the butter.

Separate the eggs into two bowls. Whisk the egg whites lightly, add 2 tablespoons of the sugar and continue whisking until the egg whites are stiff and shiny. Set aside.

Whisk the egg yolks with the rest of the sugar until fluffy. Add the lemon zest, flour, milk, melted butter and, lastly, the lemon juice to the egg yolk mixture.

Fold in about half of the egg whites and then carefully add the rest. Pour the batter into the dish or dishes.

Bake for 15 minutes if using small dishes, and 30-35 minutes for one large dish. The pudding should turn lightly golden when cooked. Allow to cool slightly and serve with the cream.

Crema catalana

Crema catalana is a much-loved Spanish dessert – it resembles crème brûlée, but is flavoured with citrus and cinnamon under its crunchy caramelised sugar crust. A real treat!

SERVES 4:

½ organic lemon or orange
4 egg yolks
100 g caster sugar
600 ml full-fat milk
100 ml pure (whipping) cream
2½ tablespoons cornflour
1 small piece cinnamon stick
1 teaspoon vanilla essence
3-4 tablespoons sugar for the crust

· Wash and dry the lemon or orange, and cut thin strips of the outermost peel with a sharp knife or potato peeler. Set aside. Whisk the egg yolks and sugar, and set aside.

Put the milk, cream and cornflour into a saucepan. Add the citrus peel and cinnamon stick and bring to the boil. Set aside to infuse for about 10 minutes.

Remove the cinnamon stick and citrus peel, put the saucepan back on the stovetop and bring the milk to the boil once more. Lower the heat to the lowest setting. Stir in the egg yolk mixture and vanilla essence. Simmer over very low heat, stirring continuously until the cream thickens.

Pour the mixture into individual, ovenproof dishes and let cool. You can prepare the recipe up to this point one day in advance.

Just before serving, preheat the oven grill. Sprinkle the puddings with a bit of sugar, and grill until the crust turns brown and starts to bubble (or use a chef's blowtorch to do this). Serve as soon as the sugar is caramelised.

Vanilla citrus salad

Fresh and tangy citrus fruits dressed in vanilla-scented syrup.

• Bring 150 ml water to the boil with ¼ vanilla pod and 3-4 tablespoons sugar. Simmer the syrup, uncovered, for about 5-6 minutes, and then flavour with a splash of fresh orange juice. Set aside to cool.

Peel and cut out membrane-free segments from 2 sweet navel oranges, 1 pink or white grapefruit and perhaps a tangerine or two. Arrange the fruit in small glasses, drizzle with the syrup and garnish with fresh mint. Serves 4

Oranges with pomegranate

This is a striking and fairly effortless dessert with exotic flavours. You can find halva in Middle Eastern or Greek speciality food stores. (Photo, page 218)

• Use a knife to peel a few sweet oranges, removing all traces of bitter white pith, and then slice and arrange them on a platter. Place pomegranate seeds (all the bitter white membrane removed) in a small bowl, combine with just a hint of orange-blossom water, a dusting of cinnamon and a little sugar or honey, to taste. Sprinkle the pomegranate seeds over the oranges, and add some roughly chopped unsalted pistachios as well. Then finish by scattering with small cubes of halva.

Left: Passionate oranges

Passionate oranges

Oranges and passionfruit complement each other beautifully. This luscious and healthy dessert is quite a favourite of ours, and it's a breeze to make.

• Carefully peel really sweet oranges, removing the bitter white pith with a sharp knife. Slice and arrange the oranges in a single layer on a platter, and spoon the pulp of a few perfectly ripe passionfruit on top. Done!

Moroccan oranges

Sweet oranges with crunchy almonds and a light dusting of cinnamon.

SERVES 4:
5-6 sweet oranges
75 g unblanched almonds
3 tablespoons honey
a scant ½ teaspoon ground cinnamon
sifted icing sugar

• Use a sharp knife to peel the oranges, leaving no traces of the bitter white pith. Thinly slice the oranges and arrange them on a large serving platter or dish.

Roughly chop the almonds and lightly toast them in a dry frying pan. When the almonds start to colour, it's time to trickle over the honey. Keep stirring for just a minute or so, until the honey caramelises around the almonds. Tip onto a non-stick baking sheet and leave to cool.

Just before serving, lightly dust the orange slices with cinnamon, scatter with the honeyed almonds and sift the icing sugar on top. This is especially nice with vanilla ice cream.

Oranges with pomegranate, page 217

Simple citrus yoghurt deluxe, page 222

Lemon delicious, page 215

Stunning saffron oranges, page 220

Stunning saffron oranges

This somewhat unusual dessert with exciting flavours has become one of our absolute favourites. A friend of ours created the recipe one Christmas, but the oranges can be enjoyed all year round. Serve them with a dollop of lightly whipped cream. (Photo, pages 184 and 219)

SERVES 4:
6–7 large, sweet and juicy oranges, preferably navel oranges
lightly whipped cream, to serve

SPICY SYRUP:
200 ml water
180 g caster sugar + an extra pinch
a pinch of saffron threads
3 star anise
1 small cinnamon stick
4 whole cloves (optional)

· Start by using a sharp knife to cut the peel off the oranges, removing the bitter white pith as well. Then segment the oranges (see page 187) and place them in a bowl.

To make the syrup, bring the water and sugar to the boil in a small saucepan. Let it bubble for a couple of minutes without a lid. Lightly grind the saffron with the extra pinch of sugar in a mortar, and add to the syrup. Add the star anise, cinnamon stick and cloves, if using. Let the syrup continue to simmer, uncovered, for another 5 minutes. Let it cool a little and then pour the syrup over the orange segments. Set aside and leave to steep for at least 1 hour before serving the saffron oranges with lightly whipped cream.

Old-style lemon mousse

This old-fashioned and virtually forgotten dessert is very pretty when served in individual glasses, or tipped onto a plate and topped with seasonal berries. (Photo, page 212)

SERVES 6–8:
1 large lemon
3 medium eggs
5 gelatine leaves or a scant 1 tablespoon gelatine powder
160 g caster sugar
300 ml pure (whipping) cream

· Scrub the lemon in warm water and dry well. Finely grate the yellow lemon peel (you only need the grated zest from half of the lemon). Squeeze the juice.

Separate the egg yolks and egg whites into two bowls. Soak the gelatine leaves in cold water for 5 minutes. *Note!* If using powdered gelatine, see below.

Beat the egg whites until almost stiff, then add 2 tablespoons of the sugar and continue beating until stiff. Set aside for now.

Beat the egg yolks with the rest of the sugar until fluffy. Stir in the lemon juice and zest.

Drain the gelatine leaves and dissolve them in a small saucepan with 50 ml water over low heat. If using the gelatine powder, dissolve in 100 ml hot water. Stir the dissolved gelatine into the fluffy egg yolks. Lightly whip the cream and fold it in as well. Carefully fold the beaten egg whites into the mixture.

Pour the mousse into glasses, rinsed with cold water. Refrigerate for 3–4 hours, or until the next day if possible, before serving.

Mousse with limoncello

When you want a small yet luxurious dessert, this one is easy to whip up. You will need lemon curd – either homemade using the recipe on the right, or good-quality store-bought – and a bit of sweet Italian lemon liqueur.

SERVES 8:
250 g mascarpone
150 ml lemon curd
200 g low-fat crème fraîche (15%)
2 tablespoons fresh lemon juice
1-2 tablespoons honey
1 egg white
2 tablespoons limoncello (lemon liqueur)
crushed amaretti biscuits, to serve

· Combine the mascarpone and lemon curd, both at room temperature, with the crème fraîche. Flavour with the lemon juice and honey.
  Beat the egg white until stiff and then carefully fold into the mascarpone mixture. Spoon into small individual glasses, cups or bowls. Top with a small splash of limoncello, then sprinkle with crushed amaretti biscuits.

Irresistible lemon curd cream

A fabulous and quick lemon cream to serve with strawberries, blackberries or other summer berries, or with a fruit salad, or on top of the Lemon pavlova with berries on page 338.

· Combine 300 g thick Greek yoghurt with about 100 ml room-temperature lemon curd, and sift in a little icing sugar, to taste.

Lemon curd

This British classic is lovely on biscuits with a cup of tea, as a luscious cake filling or in the desserts on the left.

YOU WILL NEED:
3 organic lemons
200 g sugar cubes + 80 g caster sugar,
  or 280 g caster sugar
150 g butter, at room temperature
6 eggs, lightly beaten

THE CLASSIC WAY: Wash and dry the lemons well. Over a small stainless steel saucepan, roughly rub the sugar cubes against the lemon peel until the sugar starts to dissolve into the pan. Add the extra 80 g sugar.

THE EASY WAY: Measure out 280 g caster sugar into a medium stainless steel saucepan. Wash and dry the lemons, then finely grate the zest of 2 lemons, and add the zest to the sugar.

IN BOTH CASES, CONTINUE THIS WAY: Squeeze all 3 lemons. Pour the juice into the saucepan with the sugar, add the soft butter in pieces and the lightly beaten eggs.
  Place the smaller saucepan into a larger one, partly filled with hot water (a bain marie/double boiler) and simmer until the cream begins to thicken. Stir constantly with a wooden spoon. *Note!* Never allow the curd to boil; it should only simmer very gently.
  Ladle the lemon curd into perfectly clean jam jars. Close the lids tightly and store in the fridge. Lemon curd is perishable because of the eggs, so don't store it for more than 2 weeks.

Pancakes with lime

Next time you make thin pancakes or crêpes, try serving them with lime wedges and sweetened condensed milk (from a tin). Simply drizzle a bit of condensed milk over the pancakes, squeeze over some lime juice and dust with a bit of caster sugar. Roll up and enjoy!

Alternatively, serve the pancakes with squeezed lemon or lime and a little sugar.

Lime-marinated berries

Lime and berries are such a wonderful match, and a hint of lime can really enhance all kinds of berries, such as strawberries in slices or chunks, blueberries or juicy blackberries.

For 500 g berries, use the juice and grated zest of 1 large lime and about 3 tablespoons sifted icing sugar, or to taste.

· Wash and dry the limes well. Finely grate the peel. Tip the berries into a bowl, squeeze over the lime juice, dust with icing sugar and then sprinkle with lime zest. Taste to see if you need a bit more icing sugar. Serve the berries with vanilla ice cream or just vanilla yoghurt. Or serve on top of a cheesecake or mousse.

Right: Pancakes with lime and condensed milk

Simple citrus yoghurt deluxe

It doesn't get any easier than this! And the citrusy yoghurt is simply delectable on raspberries, blueberries or strawberries; or merely on its own, chilled in small glasses and served with almond biscotti or a wafer. (Photo, page 218)

WITH LEMON: Combine 300 g thick Greek yoghurt with about 4-5 tablespoons sifted icing sugar and the finely grated zest of 1 well-washed organic lemon. Serves 3-4

WITH LIME: Combine 300 g thick Greek yoghurt with about 4-5 tablespoons sifted icing sugar and the finely grated zest of 1-2 well-washed limes. Add extra sugar if needed, to taste.

WITH ORANGE: Combine 300 g thick Greek yoghurt with about 4-5 tablespoons sifted icing sugar and the finely grated zest of 1 well-washed organic orange.

Fragrant lime sugar

Wash 2-3 limes in warm water and dry well. Grate the outermost green peel using a fine grater. Combine the zest with 100 g caster sugar in a jar. Delicious sprinkled over fresh strawberries, blueberries, pineapple or mango, or on a tropical fruit salad.

nuts and
seeds

our graceful old walnut tree…

… gives us so much joy. Its leaves usually don't come until early summer, but once they do, they are large, lush green and beautifully jagged. Some years the huge tree is literally covered with thousands of walnuts, and others it barely yields a handful. In good years, we indulge in all kinds of delicacies and have walnuts drying in baskets all over the house. The nuts may be slightly smaller than the Mediterranean ones, but they are full of flavour and pleasant crunchiness. We use them in desserts and biscuits, of course, but also in salads, breads, pasta dishes and sauces, giving everything that rich, slightly coarse, walnut flavour.

Nuts and seeds are exceptionally wholesome. They are meant to give life to new plants and are loaded with energy. They contain the best kind of fat and plenty of vitamins and minerals. Eating nuts and seeds on a regular basis can help lower your cholesterol, and they are a great source of B vitamins and vitamin E. Make sure you use only perfectly fresh nuts and seeds, and enjoy them either as they are or gently toasted at home. Many store-bought nuts are heavily salted, and contain additives and hydrogenated fats. It's easy to make healthier snacks and delicious seed mixes yourself, and the combinations are practically endless.

Above: Pecans; Freshly toasted Brazilian cashews. Left, clockwise from top: Pistachios, salted pumpkin seeds and other mixed nuts; Pine nuts from Siberian cedar trees; Walnuts from our garden and some almonds from the local market; Spicy almonds with garlic, page 235

cashews, pecans, pistachios and almonds…

WALNUTS, *Juglans regia*, grow on tall, magnificent trees, with the brown-shelled nuts hidden inside bright green fruits. The walnut tree is thought to have grown wild in Asia Minor, and then spread to large parts of Europe and all the way to China. Wild walnuts have been gathered from time immemorial, but eventually walnuts began to be cultivated in Persia (present-day Iran), among other places. They soon became widely popular, and in Ancient Greece, walnuts and walnut oil were common goods. The nut became a fertility symbol to the Romans, whose tradition was to throw walnuts at newlyweds to wish them luck. Walnuts were also grown early on in China, where walnut farming continues to this day. The true European walnut enthusiasts were the French, who still cultivate many lovely varieties, and the French word for nut, *noix*, also became synonymous with the walnut. Walnuts yield a very tasty oil, which is fabulous in dressings. Fresh, undried walnuts are delicious preserved or pickled, which is a common sweet in the Middle East, or enjoyed as they are with a nice, creamy cheese. Walnuts are terrific in salads, bread, baked goods, sweets and desserts. However, they can quickly turn rancid at room temperature, and should preferably be stored in the fridge or even the freezer. Walnuts are regarded as one of the 'superfoods' because of their high levels of antioxidants and valuable fatty acids.

PECANS, *Carya illinoinensis*, are native to North America and are related to walnuts. Pecans have a shiny, reddish shell, and the nut itself resembles an oblong walnut. It is cultivated primarily in the United States and Mexico, but also grows wild. Pecans are sweet and mild, and are mainly used in desserts, sweets and ice cream.

ALMONDS, *Prunus dulcis*, are the seeds of a lovely flowering tree that is native to Afghanistan and Iran, and is closely related to the peach tree. Botanically, the almond is not a true nut, but is termed a 'drupe'. The almond fruit resembles a fuzzy little bluish-green peach, inside which the nut itself is encased in a hard shell. Almonds have been cultivated for at least 7000 years. The tree spread from western Asia to the Mediterranean region, and these days both Spain and Italy are avid almond cultivators. Almonds are a rich source of many essential nutrients, including vitamin E and magnesium.

HAZELNUTS, *Corylus avellana*, are native to Europe and Asia Minor, and although hazel trees grow wild in many areas, Turkey is one of the largest producers of cultivated hazelnuts. The nuts grow inside small fibrous husks on a large shrub, and the shells eventually become brown and hard. Hazelnuts are used in baked goods, confectionery, nougat and desserts, but are also great in salads and bread, and a little hazelnut oil can really boost a salad dressing.

PISTACHIOS, *Pistacia vera*, are precious green nuts that have been cultivated for thousands of years in the Middle East and Mediterranean regions. The pistachio grows inside a hard, almond-shaped shell that splits open at one end when the nut is ripe. Pistachios are often used in pilaf rice and desserts from the Middle East and India, but also in Italian mortadella sausage, cassata and pistachio ice cream. Large-scale pistachio production currently exists in Iran, Turkey and California, as well as in Italy and Australia.

PINE NUTS, *Pinus*, are actually the seed kernels found in the cones from certain pine trees. These pines (conifers) are native to many regions around the world, which is why pine nuts are used in a variety of ways in different local cuisines. For instance, pine nuts are a given ingredient in Italian pesto, Turkish dolmas and Tunisian tea, and they are also marvellous in a pie filling, sprinkled over a salad or on a cake.

PEANUTS, *Arachis hypogaea*, aren't nuts at all, but leguminous plants with flowering stalks that bend down and force their way underground for the pods to mature. The peanut originally came from South America, and was brought to Europe by Columbus and other explorers, and then spread around the world. Today peanut farming is a massive industry in the United States, China and India. Peanuts and peanut oil are used in many cuisines worldwide.

MACADAMIA NUTS are round, white, delicious nuts native to Australia. The nuts grow in clusters on evergreen trees, *Macadamia integrifolia* and *M. tetraphylla*. The Aborigines had known about these exquisite nuts for thousands of years, but they were otherwise unknown until a couple of botanists came across them in the mid 1800s. At the end of the 19th century, the nut was taken to Hawaii, which is now the largest macadamia nut producer in the world. Macadamia nuts are high in fat, which is why they can go rancid quickly. The nuts are often used in desserts, ice cream and biscuits, or eaten as a snack.

CASHEW NUTS, *Anacardium occidentale*, grow on medium-sized tropical trees. Believed to be native to Brazil, cashew nuts are now produced all over the tropics. The nuts hang under a large, edible fruit called a cashew apple, which in some countries is just as popular as the nut itself. Cashew nuts are appetising, kidney-shaped nuts that are wonderful toasted, and very popular in Southeast Asian and Indian cooking.

BRAZIL NUTS, *Bertholletia excelsa*, obviously come from Brazil, primarily from the Para region. The nuts themselves are actually the seeds of one of the tallest trees in the Amazon rainforests, and are only harvested from wild trees. Brazil nuts grow inside large fruits the size of a football, with each fruit containing up to 25 nuts, and are eaten as snacks and used in baked goods.

and a few tasty seeds...

SESAME SEEDS, *Sesamum indicum*, originate from Africa, and have been cultivated for a very long time. The word 'sesame' allegedly goes all the way back to the Egyptian word *sesemt*. Sesame seeds were taken to India very early on, and are now grown in many parts of the world. Unpeeled sesame seeds can be white, black, brown, red or yellow, and grow in oval-shaped pods on a tall, annual plant. The seeds are used in cooking, bread and baked goods in many different cultures, and are also pressed into oil and ground into tahini, a sesame paste, which is a staple of Middle Eastern cuisine.

PUMPKIN SEEDS, *Cucurbita pepo*, when peeled are pale green seeds that are excellent in salads, breads or in muesli, while salted, unpeeled pumpkin seeds are a popular snack around the Mediterranean. Pumpkin seeds contain a number of essential vitamins and minerals.

SUNFLOWER SEEDS, the tasty and nutty seeds from the sunflower, *Helianthus annuus*, are also very rich in vitamins and minerals. Toast and sprinkle the seeds on a salad, or enjoy them lightly salted as a snack. Sunflower seeds are also great in muesli, breads, cakes or biscuits.

Right, from top left: Sesame salt, page 234; Black sesame seeds; Cashew fruits in Brazil

An aromatic broth with noodles, page 171   *Nuts and seeds for a salad*

Chicken salad from Laos, page 245

Crunchy carrot salad, page 245

Toasting nuts and seeds

Toasted nuts and seeds are equally enjoyable whether sprinkled over a salad, on plain yoghurt or in desserts.

IN A FRYING PAN: Place the nuts or seeds in a warm, dry frying pan. Toast them gently over medium heat, stirring frequently. *Note!* Some nuts and seeds, such as sesame seeds, toast very quickly and can easily burn. Others, such as pine nuts, take longer at the start and then suddenly toast very rapidly. Don't overfill the pan — it's better to toast them in batches in a single layer. Once the nuts or seeds are nicely coloured, tip them onto a plate and leave to cool.

IN THE OVEN: Whole hazelnuts, cashew nuts and almonds turn out better when toasted in the oven. Spread the nuts out on a baking tray and toast them at 200°C/400°F for about 8 minutes, or until golden brown. Allow the nuts to cool on a plate.

Toasted seed mix

BREAKFAST MIX: Toast equal parts sunflower seeds and pumpkin seeds in a dry frying pan. Leave to cool on a plate and then combine with I part whole linseeds, roughly chopped dried apricots or figs, and some raisins or sultanas. Store in an airtight jar. Delicious sprinkled on natural yoghurt or a fruit salad.

SALAD MIX: Toast equal parts unpeeled sesame seeds, peeled sunflower seeds and pumpkin seeds in a dry frying pan. Stir in a pinch of crumbled sea salt flakes, let cool on a plate and store in an airtight jar. Perfect for leafy green salads or crudités.

Crunchy oat mix

This all-natural muesli is great with creamy yoghurt or scattered over a fruit salad.

FOR ONE BATCH:
100 g almonds or walnuts
100 g peeled sunflower seeds
250 g organic rolled oats
90 g raw (demerara) sugar
150 ml water
3 tablespoons vegetable oil
  (not olive oil)

• Preheat the oven to 200°C/400°F. Roughly chop the almonds or walnuts. Combine the chopped nuts in a bowl with the sunflower seeds, rolled oats and sugar.

  Mix the water and oil, splash it over the oat mix and then squeeze with your hand to lightly moisten the muesli. Line a large baking tray with non-stick baking paper and spread the muesli on top.

  Toast in the oven for 25 minutes, or until golden, stirring occasionally. Remove the tray from the oven and allow the muesli to cool. Store in an airtight jar for up to I month.

Sesame salt

Sprinkle a pinch of this sesame salt over a potato and leek soup, or perhaps on an avocado sandwich. (Photo, page 231)

• Toast 100 g white sesame seeds in batches in a dry frying pan (don't overfill the pan). Leave to cool, then grind with 3-4 teaspoons of sea salt in an electric spice grinder, or use a mortar and pestle. Store the sesame salt in an airtight jar.

Indian chilli nuts

YOU WILL NEED:
2 tablespoons vegetable oil
1 teaspoon ground turmeric
1-2 teaspoons garam masala
¼ teaspoon chilli powder
200 g almonds, blanched and peeled
200 g cashew nuts
1-2 teaspoons sea salt flakes
6-7 small dried chillies for garnish
  (optional)

• Heat the oil in a wok or frying pan and add the turmeric, garam masala and chilli powder. Stir and then add the almonds and cashews. Sauté for 4-5 minutes over medium heat while stirring. Crumble over the sea salt flakes and stir again. Pour the nuts into a bowl and let cool. Garnish with the dried chillies if you like.

Holiday mixed nuts

YOU WILL NEED:
1 egg white
200 g almonds, blanched and peeled
100 g walnuts
50 g raw (demerara) sugar
½ teaspoon ground cinnamon
½ teaspoon ground ginger
½ teaspoon ground cardamom

• Preheat the oven to 200°C/400°F. Lightly whisk the egg white in a bowl until slightly foamy. Stir in the almonds and walnuts, then place on a baking tray lined with non-stick baking paper. Combine the sugar and spices and sprinkle the mixture over the nuts. Toast for 10-12 minutes until the almonds are nicely coloured. Tip them onto a plate and cool.

Salted almonds

YOU WILL NEED:
200 g almonds
½-1 tablespoon vegetable oil
1 teaspoon fine salt (iodine-free)

• Preheat the oven to 200°C/400°F. Blanch and peel the almonds (bring some water to the boil in a saucepan, add the almonds and let them boil for just 1 minute, then drain in a colander. Peel by squeezing them out of their skins). Put the almonds in a small bowl, pour over the oil and stir until coated. Spread the almonds on a baking tray lined with baking paper and toast in the oven for 10-12 minutes, or until nicely coloured. Sprinkle with the salt and stir to combine. Cool on a plate.

Spicy almonds with garlic

YOU WILL NEED:
1 tablespoon chopped fresh rosemary (optional)
200 g almonds, blanched and peeled
1 tablespoon olive oil
1 teaspoon dried rosemary
a scant ½ teaspoon cayenne pepper
1 teaspoon crumbled sea salt
1 teaspoon brown sugar or raw (demerara) sugar
1 garlic clove, crushed

• Preheat the oven to 200°C/400°F. Finely chop the fresh rosemary leaves, if using. Mix the almonds and olive oil in a small bowl. Add all the other ingredients and stir well, making sure to coat the almonds with the spices.

  Spread the almonds out on a baking tray lined with non-stick baking paper, and toast them in the oven for 10-12 minutes, or until golden brown. Tip the almonds onto a plate and leave to cool. (Photo, page 226)

Chèvre and walnut nibbles

These nibbles are truly tasty and absolutely effortless — and always a hit at parties.

• Finely chop perfectly fresh walnuts. Remove the rind of a tasty soft goat's cheese or, if using chèvre covered in a thin layer of ash, you can use the entire cheese.
  Roll the cheese into grape-sized balls. Pour the chopped walnuts onto a plate and then roll the cheese balls in the nuts until they are coated all over.

Cheese, nuts and dried fruit

Both pleasant and simple, and perfect with a glass of wine. Decorate the cheese platter with a few pretty leaves (we like to use pear or grape leaves, or just a large walnut leaf or two).

• Arrange dried fruit on a platter, perhaps some apricots, figs or a few dates on a twig. Place a few small bowls of nuts (such as fresh walnuts, toasted almonds and pecans) on the table as well. Add a couple of flavourful cheeses, for instance Taleggio, a piece of Brie de Meaux or a rustic country goat's cheese.

Right: The sweet-tasting nutty fruit bread; Chèvre and walnut nibbles; Manchego cheese and dates on a twig

Nutty fruit bread

This slightly sweet fruit bread is easy to bake, and is a perfect match with mild blue cheese, tasty Vacherin or an aged, peasant-style hard cheese.

FOR 1 LOAF:
soft butter + a little flour for the tin
150 g wholemeal flour
250 g plain flour
2 teaspoons salt
2 level teaspoons bicarbonate of soda
80 g sultanas
8 dried apricots, roughly chopped
6 dried figs, roughly chopped
150 g walnuts or hazelnuts
500 g natural yoghurt
100 ml treacle or honey

• Preheat the oven to 160°C/320°F. Grease a loaf tin (about 1.5 litre capacity) and dust with a little flour. Line the base of the tin with a piece of non-stick baking paper.
  In a bowl, combine both types of flour with the salt and bicarbonate of soda. Stir in the sultanas, dried fruit and walnuts or hazelnuts. Lastly, pour in the yoghurt and the treacle or honey, and work into a sticky dough. Pour the dough into the prepared tin.
  Bake for about 1 hour 35 minutes. Allow the bread to cool slightly before you knock it out of the tin and wrap it in a thick tea towel to cool completely. You can serve the fruit bread once cool, but it's better if you let it rest for 24 hours in a plastic bag (tea towel and all).

Olive and almond biscotti

These rather unusual, savoury biscotti are good to nibble on, perhaps with a glass of wine. The quickest way to make the dough is to use a food processor.

FOR ABOUT 450 G THIN BISCOTTI:
30 good-quality black olives
2 tablespoons red wine vinegar
1 tablespoon fresh lemon juice
1 tablespoon caster sugar
1 heaped teaspoon salt
4 tablespoons olive oil
1 medium egg
200 ml lukewarm water
about 350 g plain flour
  + some for sprinkling
1½ teaspoons baking powder
60 g almonds

• Preheat the oven to 200°C/400°F. Line a baking tray with non-stick baking paper.

If you don't have pitted olives, pit them with a small sharp knife. Put half of the pitted olives in the food processor, and reserve the rest. Add the vinegar, lemon juice, sugar, salt, oil, egg and water. Pulse quickly to chop the olives into little pieces.

Mix the flour with the baking powder and add both. Work into a dough, adding a bit more flour if the dough seems too sticky.

Tip the dough onto a lightly floured surface, flatten it by hand and scatter with the almonds and reserved olives. Quickly knead the dough to work in the olives and almonds. Divide the dough into four pieces, and roll them into thin lengths (about as long as the baking tray). Put the dough lengths onto the tray.

Place the tray in the middle of the oven and bake for 25 minutes. Remove the tray and allow the lengths to cool completely.

Use a sharp knife to thinly slice the lengths. Arrange the slices in a single layer on two baking trays lined with baking paper. Toast at 190°C/375°F for about 10 minutes, or until lightly golden.

Let the biscotti cool on the tray, and then store in airtight jars once cooled. It will take an additional 24 hours for the flavours to truly develop.

WITH PESTO: Add 100 ml pesto to the dough instead of olives, or use both olives and pesto, a great combination. If so, you will need about 50 g more flour, but otherwise just follow the recipe.

WITH ANCHOVIES: Make the dough with olives, but only use ½ teaspoon salt. Add 1 tin (50 g) anchovies in oil (discard the excess oil), and mix with the olives in the food processor as per the recipe. You might need a little more flour.

Sesame cream cheese

Spread this cream cheese mix on thin crackers as a little appetiser.

• Toast 5 tablespoons sesame seeds (see page 234), and then set aside 2 tablespoons of the seeds. Combine the remaining sesame seeds with 200 g Philadelphia cream cheese at room temperature and 2-4 teaspoons soy sauce.

Spread the cheese on crackers and sprinkle with the reserved sesame seeds.

Poppy seed breadsticks

These crispy breadsticks dusted with sweet paprika, mixed seeds and grated cheese provide a pleasant crunch alongside a soup, or simply with a welcome drink.

FOR ABOUT 30 BREADSTICKS:
1 egg
200 g plain flour
½ teaspoon salt
150 g fridge-cold butter, in cubes
3 tablespoons water + 1 teaspoon vinegar
2 tablespoons black poppy seeds
3 tablespoons sesame seeds
1 teaspoon sweet paprika
4 tablespoons grated parmesan
  or cheddar cheese

· Preheat the oven to 180°C/350°F. Crack the egg into a glass and beat lightly with a fork. You will need half the egg for the dough, and the other half for brushing the breadsticks.

Measure out the flour, salt and butter into a food processor, and pulse into a crumbly mixture. Add just about half the egg plus the water mixed with the vinegar, and quickly pulse into a dough.

Place the dough between two pieces of non-stick baking paper and roll it into a large square. Transfer everything to a baking tray and pull off the top paper. Brush the dough with the rest of the beaten egg.

Sprinkle a mix of poppy and sesame seeds, paprika and cheese on top. Cut the dough into thin strips, no more than 2 cm wide, but don't separate them until after baking. Cut once across as well, or the breadsticks will be too long. Bake for about 25 minutes. Leave to cool on the tray, and then break the breadsticks apart.

Mini crispbread crackers

You can vary the seeds on these little crackers, which are ideal for cheese platters.

FOR ABOUT 80 CRACKERS:
300 ml lukewarm water
4 tablespoons olive oil
25 g fresh (compressed) yeast
1 teaspoon salt
1 tablespoon sugar
175 g wholemeal flour
60 g rye flour
175 g plain flour
1 teaspoon baking powder
1 lightly beaten egg white for brushing
3-4 tablespoons each of sesame seeds,
  sunflower seeds, pumpkin seeds and linseeds
a small pinch of sea salt

· Mix the lukewarm water with the oil. Crumble the fresh yeast into a bowl, sprinkle with the salt and sugar, and pour in a bit of the warm water. Stir to dissolve the yeast, then pour in the rest of the water. Add all of the flour combined with the baking powder and work into a smooth dough. Cover and let it rise until doubled in size, which will take about 1 hour.

Preheat the oven to 225°C/435°F. Tip the dough out onto a lightly floured surface and knead gently. Divide the dough into three pieces, and then thinly roll out each piece. Use a knife or pastry wheel to cut out square crackers, roughly 4 x 4 cm. Place the crackers on a baking tray lined with non-stick baking paper and prick them with a fork. Brush with the egg white and sprinkle with the combined seeds and a touch of salt. Bake the crackers in the middle of the oven for 10-12 minutes. Allow them to cool on the tray.

Walnut bread from Gotland

A rustic bread with a delicate walnut flavour. A few drops of walnut oil in the dough gives an added dimension, but make sure the oil is perfectly fresh.

25 g fresh (compressed) yeast
200 ml lukewarm water
200 g thick Greek yoghurt
175 g wholemeal flour

YOU WILL ALSO NEED:
another 200 ml lukewarm water
2 heaped teaspoons salt
3 tablespoons honey
3 tablespoons walnut or olive oil
100 g whole walnuts
550 g plain flour + 100-150 g extra

· Crumble the yeast into a bowl, pour over the lukewarm water and stir until the yeast dissolves. Add the yoghurt and flour and stir once more. Cover and let stand for 1 hour.

Next, combine the dough with the lukewarm water, salt, honey and oil. Add the walnuts and the 550 g of flour, and then work the dough briskly with a wooden spoon. Work in the rest of the flour, cover and let rise for about 1 hour.

Turn out the dough onto a lightly floured work surface and knead gently with floured hands. Shape into a large loaf and place it on a baking tray lined with non-stick baking paper. Let the loaf rise for 30 minutes.

Preheat the oven to 250°C/480°F. Score the bread with a knife and bake for 10 minutes at first, then lower the heat to 160°C/320°F and bake for another 40 minutes or so. Let the bread cool under a tea towel.

Sunday breakfast buns

These wholesome breakfast buns are a cinch to make. Just let the dough rise, turn it out and cut it into pieces.

FOR 12 BUNS:
25 g fresh (compressed) yeast
2 tablespoons honey
1 heaped teaspoon salt
400 ml lukewarm water
50 g walnuts or sunflower seeds
4 tablespoons linseeds (optional)
40 g rolled oats
75 g crushed wheat
550 g plain flour

· Crumble the yeast into a bowl. Drizzle with the honey and sprinkle with the salt. Pour in some of the lukewarm water and stir to dissolve the yeast. Pour in the rest of the water and add the walnuts or seeds, linseeds if using, oats and crushed wheat. Stir again, then add the flour and work into a loose dough. Cover the bowl and let the dough rise for about 1 hour.

Preheat the oven to 250°C/480°F. Grease a baking tray or line it with non-stick baking paper. Turn out the dough onto a work surface liberally sprinkled with flour, as the dough will be quite loose. Sprinkle a bit of flour on top of the dough and lightly flatten it with your hand. Use a sharp knife or dough scraper to cut the dough into 12 even-sized square pieces, then transfer them to the baking tray. Leave to rise for 10-15 minutes.

Place the tray in the middle of the oven and bake for 12-15 minutes. If you want a crispy crust, let the buns cool on a wire rack. If you prefer softer bread, cover the buns with a tea towel while cooling. The buns also freeze well.

Bread from Sacré Cœur

We once bought fabulous bread flavoured with fennel seeds and cumin from a little bakery in Paris, near Sacré Cœur. We don't know how the baker on rue Lepic baked his bread, but this comes quite close.

FOR 8-10 MINI BAGUETTES:
4-5 tablespoons each of sunflower
  and sesame seeds
2 tablespoons black poppy seeds
2 teaspoons whole cumin seeds
2 teaspoons whole fennel seeds
25 g fresh (compressed) yeast
2 scant teaspoons salt
600 ml lukewarm water
2 tablespoons olive oil
650-700 g plain flour
  + extra for sprinkling
1 egg white, lightly beaten, for brushing

· Measure out all the seeds and spices into a cup. Stir them and set aside.

Crumble the yeast into a bowl. Add the salt and some of the water, and stir to dissolve the yeast. Pour in the rest of the water, oil and half of the seed mix. Add almost all the flour and work into a smooth dough, adding a bit more if necessary. Cover and let rise for about 1 hour.

Line two baking trays with baking paper. Turn out the dough onto a floured surface and knead gently. Divide the dough in half and cut each half into 4 or 5 pieces, shaping each one into a thin mini baguette. Let the baguettes rise on the trays for about 25 minutes. Preheat the oven to 250°C/480°F. Brush the bread with the beaten egg white and sprinkle with the remaining seeds.

Bake for 10 minutes, then lower the heat to 150°C/300°F and bake for another 5 minutes, or until nicely golden. Cool under a tea towel.

Summertime bread

We bake this bread nearly every day in the summer, when many of us gather around the dining table. One day we'll add hazelnuts or walnuts to the dough, the next we might throw in both sunflower and sesame seeds instead.

FOR 1 LARGE LOAF:
25 g fresh (compressed) yeast
2 teaspoons salt
1 tablespoon honey
500 ml lukewarm water
100 ml milk
2 tablespoons olive or walnut oil
100 g wholemeal or rye flour
150 g hazelnuts or walnuts
  or 120 g sunflower seeds
600 g plain flour + extra for sprinkling
40 g sesame seeds and/or sunflower seeds
  for baking

· Crumble the yeast into a bowl, sprinkle with salt and add the honey. Pour in a little bit of the lukewarm water and stir to dissolve the yeast. Pour in the rest of the water, milk and all the other ingredients (except for the sesame or sunflower seeds). Knead until the dough comes together, then set it aside to rise for 1-1½ hours at room temperature.

Preheat the oven to 260°C/500°F. Sprinkle a bit of extra flour, the sesame seeds and/or sunflower seeds on the work surface. Turn out the dough and shape it into a single loaf.

Bake the bread for 10 minutes, then reduce the heat to 180°C/350°F and bake for another 30 minutes. Let the bread cool on a wire rack.

Right: Delicious summertime bread, baked here with hazelnuts, sunflower seeds and sesame seeds

Warm lentil salad with walnuts

For added crunch, this satisfying salad can be topped with crispy bacon bits, but is equally tasty without them.

SERVES 4-6:
350 g green lentils or Puy lentils
1 organic chicken or vegetable stock cube
1 bay leaf
2 sprigs of fresh flat-leaf parsley
2 tender sprigs of fresh thyme
2-3 hard-boiled eggs
100 g bacon, in pieces (optional)
3-4 tablespoons good-quality olive oil
2 tablespoons red wine vinegar
2 tablespoons walnut oil (optional)
a scant teaspoon sea salt
freshly ground black pepper
4 shallots, peeled and chopped
1 small garlic clove, crushed
a handful of flat-leaf parsley, chopped
frisée, watercress or rocket for garnish
100 g walnuts, very roughly chopped

· Soak the lentils in cold water for 1 hour. Discard the soaking water, and cook the lentils in fresh water with the stock cube, bay leaf, and the parsley and thyme sprigs. Soaked lentils often only need 15-20 minutes to cook, so watch them carefully to avoid overcooking. Boil the eggs. Fry the bacon pieces if using, and drain them on paper towels.

Drain the lentils, then return them to the saucepan and drizzle with the olive oil, vinegar and walnut oil, if using. Season with salt and pepper, and fold in the shallots, garlic and chopped parsley. Transfer to a large platter and garnish with the leafy greens, walnuts and bacon pieces. To finish, add half a boiled egg per person and serve with crusty bread.

A colourful bean salad

A filling, multi-coloured salad, ideal for a light lunch, with a barbecue or to accompany roast lamb or chicken.

SERVES 4-6:
4-5 tablespoons sesame seeds
  or 50 g pine nuts
600 g home-cooked beans, such as large white beans,
  cannellini beans and small black beans (about 250 g
  dried beans)
  or 2 x 400 g tins mixed beans
1 large bunch rocket
2 carrots
1 red capsicum (pepper)
2 avocados
200 g fridge-cold crumbled soft goat's cheese
mild red wine vinegar for drizzling
olive oil for drizzling
sea salt + freshly ground black pepper

· Start by toasting the sesame seeds or pine nuts in a dry frying pan until lightly golden. Leave to cool on a plate.

Pour the home-cooked or tinned beans into a colander and rinse with cold water. Drain well and tip them into a large salad bowl.

Rinse and trim the rocket leaves, and put half of them in the bowl. Peel and cut the carrots into very thin matchsticks (julienne strips), dice the capsicum and dice the avocado. Place half of each in the salad bowl with the beans and gently fold to combine. Add the remaining rocket leaves, avocado and carrot strips.

Finally, crumble the goat's cheese on top and scatter the remaining capsicum over the top. Drizzle with the vinegar and olive oil, and season to taste with salt and pepper. Garnish with the toasted sesame seeds or pine nuts.

Crunchy carrot salad

This is a weekday favourite of ours, jam-packed with wholesomeness. (Photo, page 233)

YOU WILL NEED:
5 tablespoons sesame seeds
100 g sunflower seeds
4 carrots
a splash of red wine vinegar + olive oil
a pinch of sea salt

· Toast the sesame seeds in a dry frying pan (see page 234). Set aside. Toast the sunflower seeds as well.

Peel and cut the carrots into very thin matchsticks (julienne strips). It requires a bit of effort, but using thinly cut carrots really makes a difference.

Place the carrot strips in a bowl, drizzle over the vinegar and olive oil and sprinkle with the toasted seeds and a little sea salt. Toss and serve right away.

Sesame snow peas

Crisp, fresh snow peas go beautifully with barbecued or stir-fried pork or chicken.

· Toast 3 tablespoons sesame seeds in a dry frying pan, then set aside. Make a dressing by combining 1 tablespoon vinegar, a scant ½ teaspoon salt, 2 tablespoons sunflower oil and 2 teaspoons sesame oil.

Rinse, top and tail 400 g fresh snow peas (mangetout). Slice them quite thinly on the diagonal and place the strips in a bowl. Sprinkle with the toasted sesame seeds, spoon over the dressing and serve more or less at once.

Chicken salad from Laos

An enticing, crunchy salad inspired by a trip to Laos. (Photo, page 233)

SERVES 4–5:
100 g unsalted cashew nuts or peanuts, chopped
4 tablespoons white sesame seeds
2 poached skinless chicken breasts (see below)
  or ½ barbecued chicken
½ cucumber, in cubes or sticks
4–5 Asian shallots, finely chopped
1–2 fresh red chillies, deseeded and chopped
a handful of fresh mint leaves, torn

DRESSING:
2 tablespoons fish sauce
2–3 tablespoons fresh lime juice
1 heaped teaspoon grated palm sugar
2 teaspoons sesame oil

· Toast the chopped cashews or peanuts in a dry frying pan, and then do the same with the sesame seeds (separately). Set aside.

Shred or tear the chicken into small strips. Rinse and prepare all the vegetables. Combine the chicken, cucumber, shallots and chilli in a bowl. Add half of the torn mint leaves and almost all of the toasted nuts and seeds.

Make the dressing in a small bowl, season to taste and pour it over the salad. Toss gently, then top with the reserved nuts, sesame seeds and a few torn mint leaves. Serve at once.

TO POACH CHICKEN: Trim 2 chicken breasts and place them snugly in a saucepan. Add 500 ml chicken stock and 5 peppercorns. Bring to the boil and simmer, covered, for 10 minutes. Remove from the heat and leave in the hot liquid for 15 minutes more.

Goat's cheese tart with pine nuts and roasted red capsicums

A savoury puff pastry tart with goat's cheese, pine nuts, fresh herbs and roasted red capsicums. The tart can be prepared a day ahead, and just reheated in a 175°C/345°F oven for 10 minutes or so before serving.

SERVES 4-5:
2-3 roasted red capsicums (peppers)
375 g puff pastry
1 tablespoon olive oil
4 tablespoons chopped fresh thyme
1-2 tablespoons chopped fresh rosemary
250 g fridge-cold soft goat's cheese
about ½ teaspoon sea salt flakes
a pinch of freshly ground black pepper
4 tablespoons pine nuts
1 egg, lightly beaten

· Begin by roasting and peeling the capsicums (see the recipe on the right).
  Preheat the oven to 200°C/400°F. Cover a baking tray with non-stick baking paper, and set aside for now.
  On a lightly floured work surface, roll out the puff pastry into a 3 mm thick rectangle or circle (depending on the type you are using). Place the pastry on the lined baking tray.
  Softly score a line 1 cm inside the outer edge of the puff pastry, *without* cutting all the way through. Brush a little olive oil on the pastry (inside the scored edge), leaving the outer edge unbrushed. Place wide strips of the roasted capsicum on the tart, leaving the edge unfilled, and scatter with some of the chopped thyme and rosemary.

Crumble the goat's cheese over the capsicum, season with the sea salt and freshly ground black pepper, and sprinkle with the pine nuts and the remaining herbs. Brush the outer, unfilled edge with the beaten egg.
  Bake the goat's cheese tart in the middle of the oven for 25-30 minutes, or until the edges are golden. Enjoy the tart while still warm or just cooled; it's an excellent little starter or light meal with leafy greens.

Roasted red capsicums

Capsicums (peppers) are amazingly sweet and mild when oven-roasted. They are lovely served on their own as a tapas dish, with just a few drops of olive oil, mild sea salt and perhaps a handful of black olives. Roasted capsicums are also delicious on bruschetta, or in a bean or lentil salad, such as the one from Arles on page 97. And simply terrific in the goat's cheese tart, on the left.

· Preheat the oven to 225°C/435°F. Halve, core and deseed some red capsicums (peppers). Arrange the capsicum halves (skin-side up) on a baking tray brushed with olive oil or lined with non-stick baking paper, and bake for about 30 minutes.
  Remove the tray from the oven and cover with foil, to keep the capsicum moist and warm. Leave for 20 minutes or so, then peel by simply pulling off the skin. Cut the capsicums into wide strips and allow to cool.

Cannelloni with ricotta

This comforting cannelloni dish is filled with ricotta, lemon, walnuts and spinach.

SERVES 4:
1 batch tomato sauce (page 42)
250 g baby English spinach
250 g ricotta cheese
1 tablespoon finely grated lemon zest
2 tablespoons olive oil
sea salt + freshly ground black pepper
50 g walnuts, chopped
50 g parmesan cheese, grated
1 garlic clove, crushed
about 300 g fresh lasagne sheets
25 g butter + extra for greasing the dish

· First make the tomato sauce and set it aside. Rinse and trim the spinach leaves. Bring lightly salted water to the boil in a saucepan, add the spinach, cover and cook for just 1 minute. Tip the spinach into a colander and rinse with cold water. Drain well, squeeze to remove any excess water and place the spinach in a food processor. Add the ricotta, lemon zest, olive oil, salt, pepper, walnuts and approximately half the parmesan cheese. Pulse, then add the crushed garlic and pulse once more.

Preheat the oven to 200°C/400°F. Grease an ovenproof dish with soft butter. Pour in half of the tomato sauce. Place the lasagne sheets on a lightly floured surface and place a line of 2-3 tablespoons of the ricotta filling in the middle of each sheet. Moisten the edges with water and then roll or fold together. Place the rolls, seam-side down, on top of the tomato sauce, preferably in a single layer. Cover with the rest of the sauce, the remaining parmesan and dot with the butter. Bake for about 25 minutes. Serve with a green salad.

Spaghetti from Verona

A rich and hearty pasta with mushrooms, porcini, fresh basil and pine nuts or walnuts.

SERVES 4:
40 g pine nuts or
  75 g walnuts, roughly chopped
10 g dried porcini mushrooms (ceps)
100 ml hot water
200 g fresh mushrooms
1 small onion
2 tablespoons olive oil or butter
200 ml pure (whipping) cream
sea salt flakes + freshly ground black pepper
pecorino or parmesan cheese, grated, to serve
about 20 fresh basil leaves, torn

· Toast the pine nuts in a dry frying pan (the walnuts don't need to be toasted, only roughly chopped), and set aside. Crumble the dried porcini mushrooms into the hot water and set aside to soak. Trim and roughly chop the fresh mushrooms, and finely chop the onion.

In a frying pan, sauté the onion for a few minutes in the olive oil or butter, add the mushrooms and sauté for 4-5 minutes. Pour in the cream, plus the porcini and their soaking liquid. Cook for 3-4 minutes, season with sea salt and freshly ground black pepper, to taste. Stir in the pine nuts or walnuts.

Toss the mushroom sauce into steaming hot spaghetti or pappardelle. Serve topped with grated cheese, torn basil leaves and a good grinding of black pepper.

Overleaf: Mette's hazelnut biscotti, page 250; Turrón, Spanish almond nougat, a store-bought delicacy

Mette's hazelnut biscotti

This is how our Danish aunt Mette always baked her sweet rusks. (Photo, page 248)

FOR ABOUT 70 SMALL BISCOTTI:
100 g hazelnuts
250 g butter, at room temperature
200 g caster sugar
½ teaspoon pure vanilla extract
¼ teaspoon salt
550 g plain flour
2 teaspoons baking powder
200 ml full-fat milk
1 medium egg

• Preheat the oven to 200°C/400°F. Roughly chop the hazelnuts, then set aside. Cream the butter, sugar, vanilla and salt until fluffy in a food processor.

Combine the flour and baking powder, and gradually add it to the mixture, alternating with the milk and the egg. Add the chopped hazelnuts. At this point, it's easier to turn out the dough onto a lightly floured surface and work the hazelnuts into the dough by hand.

Divide the dough into eight pieces. On a lightly floured surface, shape the pieces into lengths, flatten a bit with your hand and place them on baking trays lined with baking paper.

Bake for about 20 minutes. Allow the lengths to cool for 15 minutes or so, and then cut them into roughly 3 cm pieces with a serrated knife. Dry into rusks at 100°C/200°F for 1-2 hours.

CHOCOLATE NUT BISCOTTI: Follow the recipe above, but when adding the nuts, also add 75 g chopped dark chocolate (70%).

Almond biscotti

This recipe comes pretty close to the Italian original, although it's always a bit tricky to achieve that perfect crunchy-yet-soft biscotti crust. Nonetheless, these biscotti always turn out a real treat.

FOR ABOUT 80 BISCOTTI:
3 medium eggs
180 g caster sugar
¼ teaspoon salt
1 tablespoon finely grated orange zest
½ teaspoon bitter almond extract
100 ml mild olive oil
350 g plain flour
1 teaspoon baking powder
200 g whole almonds
egg wash (1 egg lightly beaten with
* 1 teaspoon sugar + 1 tablespoon water)*

• Preheat the oven to 190°C/375°F. Beat the eggs and sugar until fluffy. Add the salt, orange zest, almond extract, oil and, last of all, the flour mixed with the baking powder. Work into a dough, then turn out onto a lightly floured surface. Knead in the whole almonds with a bit of extra flour.

Divide the dough into three pieces, and shape each into a long roll. Transfer the rolls to a baking tray lined with non-stick baking paper and brush liberally with the egg wash.

Bake for 30 minutes. Allow the lengths to cool for about 15 minutes, then use a serrated knife to slice them into roughly 2 cm pieces. Transfer the pieces, cut-side up, onto lined baking trays. Dry into rusks at 100°C/200°F for 1 hour or a bit more.

Tosca pie with walnuts

A delicious caramel and walnut pie, which actually freezes well. Excellent party fare.

DOUGH:
120 g plain flour
1 tablespoon caster sugar
75 g cold butter, in cubes
2 tablespoons cold water

FILLING:
200 g walnuts
120 g caster sugar
2 tablespoons plain flour
2 tablespoons golden syrup
75 g butter, at room temperature
2 tablespoons milk

· To make the dough, combine the flour and sugar, ideally in a food processor. Add the butter and pulse into a crumble. Pour in the water and quickly work into a dough. Place the dough in the fridge for 30 minutes.

Preheat the oven to 190°C/375°F. Toast the walnuts on a baking tray for 5-7 minutes, then remove from the oven and set aside.

Roll out the dough until nice and thin, and press it into a 20-22 cm loose-based fluted pie tin. Place the pastry shell in the oven and bake for 12-15 minutes.

In the meantime, prepare the caramel. In a small saucepan, measure out the sugar, flour, golden syrup, butter and milk. Gently melt the mixture while stirring, never allowing it to boil. Last of all, stir in the toasted walnuts. Pour the mixture into the pie shell and bake for 15 minutes, or until nicely golden.

Frangipane tart with fruit

You can use many kinds of fruit to fill this French almond tart: cherries, plums, apricots, nectarines, peaches, pears...

DOUGH:
150 g plain flour
2 tablespoons caster sugar
125 g cold butter, in cubes
1 egg yolk (reserve the egg white)
1 tablespoon water

FILLING:
800 g pitted cherries, or 8 medium plums
  or apricots in halves, or 3 cored pears
  or 3-4 nectarines in large wedges
100 g caster sugar
50 g butter, melted
2 medium eggs
100 g almonds, blanched and ground
1-2 tablespoons cognac (optional)

· Sift the flour into a bowl and add the sugar. Add the butter and use your fingers to crumble everything together. Next, add the egg yolk and water and quickly work into a dough. Use floured fingers to press the dough into a 22-24 cm loose-based pie tin. Place the tin in the freezer for 10 minutes.

Preheat the oven to 200°C/400°F and then prebake the cold pastry shell for 15 minutes. Meanwhile, prepare the fruit.

Make the filling by stirring together the sugar and melted butter. Add one egg at a time, followed by the reserved egg white and then the ground almonds. If you like, add a splash of cognac. Arrange the fruit in the pie tin, pour over the almond mixture and bake for 30-35 minutes at 180°C/350°F.

Crisp butterscotch thins

Delicate, brittle wafers with flaked almonds. Sometimes we use these thins to liven up a fruit salad – making it instantly more sophisticated – or simply serve them with ice cream.

FOR ABOUT 40 THINS:
150 g butter
130 g caster sugar
3½ tablespoons golden syrup
3½ tablespoons milk
3 tablespoons plain flour
50 g flaked almonds

· Slice the butter and put it in a small saucepan together with the sugar, golden syrup, milk and flour. Wait before you add the almonds.

Preheat the oven to 200°C/400°F. Line two baking trays with non-stick baking paper. Carefully melt and *just* bring the butterscotch mixture to a gentle simmer, never allowing it to boil. Take the pan off the heat and fold in the flaked almonds.

Drop the butterscotch mixture by the spoonful (about 1 tablespoon each) onto the prepared trays. Bake in the middle of the oven for 5-6 minutes, or until golden. *Note!* Watch the butterscotch thins carefully, as they burn quite easily. Allow the thins to cool a little before lifting them off the paper with a spatula.

Store in an airtight container with non-stick baking paper between the layers. The wafers will keep for up to 2 weeks.

Almond blueberry muffins

These luscious pastries are neither Swedish *mazarines* nor regular muffins, but something in between. Bake them in a non-stick muffin tin for 10-12 muffins or use individual baking tins. (Photo, page 255)

YOU WILL NEED:
soft butter for the tin
150 g butter
2 tablespoons finely grated lemon zest
100 g almonds, blanched
130 g sifted icing sugar
2 medium eggs
90 g plain flour
about 200 g blueberries

· Grease a 12-hole muffin tin with a bit of soft butter. Slowly melt the butter for the dough and set aside. Finely grate the lemon peel. Preheat the oven to 190°C/375°F.

Grind the blanched almonds in an almond grinder, or use a food processor with a steel blade. (If so, add a bit of the icing sugar halfway through grinding to make them less oily.) Tip the ground almonds into a large bowl.

Stir in the icing sugar and lemon zest, and then add the eggs, one at a time, stirring vigorously after each egg. Add the flour and then the melted butter. Stir to combine the mixture, then pour it into the greased muffin tin. Place a few blueberries on top of each muffin. Bake for 15-20 minutes. Cool slightly in the tin before carefully tipping them out. Store the muffins in an airtight container or freeze them for up to 1 month.

Mallorcan almond chews

Irresistible, chewy almond biscuits with a hint of orange. This recipe came about during a trip to Mallorca, where the almonds are simply fabulous. (Photo, page 254)

FOR ABOUT 40 BISCUITS:
200 g almonds
150 g sifted icing sugar + extra for dusting
1 tablespoon finely grated orange zest
2 medium egg whites (see note)
30 g flaked almonds

· Blanch and peel the almonds. Use a food processor to make the dough: grate the almonds with the shredding disc, stop the machine and switch to the steel blade. Now add half of the icing sugar, and mix until the almonds are finely ground (the sugar makes the almonds less oily). Stop the machine once more and add the rest of the icing sugar, the orange zest and the (unbeaten) egg whites. Mix briefly.

Preheat the oven to 180°C/350°F. Line two baking trays with non-stick baking paper. Drop heaped teaspoonfuls of almond dough onto the prepared trays, with the help of a second teaspoon. Scatter the flaked almonds over each biscuit.

Bake the biscuits in the middle of the oven for 11-12 minutes. When slightly cool, dust with extra sifted icing sugar and allow them to cool completely.

Note! Don't use egg whites from large eggs: it will be too much, and the biscuits will flatten and spread during baking.

Festive almond slices

These crispy puff pastries are topped with cream cheese, apricot jam and almond paste. (Photo, page 254)

FOR 12-15 PASTRIES:
200 g almond paste or marzipan
100 g Philadelphia cream cheese,
  at room temperature
60 g sifted icing sugar + extra for dusting
½ teaspoon pure vanilla extract
1 lightly beaten egg (half for the mixture,
  half for brushing)
375 g puff pastry
100 ml apricot jam
50 g flaked almonds

· Coarsely grate the almond paste or marzipan. Mix the almond paste with the cream cheese, icing sugar, vanilla and half the egg, either by hand or with a stick blender. Set aside.

Preheat the oven to 200°C/400°F. Line a baking tray with non-stick baking paper. Roll out the puff pastry until 3 mm thick. Cut the pastry into two rectangles, about 25 x 15 cm, and transfer them to the baking tray. Fold up the edges of the long sides of each pastry sheet. Spread a thin layer of apricot jam over the pastry, then spread a layer of the almond and cheese mixture on top. To finish, brush the pastry edges with the rest of the lightly beaten egg, and sprinkle the flaked almonds over the filling. Bake for 20-25 minutes, or until nicely coloured. Cool before cutting into pieces and dusting with sifted icing sugar.

Mallorcan almond chews, page 253

Festive almond slices, page 253

Walnut baklava, page 256   *Almond blueberry muffins, page 252*

Walnut baklava

Sweet little pastries filled with walnuts, pistachios, honey and cinnamon. Divine in small doses. (Photo, page 255)

FOR ABOUT 24 BAKLAVA:
100 g butter
4 tablespoons caster sugar
¾ teaspoon ground cinnamon
75 g unsalted pistachios,
  finely chopped
    + 2–3 tablespoons, extra, finely chopped
75 g walnuts, finely chopped
4 large sheets filo pastry
120 ml honey
100 ml water
1 thin ribbon of lemon peel
1 small cinnamon stick
1 tablespoon fresh lemon juice

• Preheat the oven to 180°C/350°F. Melt the butter over low heat, then use some of the butter to grease a small baking tray, about 30 x 20 cm, and set the remaining butter aside. Blend the sugar and cinnamon with the chopped nuts and set aside as well.

Carefully spread out a sheet of the delicate filo pastry (long side horizontal), brush with the melted butter and place another sheet on top. Cover the rest of the filo with a slightly damp tea towel (otherwise the filo will dry up and break apart).

Spread about half of the filling all across the buttered filo sheet, nearly all the way to the edges. Then roll it up like a narrow Swiss roll, liberally brushing with melted butter on top of the roll as you go. Make a second baklava roll the same way.

BAKE THIS WAY: Cut each roll in two and place them snugly on the greased tray. Use a sharp knife or metal pastry scraper to cut them into 5–6 cm pieces. Bake the baklava in the oven for about 25 minutes, or until golden.

Meanwhile, heat the honey, water, lemon peel and cinnamon stick in a small saucepan. Simmer the syrup, uncovered, for 8 minutes, then flavour it with the lemon juice.

To finish, spoon the syrup over the freshly baked, still hot baklavas. Sprinkle with the extra finely chopped pistachios and let the baklavas sit for at least a couple of hours before serving.

Yoghurt with honey and nuts

We always relish this simple Greek dessert with toasted nuts and honey.

SERVES 4:
100–150 g assorted nuts, such as walnuts,
  blanched almonds, pistachios, hazelnuts
about 100 ml honey (thyme or orange blossom honey,
  if available)
500 g thick Greek yoghurt
a touch of ground cinnamon (optional)

• Preheat the oven to 200°C/400°F. Toast the nuts on a baking tray for 6–8 minutes. Cool on a plate. Roughly chop the nuts and stir in the honey.

Spoon the yoghurt into small glasses or bowls, and top with the honey nuts. Or even simpler: top the yoghurt with natural nuts and just trickle the honey on top. You may even wish to dust with cinnamon.

Almond brittle

Almond and nut brittle crumbled over really good ice cream or chocolate mousse is simply scrumptious. Hazelnuts, walnuts, blanched almonds or pecans all work well too.

· Toast 100 g nuts and/or blanched almonds until nicely coloured (see page 234). Line a small baking tray with baking paper.

Combine the toasted nuts with 100 g sugar in a small, heavy-based saucepan, melting and caramelising the sugar over medium heat.

When the sugar turns nice and golden, add 1 tablespoon butter and give it a little stir. Next, very carefully pour the very hot mixture onto the paper-lined baking tray. Leave to cool down slightly before putting the tray in the freezer for 5-6 minutes.

Crush the brittle in a mortar. Store in an airtight container at room temperature.

Pecan caramel sundae

Vanilla or chocolate ice cream smothered in a caramel sauce and topped with toasted pecans.

· Toast about 100 g pecans until nicely golden (see page 234). Chop and set aside.

Slowly melt 50 g butter, 3 tablespoons golden syrup, 3 tablespoons caster sugar and 200 ml pure (whipping) cream in a small, heavy-based saucepan. Simmer over low heat for 20-25 minutes, uncovered, stirring regularly until it thickens.

Drizzle the warm or just-cooled caramel sauce over ice cream, and sprinkle the toasted pecans on top. Serves 4-5

Hazelnut parfait

A quick-and-easy parfait with a delicate nutty flavour. The key is to carefully toast the hazelnuts in the oven, creating that perfectly nuanced nuttiness.

PARFAIT FOR 8-10:
200 g hazelnuts
4 eggs
300 ml pure (whipping) cream
90 g caster sugar

· Preheat the oven to 200°C/400°F. Put the nuts on a large baking tray and toast them in the middle of the oven for 6-8 minutes, watching them carefully. Let the hazelnuts cool down a bit, and then rub off most of the brown skin (don't worry if you can't get it all off). Finely chop half of the nuts, and roughly chop the other half. Set aside.

Separate the egg yolks and egg whites into two bowls. Whip the cream until thick but not stiff.

Beat the egg yolks and sugar until nice and fluffy. Fold in the chopped nuts and the whipped cream.

Finally, beat the egg whites until stiff, using a perfectly clean whisk (the slightest trace of egg yolk or cream on the whisk or in the bowl will prevent the egg whites from stiffening). Use a spatula to gently fold half of the beaten egg white into the nut mixture, then gradually and gently fold in the rest.

Pour into a loaf tin (about 1.5 litre capacity) and freeze. Cut into slices to serve.

Apple wedges à la maison

In the autumn, a baking tin filled with the most wonderful baked apple wedges is a long-standing family favourite. The apples are just as good when eaten warm, lukewarm or even cold the next day.

SERVES 6-8:
100 g butter, at room temperature
120 g almonds
8 red apples (about 1 kg)
100 g caster sugar
50 g desiccated coconut
1 teaspoon ground cinnamon
50 g raisins
vanilla ice cream, for serving

• Preheat the oven to 200°C/400°F. Grease a large baking tin with some of the butter. Roughly chop the almonds.

Halve and core the apples, then cut each half into 3-4 wedges. Place them higgledy-piggledy in the baking tin and sprinkle with the sugar, coconut, cinnamon, raisins and almonds. Dot the remaining butter on top.

Bake for about 25 minutes. As the apples are baking, the kitchen fills with an enticing aroma. Serve these delicious apples with vanilla ice cream.

Baked walnut apples

During the apple season, old-fashioned baked apples are a homely Sunday dinner dessert. Always appreciated, particularly if served with pouring custard, ice cream, or crème fraîche sweetened with a touch of sifted icing sugar.

SERVES 4:
50 g walnuts, almonds, hazelnuts or pecans
2 tablespoons butter, at room temperature
  + a little extra for topping
2 tablespoons honey or brown sugar
4 large or 8 small apples

• Preheat the oven to 225°C/435°F. Roughly chop the nuts. Cream the butter with the honey or sugar, then add the nuts. Set aside.

Rinse and core the apples with an apple corer. If you wish, use a potato peeler to remove a thin ribbon of peel all the way around the middle of each apple (as a 'waist'), to prevent the fruit from splitting in the oven.

Arrange the apples snugly – holes up – in a lightly greased ovenproof dish. Fill the holes with the butter and nut mixture. Put a small knob of extra butter on top of each apple.

Place the dish in the middle of the oven and bake for 15-20 minutes, or until the apples are tender.

coconut

coconuts and coconut peaks

The wind rustling through the palm trees, the gentle sway of the hammock and a cool, refreshing coconut in your hand... It's hard to think about coconuts without picturing a tropical beach paradise. But to us, coconuts also bring to mind the luscious old-fashioned coconut balls from Augusta Jansson's legendary confectionery factory in Stockholm, or the juicy coconut peak biscuits from our favourite café. Not to mention all the wonderful food memories from travels in countries where coconut is a staple of the local cuisine.

The coconut palm, *Cocoa nucifera*, plays an extremely important role in the tropics, where the nuts are consumed fresh as well as manufactured into a range of foods and beverages, including coconut oil, coconut butter, coconut milk, baked goods and drinks... The actual palm tree and its leaves, as well as the coconut's brown inner peel and fibres, are used to make everything from fuel, timber, roofing and furniture upholstery to woven baskets and trays, rope and other household utensils. The coconut palm is simply indispensable.

Above: Fruit sprinkled with desiccated coconut; Coconuts in India. Left, from top: Coconut palms on a beach in Brazil; Newly picked coconuts in their green shells, Vietnam

coconuts are picked by hand...

The coconut itself is not a nut, but a stone fruit or drupe. Its outer green husk holds a fibrous shell, and in its centre lies the hard, brown edible seed. The hollow seed contains coconut water, which is at its best when the coconut is young. That's when the coconut flesh is very tender, almost jelly-like, and marvellous to enjoy fresh. Once the coconut is fully ripe, the flesh becomes harder and perfect for grating.

DESICCATED COCONUT is dried, mature coconut flesh that comes finely shredded or in larger flakes. Desiccated coconut is primarily used for baked goods and sweets, but is also great in certain salads and savoury dishes.

COCONUT MILK is obtained by soaking and straining ripe coconut flesh. The sweet milk adds a smooth taste to curries, soups and desserts, and is an essential ingredient in Southeast Asian cuisine.

COCONUT CREAM is a thicker variety, which adds a rich, velvety texture to the dish.

CREAMED COCONUT consists of small, semi-solid blocks made out of fresh mature coconut. Mix it with water to get coconut milk or coconut cream.

COCONUT OIL AND COCONUT BUTTER are actually the same product; pure coconut oil is liquid when warm, but turns solid and opaque at temperatures below 25°C/77°F. After suffering from a bad reputation for some time, coconut oil/butter is now regarded as a very healthy source of fat.

COCONUT WATER is the clear liquid inside young coconuts. It's a popular drink in the tropics, and is sold both fresh and tinned.

COCONUT PALM SUGAR is derived from coconut blossom nectar. It has a smooth caramel taste that rounds off both savoury dishes and desserts beautifully. Coconut palm sugar is sold granulated, as a soft, sticky paste, or in coarse blocks that can be grated or crushed. *Note!* Generally speaking, palm sugar usually refers to sugar extracted from several varieties of palm trees.

Right, clockwise from top: Coconut peaks, page 272; Young coconut drink in a tin; Coconuts for sale in India

Salmon and prawn laksa

Laksa is a fragrant and spicy Malaysian soup, made here with salmon, prawns, chilli and coconut milk.

TO MAKE LAKSA FOR 4:
4 Asian shallots, thinly sliced
50 g mung bean sprouts
  or baby English spinach, trimmed
3 cm piece fresh galangal or ginger, peeled and
  thinly sliced
1 fresh red chilli, deseeded and thinly sliced
300 g skinless salmon fillet
100 g Asian rice noodles
2 tablespoons vegetable oil
1-2 tablespoons Thai red curry paste
400 ml tin coconut milk
400 ml fish stock
1-2 tablespoons fish sauce
100 g peeled cooked prawns
a small handful of fresh coriander leaves
1 lime, in wedges

· Start by preparing the vegetables and then cut the salmon into 3 cm cubes.

Just before you are about to serve, cook the noodles according to the instructions on the packet. Drain the noodles and divide them among four large bowls. Place the shallots and sprouts or spinach leaves on top.

Heat the oil in a wok and gently stir-fry the galangal or ginger over medium heat, then 'mash' in the curry paste using the back of a spoon. Let the curry paste start to bubble a little; this releases the flavours and a marvellous fragrance. Stir in a bit of coconut milk to thoroughly dissolve the curry paste, and then pour in the rest of the coconut milk and the fish stock.

Season with fish sauce and add the salmon, which only needs to simmer for 2-3 minutes at most. Add the prawns last, and season to taste. Ladle the steaming hot soup over the noodles in the bowls and serve immediately with the coriander and lime wedges.

Tom kha gai

This Thai chicken and galangal soup is loved by many, perhaps because it is so flavoursome and easy to prepare. (Photo, on the right)

SERVES 3-4:
2 lemongrass stalks
2 chicken breast fillets, sliced
2 x 400 ml tins coconut milk
½-1 organic chicken stock cube
6 kaffir lime leaves, washed and halved
5 cm piece fresh galangal, peeled and sliced
1-2 fresh red chillies, deseeded and chopped
2 teaspoons grated palm sugar
2 tablespoons fish sauce
10 cherry tomatoes, halved (optional)
juice of 1-2 limes
fresh coriander (cilantro) leaves, to serve

· Trim and lightly bruise the thick white ends of the lemongrass, and cut it into large pieces. Prepare the chicken and the rest of the ingredients as well.

Bring the coconut milk and the crumbled stock cube to the boil in a saucepan, and add the lemongrass, lime leaves and galangal. Add half of the chopped chilli, the palm sugar and fish sauce. Stir to dissolve the sugar, then add the chicken pieces. Cook for 5 minutes, or until the chicken is cooked through. Add the tomatoes, if using, the rest of the chilli and season to taste with lime juice. Ladle the soup into individual bowls, top with coriander and serve at once.

Green beef curry

This quick-and-easy curry with minute steak, snow peas and coconut milk is terrific with jasmine rice and lots of fresh coriander.

SERVES 3–4:
3 shallots, finely chopped
3 garlic cloves, finely chopped
1 fresh red chilli, deseeded and thinly sliced
3 cm piece fresh ginger, peeled and finely grated
150 g snow peas (mangetout)
250 g minute steak (topside beef)
2–3 tablespoons vegetable oil
1 tablespoon Thai green curry paste
1 teaspoon grated palm sugar
400 ml tin coconut milk
1–2 tablespoons fish sauce
fresh coriander or Thai sweet basil, to serve

· Begin by preparing the shallots, garlic, chilli and ginger. Top and tail the snow peas and then slice them on the diagonal. Cut the meat into strips barely 2 cm wide. Set everything aside.

Heat half of the oil in a wok or large frying pan and gently stir-fry the shallots and garlic until lightly golden. Add the curry paste and ginger, and keep stir-frying for 1 minute more, then transfer the fragrant mixture onto a plate and set aside for now.

Stir-fry the meat in batches in a bit more oil. Return the shallot mixture to the wok, add the palm sugar and pour over the coconut milk. Stir and bring the curry to the boil, season with the fish sauce and simmer for 2 minutes. Add the snow peas and chilli, cover and simmer for another 1–2 minutes. Top with coriander or Thai basil and serve at once.

Coconut lime prawns

These deliciously crispy, deep-fried prawns with coconut and lime are a treat to nibble on as a small starter with a welcome drink, or simply serve with a cold glass of beer.

YOU WILL NEED:
20–25 large raw prawns
40 g desiccated coconut
40 g panko (Japanese breadcrumbs)
finely grated zest of 1–2 limes
1 egg + 1 tablespoon water
a small pinch of salt
3 tablespoons plain flour
vegetable oil for deep-frying

TO SERVE:
lime, in wedges
Thai sweet chilli sauce

· Peel and devein the prawns but leave the tail tips on. Set them aside for now.

Mix the coconut and the panko with about half of the lime zest in a bowl. Lightly beat the egg with the water and a touch of salt in a separate bowl. Put the flour in a third bowl.

Gently heat the oil in a wok or saucepan for deep-frying. Take the prawns by the tail, one by one, and dip them first in the flour, then in the egg and lastly in the coconut mixture.

Carefully deep-fry a few prawns at a time until cooked through and nicely golden. Remove from the oil with a slotted spoon and drain the prawns on double layers of paper towels.

Serve the prawns sprinkled with the remaining lime zest, lime wedges and a dipping sauce, such as Thai sweet chilli sauce.

Thai curry in four ways

This Thai-inspired curry can be varied in an infinite number of ways. We often make it purely vegetarian, but other times we add some salmon, prawns (or both), or pieces of chicken. The list of ingredients may seem dauntingly long, but once the vegetables are prepared, you make the curry itself in no time.

BASIC GREEN CURRY FOR 4-6:
6 shallots, finely chopped
4-5 garlic cloves, very finely chopped
5 cm piece fresh galangal, peeled and grated
6-7 cm piece fresh ginger, peeled and grated
2-3 medium carrots, in thin strips
250 g broccoli, in small florets
4 lemongrass stalks, lightly bruised and
   cut into large pieces
8 kaffir lime leaves, well washed
1 medium zucchini (courgette), halved lengthwise
   then cut into half-moon pieces
1 red capsicum (pepper), in thin strips
50 g snow peas (mangetout)
130 g tin sliced water chestnuts
2-3 tablespoons vegetable oil
1-2 tablespoons Thai red curry paste
2 x 400 ml tins coconut milk
2-3 tablespoons fish sauce
1 teaspoon grated palm sugar (optional)
juice of 1-2 limes
1 fresh red chilli, deseeded and thinly sliced
fresh Thai sweet basil or coriander leaves

ACCOMPANIMENTS:
lime wedges
200 g chopped toasted cashew nuts
   or peanuts
jasmine rice

· Start by preparing all the vegetables and then set them aside.

Heat the oil in a large wok, and gently stir-fry the shallots, garlic, galangal and ginger over medium heat. Add the curry paste, mash it around a little and stir-fry for 1 minute more until fragrant.

Add the coconut milk, fish sauce and palm sugar and bring to the boil. Then add the carrots, broccoli, lemongrass pieces and 5 of the kaffir lime leaves torn in two. Simmer for 2-3 minutes, and then add the zucchini and capsicum pieces, snow peas and sliced water chestnuts. Simmer for another 2-3 minutes, before you season with freshly squeezed lime juice and pop in the remaining 3 lime leaves. Taste it: you may want a bit more fish sauce or lime juice.

Finally, sprinkle with the chilli, a handful of Thai sweet basil leaves or plenty of chopped coriander. Serve the curry with lime wedges, toasted cashews or peanuts and jasmine rice.

WITH PRAWNS: Add 300-400 g peeled prawns for the last 2 minutes of cooking.

WITH SALMON: Cut 400 g skinless salmon fillet into 3 x 3 cm pieces, and let simmer in the wok for the last 2-3 minutes. (You can also add 150 g peeled prawns, if you want both fish and prawns in the curry.)

WITH CHICKEN: Cut 2-3 chicken breast fillets into quite small pieces. Give them a quick stir-fry before adding the coconut milk and vegetables, and then let simmer for 5 minutes, or until the chicken is cooked through.

Chickpeas Kerala-style

This aromatic yet uncomplicated stew was inspired by a trip to Kerala in southern India. The green spinach leaves provide a nice splash of colour.

SERVES 3-4:

1 fresh green or red chilli
1 medium onion
3 garlic cloves
3 cm piece fresh ginger
600 g home-cooked chickpeas (about 250 g dried
  chickpeas) or 2 x 400 g tins chickpeas
2 tablespoons vegetable oil
2 teaspoons curry powder
400 ml tin coconut milk
100 g baby English spinach, rinsed
12 cherry tomatoes, halved
juice of 1 lime, or to taste
a pinch of sea salt
fresh coriander leaves, to serve

· Deseed and chop the chilli. Peel and roughly chop the onion. Peel, gently bruise and then chop the garlic cloves (don't use a garlic press or the taste will be too acrid). Also peel and grate the ginger.

Put the chickpeas in a colander and rinse well, then drain and set aside.

Gently sauté the chilli, onion, garlic and ginger in the oil. Sprinkle over the curry powder. Stir in the chickpeas and pour in the coconut milk. Bring the stew to the boil and simmer for a few minutes.

Fold in the spinach leaves and tomatoes. Simmer for just a few minutes more, and then season with lime juice and a touch of salt. Sprinkle with fresh coriander and serve with basmati rice.

Potato and coconut curry

Such a simple potato curry, but ever so delicious when served with basmati rice, yoghurt and naan bread.

SERVES 3-4:

6-7 medium potatoes (500 g), diced
2 large onions, halved and very thinly sliced
2 tablespoons vegetable oil
2-3 garlic cloves, finely chopped
1 tablespoon grated fresh ginger
2 teaspoons coriander seeds,
  roughly crushed
2 tablespoons brown mustard seeds
1 fresh red chilli, finely chopped
400 ml tin coconut milk
300 ml chicken or vegetable stock
2-3 star anise
sea salt, to taste

GARNISH WITH:

½ fresh red chilli, very thinly sliced
a small handful of chopped fresh coriander leaves

· Prepare the potatoes and onions. Pour the oil into a saucepan and sauté the garlic, ginger, coriander seeds, mustard seeds and chilli.

After a few minutes, add the coconut milk and stock, and then the star anise, diced potato, sliced onion and a pinch of salt.

Let everything simmer for about 10 minutes (the first 5 minutes covered), until the potatoes are tender yet firm. Season to taste, and top the curry with the chilli and chopped fresh coriander. Serve at once.

Left: Chickpeas Kerala-style

All-round fruit salad

This is a plain yet really tasty fruit salad that we enjoy making for parties or get-togethers. It's perfect with ice cream or as a refreshing addition to a dessert table. You can prepare the fruit salad a few hours in advance; just cover it with plastic wrap and store somewhere cool – but not in the fridge.

SERVES 4-6:
80 g almonds
5 sweet oranges
4 beautiful red apples
4 kiwi fruit
100 g raisins or sultanas
about 40 g desiccated coconut

· Begin by roughly chopping the almonds. Set them aside.

Cut a bit off the bottom of the oranges so that they can stand upright (set aside half an orange for later). Then use a sharp knife to trim off the peel, including the white pith. Slice and cut the oranges into pieces. Wash then cut the apples into pieces (we use bright red apples to add a nice touch of colour). Peel and cut the kiwi fruit into half-moon pieces. Put the fruit in a bowl or on a serving platter.

Sprinkle with half of the chopped almonds, raisins and coconut, then gently fold into the fruit. Squeeze the juice of the reserved orange half on top and scatter with the rest of the almonds, raisins and coconut.

Coconut peaks

Sweet, luscious coconut treats that are timeless Scandinavian classics. You can make them half the size, for a more elegant impression. No flour is used in this recipe, which makes these biscuits perfect for those who are gluten intolerant. (Photo, page 265)

FOR ABOUT 15 LARGE PEAKS
3 medium egg whites
  (100 ml egg white)
200 g desiccated coconut
200 g caster sugar
25 g butter, at room temperature

· Preheat the oven to 190°C/375°F. Line a baking tray with non-stick baking paper. Carefully measure out the right amount of egg white, and put all the ingredients in a heavy-based saucepan. Gently heat everything over low heat, stirring every now and then until the mixture thickens. Then drop the mixture by the spoonful into spiky 'peaks' on the tray.

Bake for roughly 12 minutes, or until nice and golden. If you make the coconut peaks smaller, they will be done in 8-9 minutes.

Right: All-round fruit salad

Lime and coconut ice cream

This delicious ice cream will be creamier if made in an ice-cream maker, or you can just use the freezer and stir regularly to make the texture nice and smooth.

FOR ABOUT 1½ LITRES YOU NEED:
60 g desiccated coconut
300 ml full-fat milk
400 ml tin coconut milk
finely grated zest of 2 limes
2 tablespoons lime juice
5 egg yolks
120 g caster sugar
300 ml pure (whipping) cream

· In a saucepan, measure out the desiccated coconut, milk and coconut milk and bring to the boil. Remove the pan from the heat and set aside to cool completely. Prepare the lime zest and juice, and set aside.

Beat the egg yolks and sugar until nice and fluffy. In another bowl, lightly whip the cream. Combine the coconut and milk mixture with the beaten egg yolks. Add the lime zest and juice. Last of all, use a spatula to gently fold in the whipped cream. Freeze the mixture in an ice-cream maker for the creamiest result.

If using the freezer, pour the mixture into a freeze-proof container, and give it a good stir every 30 minutes until almost frozen, to prevent the ice cream from becoming too hard.

Serve the coconut ice cream on its own, with a fruit salad, or simply with pieces of perfectly ripe mango.

Coconut crêpes

These pancakes or crêpes are slightly thicker than usual. Serve them with diced fresh mango and a drizzle of maple syrup or with a nice little tropical fruit salad and a scoop of ice cream. Or perhaps with warm bananas, quickly fried in a knob of butter and some muscovado sugar.

FOR ABOUT 10 CRÊPES:
2 medium eggs
400 ml tin coconut milk
2 tablespoons sifted icing sugar
¼ teaspoon salt
100 g plain flour
25 g desiccated coconut
30 g butter, melted + extra butter for frying
icing sugar for dusting
the topping of your choice

· Crack the eggs into a round-bottomed bowl (the round base makes it easier to whisk the mixture smooth). Pour in the coconut milk, stir in the icing sugar, salt and flour, then whisk until smooth and lump-free. Add the coconut and melted butter and whisk again.

Use about 75 ml mixture for each crêpe, and fry the crêpes in a bit of butter in a warm crêpe pan or regular frying pan. Cook until light golden, flipping them once.

Serve the crêpes dusted with icing sugar and heaps of fresh fruit, berries or with your choice of topping.

Apple and coconut crumble

This is truly an easy and quick-to-prepare dessert – the apples or pears are simply baked in the oven, then topped with coconut crumble. Serve with pouring custard or vanilla ice cream.

YOU WILL NEED:
1 tablespoon soft butter for the dish
100 g butter, in cubes
90 g caster sugar
1 teaspoon vanilla paste
80 g plain flour or a bit more
60 g desiccated coconut
4-6 medium apples or pears

• Preheat the oven to 225°C/435°F. Grease a fairly large ovenproof ceramic dish with a bit of soft butter.

Make a simple crumble topping by rubbing the butter, sugar, vanilla, flour and desiccated coconut together with your fingers. Set aside.

Peel, core and cut the apples or pears into wedges and arrange them in the dish, preferably in a single layer. Bake in the middle of the oven for 10 minutes. Take the dish out and sprinkle the crumble topping over the fruit.

Bake for another 25-30 minutes until the crumble turns nice and golden, and a lovely scent fills the kitchen. Serve the crumble either warm or cold with cream or ice cream.

Coconut cake for Susanne

A soft, moist cake flavoured with coconut and lime. Sometimes we put a cream cheese icing on top, but it is just as good without.

YOU WILL NEED:
150 g butter
1 large lime
4 medium eggs
150 g caster sugar
1 teaspoon vanilla paste
110 g desiccated coconut
120 g plain flour
1 teaspoon baking powder
cream cheese icing (optional, see below)

• Melt the butter in a small saucepan over low heat. Use some of the butter to grease a round cake tin, about 22 cm in diameter. Lightly sprinkle the inside with flour and set aside.

Preheat the oven to 175°C/345°F. Wash, dry and zest the lime, and squeeze the lime juice.

Whisk the eggs, sugar and vanilla until fluffy. Stir in the lime juice, lime zest, desiccated coconut and butter. Add the flour (mixed with the baking powder) last of all, then pour the mixture into the greased tin. Bake the cake for 40 minutes, or until nice and golden.

To make the cream cheese icing, beat 200 g room-temperature Philadelphia cream cheese with 5 tablespoons sifted icing sugar, a bit of lime juice and 1-2 tablespoons grated lime zest. Spread the icing over the cooled cake. Sprinkle a bit of extra lime zest over the top as a final touch just before serving.

cardamom

the lush green cardamom hills

In the fertile inland of southern India, the vegetation is remarkably rich and bountiful. The air is warm and moist, and the hilly landscape — with its winding roads and waterfalls — is simply stunning. Everywhere you look it's green, green, green. These verdant hills offer perfect conditions for both cultivated and wild-growing cardamom, *Elettaria cardamomum*, to thrive and bloom. Cardamom grows in large clusters, surrounded by bushy banana trees and protective jungle foliage, or in elevated plantations under tall shady trees. True cardamom is one of the world's three most precious spices, surpassed only by saffron and vanilla, and is thought to have originated here in the rainforests and mountains of the Western Ghats, part of which is also known as the Cardamom Hills.

The unique flavour of cardamom, with its refreshing notes of citrus and menthol, gives a sweet and pungent warmth to both savoury dishes and desserts. We were determined to include a chapter on cardamom in this book, since we are both very fond of Indian food as well as the traditional Swedish cardamom buns and country-style rusks... And that is essentially what this chapter contains: a little bit of India and a little bit of Sweden. Hopefully, you will find something to inspire you to grind the cardamom mill a bit more often. Just use a regular pepper mill (sans the pepper, of course) filled with cardamom seeds, ready to be freshly ground whenever you need them. Otherwise, use a mortar and pestle, because grinding or pounding the seeds yourself releases a whole new dimension of flavours and aromas in a way that can never be matched by pre-ground cardamom.

Left: A stop along the way in the breathtaking Cardamom Hills in Kerala

black, green, white or false cardamom

Cardamom is a member of the ginger family, *Zingiberaceae*, and has been around for a very long time. The ancient Greeks traded a spice believed to be cardamom as far back as the 6th century AD, and in India and Sri Lanka, cardamom has been an essential commodity for at least a thousand years. Nowadays, major producers also include Guatemala and Tanzania, among other countries. Cardamom plants have long, narrow leaves, and can grow up to 5-6 metres tall. The flowers are pale greenish-white with purple veins and centimetre-long pods that grow close to the ground. The remarkable flavour comes from the seeds inside the pods, which must be gathered before they ripen and split open. Harvesting is hard work, since the pods are hand-picked one by one. Once harvested, the cardamom pods are dried and then either allowed to keep their lovely green colour, or, as was commonly done in the past, bleached until almost white.

GREEN (TRUE) CARDAMOM, *cardamom elettaria*, is frequently used in Indian cooking, giving lots of lovely flavour to spice blends, drinks and desserts, as well as curries and certain meat or chicken dishes. Green cardamom is considered especially good for the digestion, and is often served in a sweet tea after dinner. In the Middle East, it's commonly used to flavour coffee, and in Scandinavia, cardamom is a traditional spice that goes all the way back to the time of the Vikings, who brought it back from Constantinople.

WHITE CARDAMOM is simply green cardamom pods that have been bleached. Try to avoid these and look for natural green pods instead.

BROWN OR BLACK CARDAMOM is a separate genus (*amomum*) from true cardamom. It is traditionally used in North Indian and Nepalese curries and pulaos, and is grown in the Himalayan foothills. Black cardamom is dried over an open fire, which adds a smoky, somewhat earthy flavour to its cool notes of camphor. The fragrant classic Indian spice blend garam masala usually contains both black and green cardamom.

FALSE CARDAMOM: There are also a number of other, more or less related 'false' cardamom varieties such as Javanese cardamom, Chinese cardamom, one from Ethiopia and another from Madagascar. These are not nearly as highly valued as true cardamom, but are often used regionally in traditional cuisines.

Right, clockwise from top: Black cardamom; Green cardamom; Shrikand, a fabulous Indian yoghurt dessert, with cardamom and pistachios, page 288; White (bleached) cardamom

One-pot chicken with fragrant saffron rice

Although this recipe contains several steps, none of them is difficult and they all result in a comforting Middle Eastern-inspired dish.

SERVES 4:
350 g basmati rice
50 g almonds, blanched and peeled
1 tablespoon olive oil for the rice
2 litres water + 1 teaspoon salt
15–20 saffron threads
  + 200 ml boiling water
1 tablespoon butter
2 tablespoons olive oil
6–8 chicken thighs
1 large onion, roughly chopped
50 g sultanas
10 whole green cardamom pods
1 small cinnamon stick
½ teaspoon cumin seeds
4 whole cloves
1 teaspoon salt, or to taste
about 2 tablespoons butter
2 fresh bay leaves

· Pour the basmati rice into a fine sieve and rinse thoroughly with cold water. Soak the rice for 1 hour in a saucepan with plenty of cold water.

Toast the almonds on a baking tray in a 200°C/400°F oven for about 8 minutes, or until nicely coloured. Tip the almonds onto a plate and set aside. Rinse the soaked basmati rice once more in a fine sieve.

Pour the oil, 2 litres of water and salt into a heavy-based pot, add the rice and bring to the boil. Set aside and let stand for 5 minutes. Carefully pour out the excess water not absorbed by the rice. The rice should now be half-cooked; set it aside for now.

Next, grind the saffron in a mortar and mix it with the boiling water. Set it aside.

Heat a frying pan with the butter and oil and brown the chicken thighs over medium heat. Cook the chicken until nicely browned all over, and gradually transfer the pieces and cooking juices to the rice pot. Add the chopped onion, sultanas, toasted almonds and whole spices as well. Season with salt and drizzle over the saffron water, but don't stir (this will give the rice pretty yellow stripes).

Bring to the boil, then lower the heat and simmer, covered, over *very* low heat for about 35 minutes. Dot with a few knobs of butter and garnish with the bay leaves. If you like, serve some thick natural yoghurt on the side.

Cardamom rice with nuts

This rice goes well with an Indian curry, or the chicken korma on page 285. Lightly toast the cardamom pods in a dry frying pan until fragrant, to deepen their flavour.

· Rinse and then cook 300 g basmati rice according to the instructions on the packet, adding 8-10 lightly crushed, toasted green cardamom pods to the cooking water.

In the meantime, toast a handful each of roughly chopped pistachios and blanched almonds in a dry frying pan. Set aside until the rice is cooked.

Once done, fluff up the rice and sprinkle with the almonds and pistachios. Serves 4

Left: One-pot chicken with fragrant saffron rice

Tandoori chicken

A bright red classic Indian chicken, which is traditionally cooked in a clay oven called a tandoor. At home we use the regular oven, but the flavour takes us right back to India. The marinade is also great for lamb.

TANDOORI FOR 4-6:
1 chicken (1.4 kg), jointed into 8 pieces
1 tablespoon oil for the baking dish

MARINADE:
500 g thick Greek yoghurt
2 tablespoons vegetable oil
2 garlic cloves, crushed
2 tablespoons fresh lemon juice
1 heaped teaspoon salt
1 tablespoon grated fresh ginger
1 teaspoon freshly ground cardamom
1 teaspoon garam masala
2 teaspoons ground turmeric
½ teaspoon chilli powder
red food colouring (optional)

· Combine all the ingredients for the marinade in a large bowl. Turn the chicken pieces in the marinade to coat all sides, and then cover the bowl. Refrigerate for at least 3-4 hours or even better, overnight.

Preheat the oven to 200°C/400°F. Take out the chicken (discard any excess marinade) and arrange the pieces in a baking dish. Roast for 25 minutes, then turn the pieces over and cook for another 20-25 minutes, or until the chicken is cooked through. *Note!* Spoon the cooking juices over the chicken a couple of times during roasting.

Serve the tandoori chicken with the tomato kachumber on page 39 and minted raita on page 86, ideally with some naan bread as well.

Dewi's potato curry

An aromatic vegetarian curry with potatoes and spinach, sprinkled with fresh coriander and served with basmati rice.

SERVES 4:
10 medium potatoes, peeled and in wedges
4 shallots, finely chopped
4 garlic cloves, finely chopped
1 fresh red chilli, deseeded and chopped
3 medium tomatoes, finely chopped
2 tablespoons grated fresh ginger
3 tablespoons vegetable oil
10 green + 2-3 black cardamom pods
1 small cinnamon stick
1 tablespoon coriander seeds
1 teaspoon garam masala
1 teaspoon ground cumin
300 ml pure (whipping) cream
400 g tin chickpeas
a pinch of sea salt
a large handful of baby English spinach or sugar snap peas
fresh coriander leaves, chopped

· Boil the potato wedges in lightly salted water for 5 minutes. Drain and set aside.

Prepare the rest of the vegetables and the ginger and set aside.

Gently heat the oil in a large pot or pan. While stirring, add the cardamom, cinnamon and coriander seeds and sauté for 1 minute, or until fragrant. Add the shallots, garlic, chilli and ginger, sauté for 2 minutes, then add the garam masala and cumin and stir once more. Add the tomatoes and sauté for 5 minutes or so. Pour in the cream, stir in the potatoes and chickpeas, cover and gently simmer for 10 minutes, or until the potatoes are soft.

Season with sea salt and fold in the spinach. Sprinkle with coriander and serve with rice.

Chicken korma with almonds

A smooth-tasting and creamy Indian chicken stew, seasoned with almonds and lots of spices. Nice and mild, yet full of flavour.

SERVES 4–5:

1 chicken, jointed into 8 pieces
  or 4 chicken breast fillets
4 cm piece fresh ginger
4 garlic cloves
1 medium onion
4 medium tomatoes

TOAST AND CRUSH:

½ teaspoon green cardamom seeds
3 cloves (optional)
1 teaspoon cumin seeds
1 tablespoon coriander seeds
1–2 small dried red chillies

YOU WILL ALSO NEED:

2–3 tablespoons vegetable oil
½ teaspoon ground cinnamon
200 ml chicken stock
1 bay leaf
1 teaspoon salt
50 g ground almonds
250 ml pouring (single) cream

ACCOMPANIMENTS:

desiccated coconut
steaming hot basmati rice

Joint the chicken into 8 pieces, or slice the chicken breast fillets into thin strips.

Peel and grate the ginger. Peel and finely chop the garlic and onion. Dice the tomatoes, and set everything aside.

Lightly toast the spices over medium heat in a dry frying pan until fragrant, stirring continuously to prevent them from burning. Once toasted, crush or grind the spices using a mortar and pestle.

Gently heat the oil in a large frying pan or pot, then add the crushed spices and sauté for 30 seconds while stirring. Add the onion, ginger, garlic and cinnamon, and sauté for a few more minutes. Add the tomatoes and stir once more.

Add the chicken pieces, pour in the stock and add the bay leaf and salt. Cover and cook for about 25 minutes over fairly low heat. Stir in the ground almonds (which will thicken the sauce a bit and give it a nice flavour) and the cream. Cook, uncovered, for another couple of minutes, then taste and adjust the seasoning if necessary.

Sprinkle the korma with desiccated coconut, and serve with basmati rice and a green salad.

Rice pudding can also be made with semolina, page 288   *Rhubarb compote with cardamom cream, page 289*

Spicy dried fruit compote with Earl Grey tea, page 289　　　　*Shrikand, a refreshing Indian dessert, page 288*

Shrikand

A refreshing Indian dessert made with yoghurt and pistachio, which we enjoy making over and over again. Very pretty served in small glasses or tiny bowls, topped with finely chopped nuts and freshly ground cardamom. Shrikand always elicits both surprise and delight, being so simple yet so delectable. (Photo, page 287)

SERVES 6-8:
*100 g pistachios or almonds
  (or half of each), chopped
1-2 teaspoons freshly ground cardamom
700 g thick Greek yoghurt
90 g sifted icing sugar, or to taste*

· Chop the pistachios and/or almonds, and use a cardamom mill (a regular pepper mill used for cardamom) or a mortar and pestle to coarsely grind or crush the cardamom seeds.

Combine the yoghurt with the sifted icing sugar, nearly all of the cardamom and most of the pistachios or almonds, saving some for garnish. If necessary, add extra icing sugar, to taste.

Divide the creamy mixture among 6-8 small glasses or tiny bowls. Top with the reserved nuts and a pinch of the ground cardamom. Chill before serving.

SHRIKAND WITH SAFFRON: Follow the recipe above, but add about 15 saffron threads (crushed with 1 sugar cube in the mortar, then mixed with 2 tablespoons hot water). Stir this into the yoghurt and then add the icing sugar, cardamom and almonds and/or pistachios.

Rice pudding from Amritsar

Another lovely, somewhat simplified, version of an Indian dessert, kheer. We often make it when we have leftover white rice. Sometimes we use semolina instead; it turns out just as good.

SERVES 6:
*1 litre full-fat milk
350 g cooked white rice
60 g caster sugar, or to taste
a few saffron threads, ground with a
  pinch of sugar in a mortar (optional)
2 tablespoons sultanas
1 teaspoon freshly ground cardamom
3 tablespoons chopped pistachios
3 tablespoons chopped almonds
1 tablespoon rose water (optional)*

· Start by gently bringing the milk to the boil in a heavy-based saucepan. Add the cooked rice, bring to the boil again and then simmer over low—medium heat, stirring constantly, for roughly 15 minutes until the rice turns creamy. Stir in the sugar, saffron (dissolved in a splash of hot water), sultanas and almost all of the ground cardamom, pistachios and almonds. Let simmer for another 4-5 minutes. Remove from the heat, add the rose water, if using, and spoon the kheer into serving bowls.

Serve the rice pudding just cooled or chilled, sprinkled with the reserved nuts and a pinch of ground cardamom.

WITH SEMOLINA: Instead of white rice, use 120 g uncooked semolina. Simmer while stirring for just 3-4 minutes before adding the sugar and other ingredients. Pour into ramekins and let cool. Serve the pudding sprinkled with chopped pistachios or almonds and a pinch of freshly ground cardamom. (Photo, page 288)

Rhubarb compote with cardamom cream

The season's first rhubarb is used in this tangy compote, which is doubly delicious when served with cardamom cream. (Photo, page 286)

SERVES 4-5:
1 vanilla pod
1 kg rhubarb
800 ml water
90 g caster sugar
2 tablespoons potato starch,
  dissolved in 3 tablespoons cold water

CARDAMOM CREAM:
250 g crème fraîche
3-4 tablespoons sifted icing sugar
½-1 teaspoon ground cardamom

· Split the vanilla pod lengthwise and scrape out the small black seeds. Place both pod and seeds in a stainless steel saucepan.

Cut the rhubarb into 3 cm pieces. Bring the water, sugar and vanilla to the boil in the saucepan. Add the rhubarb and let it simmer gently. When the pieces are *just about* to turn mushy, carefully stir in the potato starch (dissolved in cold water). Quickly bring the compote to the boil again and stir very gently. Pour the compote into a bowl and chill until it's time to serve.

Combine the ingredients for the cardamom cream, adding enough icing sugar, to taste.

Serve the rhubarb compote chilled, with the smooth cardamom cream and a biscuit on the side, maybe one of Mette's Danish hazelnut biscotti on page 250.

Spicy dried fruit compote with Earl Grey tea and more

In this succulent, sweet-tasting compote, the dried fruit is simmered in a syrup based on Earl Grey tea, flavoured with cardamom and vanilla. It's great with a dollop of lightly whipped cream. (Photo, page 287)

SERVES 4-6:
700 ml freshly brewed Earl Grey tea
3-4 tablespoons caster sugar
10 green cardamom pods
½ vanilla pod
12 dried soft figs
12 dried soft apricots
12 soft prunes
lightly whipped cream for serving

· Measure out the freshly brewed tea, sugar and cardamom pods in a saucepan. Split the half vanilla pod lengthwise and add it as well. Cover and cook until the liquid is syrupy, about 5 minutes.

Meanwhile, remove the small hard stems on each fig. Put the dried fruits into the syrup and continue cooking, covered and over low heat, until the fruit plumps up and softens. It takes about 10-12 minutes. Take the lid off the pan and allow the compote to cool. Serve with lightly whipped cream.

Swedish cardamom tea ring

DOUGH FOR 1 LARGE RING:

75 g butter

300 ml full-fat milk

about 425 g plain flour

2 sachets (7 g each) dry yeast

2 tablespoons coarsely ground cardamom

½ teaspoon salt

90 g caster sugar

FILLING AND TOPPING:

100 g soft butter

4 tablespoons caster sugar

1 teaspoon pure vanilla extract

1 egg, lightly beaten

2-3 tablespoons caster sugar

* + 1 teaspoon ground cardamom for dusting*

· For the dough, melt the butter in a saucepan, add the milk and gently heat until lukewarm.

Sift the flour into a large bowl. Stir in the yeast, cardamom, salt and sugar. Gradually pour in the milk and combine to a rather soft dough. Work the dough with a wooden spoon until smooth and elastic. Cover and let rise for about 1 hour.

Preheat the oven to 200°C/400°F. Line a baking tray with non-stick baking paper. Sprinkle a bit of flour on the work surface and turn out the dough. Gently knead the dough until smooth. Add a bit more flour if needed.

Roll out the dough into a large rectangle, and spread a mix of butter, sugar and vanilla on top. Roll it up like a Swiss roll, joining the two ends to form a ring, and place it on the tray, seam-side down. Use kitchen scissors to cut small notches on the top of the ring. Set aside to rise for 30 minutes. Brush with the beaten egg and sprinkle with the combined sugar and cardamom. Bake in the middle of the oven for 25-30 minutes. Let cool under a tea towel.

Our best vega buns

Wonderfully moist and buttery buns, redolent of sweet cardamom. (Photo, on the left)

FOR ABOUT 20 BUNS:

1 batch of dough as per the previous recipe

* + 50 g butter at room temperature*

FILLING:

1 tablespoon coarsely ground cardamom

100 g butter, at room temperature

5 tablespoons caster sugar

1 teaspoon pure vanilla extract

LAST OF ALL:

1 egg, lightly beaten

1-2 tablespoons caster sugar

* + 1 teaspoon ground cardamom for dusting*

· Prepare the dough according to the previous recipe, kneading 50 g extra butter into the dough. Cover and let the dough rise for 1-1½ hours. Meanwhile, combine the filling ingredients.

Preheat the oven to 225°C/435°F. Line baking trays with non-stick baking paper. Turn out the dough onto a lightly floured work surface and knead it gently until smooth.

Divide the dough into 2 pieces. Roll out each piece into a rectangle, about as thin as a pizza base. Spread the cardamom filling evenly over the 2 pieces, then roll them up like Swiss rolls. Place the rolls with the seam facing down, and cut them into 5-6 cm wide pieces. Place them, seam-side down, on the trays. Use something narrow, like the handle of a table knife, to press down fairly hard along the centre of each bun, creating something of a butterfly shape. Let the buns rise for 15 minutes.

Brush with beaten egg and sprinkle with sugar and cardamom. Bake for 12-15 minutes until nice and golden. Let cool under a tea towel.

Country cardamom cake

This delicious homely cake is made without eggs. Use coarsely ground cardamom in the dough, and sprinkle liberally with chopped almonds and extra cardamom on top.

YOU WILL NEED:
225 g plain flour
130 g caster sugar
2 tablespoons coarsely ground cardamom
1½ teaspoons baking powder
150 g butter
200 ml full-fat milk

TOPPING:
a scant teaspoon ground cinnamon
2 tablespoons caster sugar
1 teaspoon coarsely ground cardamom
75 g almonds, chopped

· Preheat the oven to 190°C/375°F. Grease a 22 cm round cake tin, and sprinkle with sifted flour.

Measure out the flour, sugar, cardamom and baking powder in a big bowl. Cut the butter into small cubes straight into the flour. Use your fingertips to rub the flour and butter into a dough, or use an electric mixer with dough hooks. The butter shouldn't be completely worked into the flour; leave some visible small knobs of butter. Stir in the milk last of all.

Transfer the rather sticky dough into the cake tin, and flatten the dough out just a tiny bit. Sprinkle with cinnamon, sugar, cardamom and lastly, the almonds. Bake in the middle of the oven for 35-40 minutes until golden. Allow to cool.

Sister Sara's biscuits

Nice and crunchy, easy-to-bake biscuits with almonds and cardamom. We like them with lots of cardamom, but choose the smaller amount if you prefer milder tasting biscuits.

FOR ABOUT 30 LARGE BISCUITS:
50 g almonds
100 g butter, at room temperature
90 g caster sugar
2 tablespoons golden syrup
150 g plain flour
½ teaspoon bicarbonate of soda
½-1 tablespoon coarsely ground cardamom

· Preheat the oven to 175°C/345°F. Lightly grease or line a baking tray with non-stick baking paper.

Roughly chop the almonds and set aside. Cream the butter with the sugar and golden syrup until smooth. Combine the flour with the bicarbonate of soda, almonds and ground cardamom, and add it all to the creamed butter. Quickly work into a dough.

Divide the dough into 2 pieces, then roll the pieces into lengths and transfer to the tray. Flatten the lengths quite a bit with your hand and groove them with a fork.

Bake for about 15-20 minutes, or until golden brown. Allow the lengths to cool slightly, but not completely, before slicing them on the diagonal into 3-4 cm biscuits. Leave to cool on the tray.

Small sweet rusks

Something in between small biscuits and rusks. An old-fashioned Swedish classic that is great to have in the kitchen pantry.

FOR ABOUT 80 SMALL RUSKS:
550-600 g plain flour
2 teaspoons baking powder
3 tablespoons freshly ground cardamom
250 g butter, at room temperature
200 g caster sugar
1 teaspoon pure vanilla extract
½ teaspoon salt
1 medium egg
200 ml full-fat milk

· Preheat the oven to 200°C/400°F. Line two baking trays with non-stick baking paper. In a bowl, combine the flour with the baking powder and cardamom. Set aside.

Cream the butter, sugar, vanilla and salt until fluffy, and then add the egg, milk and the flour and cardamom mixture. Work into a soft dough. At this point, it may be easier to turn out the dough onto a lightly floured work surface and work it by hand.

Divide the dough into 8 pieces. On a lightly floured surface, use your hands to gently roll the pieces into fairly narrow rolls. Place the rolls on the baking trays. Don't flatten the rolls; they should be baked just as they are.

Bake in the middle of the oven for about 20 minutes (the rolls should still be quite pale). Allow to cool for 10 minutes, and then use a serrated knife to cut the rolls into roughly 2 cm pieces. Place them on the trays, pop them back into the oven and dry into rusks at low heat, 75°C/165°F, for 1-2 hours.

Rusks from the farm

Country-style cardamom rusks to go with cheese or marmalade and a nice cup of tea.

YOU WILL NEED:
600 ml full-fat milk
100 ml canola oil or mild olive oil
90 g caster sugar or honey
250 g wholemeal flour
550-600 g plain flour
2 sachets dried yeast (7 g each)
2 teaspoons salt
3 tablespoons coarsely ground cardamom
1 teaspoon baking powder

· Warm the milk and oil until lukewarm in a saucepan. Add the sugar or honey.

Combine the wholemeal and plain flours with the yeast, salt, cardamom and baking powder in a large bowl. Gradually stir in the milk and mix with a wooden spoon until the dough comes together. Cover with a tea towel and let rise for about 1 hour.

Turn out the dough onto a lightly floured work surface and knead gently. Cut the dough into 4 pieces, shape them into rolls and then cut each roll into about 6 pieces. Arrange the pieces on baking trays lined with non-stick baking paper, and let rise for 15 minutes.

Meanwhile, preheat the oven to 225°C/435°F. Bake the buns for 15 minutes and then leave them to cool. Use a serrated knife to divide each bun into a top and a bottom half. Bake the halves, cut-side up, for 5-7 minutes until they get a bit of colour, then remove the trays from the oven. Lower the heat to 100°C/200°F and dry the buns into rusks for 1-2 hours, switching the position of the trays once while drying. Store in an airtight container.

pears

pears need tender loving care...

Somehow pears seem slightly more sophisticated than their rather robust cousins, the apples. A perfectly ripe pear is a delicacy in itself, whether it is a modest little pear or an elegant Williams or Beurre Bosc pear. Pears are also beautiful to behold, and have been depicted in paintings and still lifes for centuries. They are more delicate than many other fruits and must be handled gently because they bruise easily. Pears should be harvested before they are perfectly ripe, stored in a cool place and then allowed to ripen at room temperature.

The common pear, *Pyrus communis*, is believed to have originated in the Caucasus and spread both east and west through migration. Pears have been cultivated in China for over 4000 years, and were prevalent in Ancient Greece as well. The Romans developed about fifty different pear varieties, while only having a handful of apple cultivars. The pear became a valued commodity, and the rest of Europe soon caught on. Pears had their heyday in France during the late 17th century. King Louis XIV adored pears, which led to new varieties being developed and pear trees being trellised even throughout central Paris. Many of our most popular pear types came about during this time.

Above: Packham pears; Kaiser Alexander pears go well with cheese; Alexander Lucas pears. Left: An unknown pear cultivar from our own garden. Previous page: Pear and pistachio squares, page 308

small pears from our old tree

On our farm on the island of Gotland we have a pear tree that is nearly 400 years old. It may not be all that beautiful, but it certainly deserves our respect. Around 20 years ago, a storm blew down half of the (then enormous) crown, but the surviving half still sprouts plenty of shoots. The trunk is covered in ivy and measures all of 4.5 metres across. The pears are small and round, and the branches are full of thorns hidden under the leaves. There is a gentle sense of peace surrounding the old pear tree.

Older pear varieties, in particular, tend to have thorns and yield quite small fruits. After centuries of cross-cultivation, there are now thousands of pear varieties, with two main groups: the European and the Asian pear, and they differ both in taste and in appearance.

European pears generally have a fine-grained, juicy flesh, and are often sweet yet slightly tart. They are usually classically pear-shaped, while Asian pears tend to be larger, chubbier or more apple-shaped. The flesh of the Asian pears is crisper and more coarse-grained (which is why they are sometimes called 'sand pears') but still wonderfully succulent. Asian pears are very refreshing, and their mild, sweet flavour and crispy texture make them an excellent choice for salads.

herzogin elsa, clara frijs and kaiser alexander...

ANJOU is a yellowish-green pear with a thin skin, and its flesh is soft, sweet and very juicy. It is largely cultivated in Chile and the United States. A delicious pear that is great also for tarts and pastries.

BEURRE BOSC, also known as Kaiser Alexander, is a very flavoursome pear, easily recognised by its yellowish-brown colour and long, narrow shape. Beurre Bosc pears have a crisp, light-coloured and very aromatic flesh that goes beautifully with peppery or slightly bitter leaves such as watercress and radicchio. This pear type goes well with cheese, perhaps a mature Vacherin or Morbier.

CONFERENCE is a popular English pear, long and slender and often slightly curved. It was named after the National British Pear Conference in 1885, where it won first prize. Its flesh is sweet and fragrant, and it's fabulous with all kinds of cheese.

HERZOGIN ELSA is a quite large pear cultivar with blushing cheeks. Lovely and sweet with soft and smooth flesh, this is an incredibly tasty pear.

WILLIAMS OR BARTLETT pears are slightly more robust with a somewhat peppery taste. They are often light green with a fair blush on one side. The Williams pear is called Bartlett in Australia and the United States, and comes in many varieties such as Red Williams. It's delicious on its own, in a salad or to accompany blue cheeses.

PACKHAM pears have a beautiful yet irregular shape. The pears have a greenish-yellow skin and firm, sweet and juicy flesh with a wonderful aroma. Packham pears are well suited for poaching.

GREY PEAR is a small, old-fashioned variety often found in Northern Europe. The trees are usually quite large and are frequently found in old gardens. The pear itself is greyish-green with flavoursome yet granular flesh and a rough skin.

ALEXANDER LUCAS is a large and round pear variety, which is both luscious and sweet. It is good for poaching and baking.

CLARA FRIJS is a soft and juicy pear with a yellowish-green skin, commonly grown in Scandinavia. Lovely in a tart or to eat fresh.

NASHI (ASIAN) PEARS are beautifully round, yellowish-brown pears with a slightly spotted skin, resembling elegant sculptures. Nashi pears are succulent and crisp, with firm white flesh. They are commonly grown in Japan, Korea, Australia and New Zealand. Asian pears are very tasty in leafy green salads or mixed fruit salads.

CHINESE WHITE PEAR is a large, whitish or pale yellow pear originally from Northern China. It has crisp, deliciously juicy flesh and is a subspecies of the Nashi pear, but with a more classic pear shape.

Herzogin Elsa pears

Pears, crackers and soft goat's cheese

Small round pears from our ancient pear tree
Fresh dates and stylish Mallorcan pears with lacquered stems

Hélène's salad with Gruyère

Our friend Hélène often makes this elegant, fresh salad with thin batons of Emmental or Gruyère cheese, topped with neatly cut pears.

SERVES 4:
1 bowl of mixed tender leaves, such as
  round lettuce, mâche lettuce and
  witlof (chicory or Belgian endive)
a good handful of watercress
200 g aged Emmental
  or Gruyère cheese
2 celery stalks
creamy mustard dressing (page 61)
1–2 firm yet ripe pears

· Arrange the lettuce leaves (rinsed and spun in a salad spinner, or lightly dried) in a large serving bowl or on a platter. Add the watercress and a few witlof leaves cut lengthwise.

Cut quite thin sticks of Swiss cheese, such as Emmental or Gruyère (or other mature cheese of your choice), and scatter over the leaves. For an added bit of crunch, add a few thin slices of celery.

Pour over the creamy mustard dressing and, when you are about to serve, place thinly sliced pears on top. Spoon over a bit more dressing just before serving.

Left: Rimini-style pear salad

Rimini-style pear salad

Pears and blue cheese are nearly always well-suited. For this salad we like a cheese with a balanced flavour, perhaps a mild Gorgonzola Dolcelatte, which won't overshadow the delicate flavour of the pears.

SERVES 4:
mixed crisp lettuce leaves of
  round or mâche lettuce, rocket,
  baby English spinach and radicchio
4–8 witlof leaves (chicory or Belgian endive) (optional)
150 g mild blue cheese
2 anjou or nashi pears
a pinch of sea salt
freshly ground black pepper
2 tablespoons aged balsamic vinegar
4 tablespoons mild olive oil
30 g pine nuts, toasted

· Rinse the lettuce leaves well and spin them in a salad spinner, or pat them dry with a tea towel. Arrange the leaves on a large platter. If you like, add a few witlof leaves cut lengthwise as well.

Crumble fridge-cold blue cheese on top. Cut the pears in half (no need to peel them unless the skin is very coarse), and use a small sharp knife to core them. Slice the pears thinly and spread them out on the lettuce.

Season lightly with salt and pepper, and drizzle with the balsamic vinegar and olive oil. Sprinkle with toasted pine nuts (toasted for just a few minutes in a warm, dry frying pan). Serve right away with delicious bread on the side.

Pear crostini with chèvre

Sourdough bread with grilled pears, frisée or radicchio and pieces of tasty soft goat's cheese is — in all its simplicity — a perfect little meal. Serve with a nice glass of wine.

SERVES 4:
60 g hazelnuts, roughly chopped
2 tablespoons olive oil
1 garlic clove, crushed
4 large slices of sourdough bread
2–3 not-too-ripe pears
sea salt flakes + freshly ground black pepper
150 g soft goat's cheese, in pieces
radicchio or other slightly bitter lettuce
balsamic vinegar and mild olive oil
a small trickle of honey (optional)

• Preheat the oven to 200°C/400°F. Line a baking tray with non-stick baking paper. Spread the hazelnuts out on the tray. Bake for 5-6 minutes, or until golden brown, and cool on a plate.

Combine the olive oil and crushed garlic, and lightly brush the bread with the garlic oil. Place the bread slices on the tray and toast for 6-7 minutes.

Meanwhile, cut the unpeeled pears into fairly thick slices and put the slices on the oven-toasted bread. Season lightly with salt and pepper. Turn on the oven grill and grill the pear crostini for about 5 minutes. Top with the goat's cheese and grill for 1 or 2 minutes more.

Arrange the crostini on individual plates, with a few crisp lettuce leaves on the side. Drizzle a bit of balsamic vinegar and mild olive oil over both the crostini and lettuce.

Add the toasted hazelnuts last, perhaps with a trickle of honey, if you like. Serve the crostini while warm, with black pepper and sea salt flakes on the table.

A delicate pear marmalade

This marmalade goes beautifully with rusks, toast or crispy crackers, and perhaps a bit of Italian Taleggio, soft goat's cheese or other tasty cheese.

YOU WILL NEED:
1 large lemon
1.2 kg ripe but firm pears
200 ml water
500 g caster sugar
3 knobs of preserved ginger (optional)
100 g walnuts, roughly chopped

• Wash and dry the lemon. Grate the lemon peel (you need 2 tablespoons finely grated zest) and squeeze the lemon juice.

Rinse the pears and remove the stems, then cut each pear into quarters. Core and dice the pears, and put the pieces in a heavy-based casserole dish or pot. Pour over the lemon juice and stir to coat all the pieces with lemon. Pour in the water and stir in the sugar. Cover and slowly bring to the boil, stirring regularly to dissolve the sugar. Lower the heat, remove the lid and simmer very gently for 30 minutes, stirring at least once every 5 minutes.

Peel and dice the preserved ginger, if using, and add to the dish, together with the chopped walnuts. Bring the marmalade to the boil again, and then let it simmer, uncovered, for another 15-20 minutes. Watch *carefully* to make sure it doesn't burn. You may need to add a bit more water. Remove from the heat and let the marmalade stand for 10 minutes, stirring occasionally. Scoop the still-warm jam into perfectly clean jars, and cover with lids once the jars have cooled down a bit.

Right: Pear marmalade with creamy cheeses, served with crispbread crackers, page 240

306 UNDER THE WALNUT TREE

Granny's French pear and almond cake

Although this cake is frequently made with apples, we find it even more irresistible with pears. It can also be made in small individual dishes, which requires less time in the oven.

SERVES 4-5:
100 g almonds or ground almonds
2 tablespoons soft butter for the dish
4 large, firm pears
100 g butter, at room temperature
100 g caster sugar
2 medium eggs
2 tablespoons fresh lemon juice

· Start by grinding the almonds (no need to blanch them first), or use store-bought ground almonds. Grease an ovenproof dish with a bit of soft butter, and preheat the oven to 200°C/ 400°F. Peel and core the pears, cut them into thick wedges and arrange them in a single layer in the dish.

Bake the pears in the oven for 10-20 minutes, or until almost soft. Meanwhile, prepare the almond mixture.

Cream the butter and sugar, and stir in the ground almonds. Add the eggs one at a time, stirring thoroughly after each egg. Lastly, add the lemon juice.

Take the dish out of the oven and spread the almond mixture over the pear wedges. Return to the oven and bake for about 15 minutes more.

Serve the pear cake warm or slightly cooled, on its own, with pouring (single) cream or vanilla ice cream.

Left: Granny's French pear and almond cake; Crisp parcels with pears, almonds and a hint of cinnamon

Crisp parcels with pears, almonds and cinnamon

Very easy to make and always appreciated. You can substitute the pears with apples.

FOR 8 PARCELS:
2-3 juicy pears
2 tablespoons butter
2 tablespoons caster sugar
½ teaspoon pure vanilla extract
50 g almonds or walnuts,
   roughly chopped
½ teaspoon ground cinnamon
375 g puff pastry
1 egg, lightly beaten
sifted icing sugar for dusting

· Rinse, halve and core the pears using a small sharp knife. Cut them into small pieces.

Melt the butter in a frying pan, add the pear pieces and cook for a few minutes. Sprinkle with the sugar and vanilla, and cook for a few minutes more while gently stirring. Add the chopped nuts and dust with cinnamon. Stir carefully to combine, then remove the pan from the stovetop and set aside to cool.

Preheat the oven to 200°C/400°F. Roll out the puff pastry until about 5 mm thick, and cut into 10 cm squares.

Place 2-3 tablespoons of pear mixture in the centre of each square. Brush the edges with a little beaten egg, fold into triangle-shaped parcels and press the edges together with a fork to seal the dough. Place the parcels on a baking tray lined with non-stick baking paper, and brush them with egg. Bake in the middle of the oven for about 20 minutes, or until light golden. Allow the parcels to cool and then dust them with sifted icing sugar.

Pear and pistachio squares

These elegant, crisp pastries with pears, almond paste, pistachios and a bit of apricot jam are so easy to make. (Photo, page 294)

FOR 8 PASTRIES:
375 g puff pastry
100 ml apricot jam
2 tablespoons water
150 g almond paste
3–4 pears, thinly sliced
4–5 tablespoons chopped pistachios
  or almonds
1 egg yolk, lightly beaten
sifted icing sugar for dusting

· Roll out the puff pastry until about 5 mm thick, and cut it into 15 x 10 cm rectangles. Place the rectangles on a baking tray lined with non-stick baking paper. Lightly score a line 1 cm inside the outer edge of each puff pastry rectangle, without cutting all the way through.

Preheat the oven to 200°C/400°F. Bring the jam and water to the boil in a small saucepan, then set aside.

Grate the almond paste and distribute it over the puff pastry inside the scored edge. Place thin pear slices (with or without skin) on top of the almond paste.

Use a pastry brush to carefully brush the pear slices with the soft apricot jam. Scatter the nuts on top, and brush the filling-free edges with lightly beaten egg yolk. Bake in the middle of the oven for 25-30 minutes. Let cool and dust with icing sugar as a finishing touch.

Teatime pear cake

This is a delightful cake with tender pear slices hidden under a walnut and sugar crust. Make it a day in advance, for the perfect consistency.

YOU WILL NEED:
150 g butter
100 g walnuts
2–3 juicy pears
3 medium eggs
200 g caster sugar
150 g plain flour
3 tablespoons raw (demerara) sugar

· Start by melting the butter in a saucepan over low heat. Fasten a piece of non-stick baking paper to the base of a 24 cm springform tin by clasping it shut over the paper, and cut off any excess paper. Use some of the melted butter to brush the side of the tin.

Preheat the oven to 180°C/350°F. Roughly chop the walnuts and set them aside.

Rinse the pears, only peeling them if necessary. Halve and quarter the pears, remove the core and then cut each quarter into 2-3 slices.

Beat the eggs and sugar until nice and fluffy, preferably using electric beaters. Fold in the flour and then stir in the melted butter. Pour the mixture into the prepared tin. Arrange the pear slices in circles on top; sprinkle with the walnuts and then with the raw sugar.

Bake for about 40 minutes; when ready it should still be slightly underdone in the centre. Allow the cake to cool, preferably leaving it to rest for 24 hours before you slice it.

Martin's exquisite pears

Delicious pears in a creamy caramel sauce. Choose nice firm pears and simmer them very slowly and gently so that they don't lose their shape. *Note!* With pears, the cooking time always varies quite a lot, depending on the variety.

SERVES 4:
4 firm and flavourful pears
½ vanilla pod
2 tablespoons butter
100 g caster sugar
100 ml pure (whipping) cream
fresh mint leaves for garnish

• Peel and halve the pears, core them with a small sharp knife, and cut each pear half into 3 wedges. Split the vanilla pod and scrape out the seeds.

Melt the butter in a frying pan, then add the pears, vanilla pod and vanilla seeds. Sprinkle with the sugar. Let the pears colour nicely and then lower the heat.

Cover, and cook or simmer the mixture over low heat until the pears are almost soft. This takes about 5-25 minutes, depending on the type of pear. Then pour in the cream alongside the fruit and cook for another 5-6 minutes, now uncovered, to make the delectable sauce.

Serve the pears either warm or slightly cooled, with a scoop of vanilla ice cream and garnished with mint leaves.

Pears in Marsala

These sophisticated pears are slowly baked in Marsala, the wonderful dessert wine from southern Italy. Serve the pears at room temperature, with a spoonful of the wine syrup and some lightly whipped cream.

SERVES 4:
50 g butter
4 quite large, firm pears
200 ml Marsala
100 g caster sugar

• Preheat the oven to 180°C/350°F. Melt the butter. Take out an ovenproof dish in which the pear halves will fit quite snugly, and brush the dish with some of the melted butter.

Peel and halve the pears, carefully coring them with a small sharp knife. Place the halves in the dish, cut-side down. Generously brush the pears with the rest of the melted butter. Pour the Marsala alongside the pears and sprinkle the sugar over the fruit.

Bake for 30-55 minutes, depending on the type of pear you are using (hard pears may require a surprisingly long time in the oven).

Use a large spoon and baste the pear halves with the wine and sugar syrup a couple of times while baking. Increase the heat to 225°C/435°F towards the very end. Allow the pears to cool down in the dish, and then serve them with the Marsala syrup and lightly whipped cream.

Swedish ginger pears

These luscious pears are cooked in a sugar syrup seasoned with fresh ginger and cinnamon. Serve with lightly whipped cream or vanilla ice cream.

SERVES 6-8:
500 ml water
180 g caster sugar
2 tablespoons finely chopped fresh ginger
1 small cinnamon stick
10 quite small, firm,
  barely ripe pears (1 kg)

· Make a sugar syrup by bringing the water, sugar, ginger and cinnamon to a quick boil. Cook, uncovered, for 5 minutes.

Meanwhile, peel the pears but leave the stems intact. Slice a tiny bit off the bottom of each pear, so they can stand upright.

Place the pears in a saucepan, standing snugly, and carefully pour over the sugar syrup. Bring to the boil and then lower the heat. Cover the pan and simmer the pears over very low heat for 25-30 minutes or more (they should become completely soft but not disintegrate).

Allow the pears to cool in the syrup. Preferably prepare the pears a couple of days in advance to allow the flavours to develop.

Saffron pears

Follow the recipe for ginger pears above, but substitute the ginger with a good pinch of saffron threads (ground in a mortar together with 1 tablespoon sugar, and then added to the syrup). Serve with a dainty raspberry coulis (page 337).

Provençal pears in red wine

Pears poached in spiced red wine, inspired by flavours from Provence. A sumptuous dessert together with some lightly whipped cream or ice cream, or a stylish accompaniment to a rustic soft goat's cheese or a creamy blue cheese.

FOR 6-8 YOU WILL NEED:
1 bottle (750 ml) red wine
1½ tablespoons dried thyme
150 ml honey, or to taste
100 ml Seville orange marmalade
8-12 not-too-ripe, quite small pears (1.25 kg)

· Find a good sized stainless steel saucepan or pot (about 3 litres), in which the pears can stand or lie quite snugly. Pour the red wine into the saucepan, and add the thyme, honey and marmalade. Bring to the boil and simmer, uncovered, for 10 minutes.

In the meantime, carefully peel the pears (we leave the stems on, which keeps the pears from falling apart while cooking). Arrange the pears in the saucepan with the red wine.

Bring to the boil again, lower the heat, cover and simmer very slowly for 20-30 minutes, or longer if necessary. The pears should be soft but not fall to pieces. If the syrup doesn't cover the pears, you need to gently turn them once or twice while cooking.

Transfer the pears to a large bowl using a slotted spoon. Continue to cook the syrup, uncovered, for about 30 minutes, or until it thickens. Pour the syrup over the pears and allow them to cool. The pears will keep in the fridge for 6-7 days.

Left: Swedish ginger pears

mango

We'll always remember the mango trees in India...

What were those magnificent trees? As the train wound its way through the Indian landscape, we passed by one lush green and exquisitely shaped tree after another. In the shade, man and beast alike would sit and rest for a while, under majestic crowns virtually groaning with fruit.

We had never seen such grand mango trees before, and were stunned by their beauty. They embodied the very image of a tree. Ever since that first, magical trip to India, the mango has found a given place as one of our favourite fruits. Not only because of its luscious, delicate sweetness and smooth texture, but also because of its sheer beauty...

There are hundreds of different types of mango. One of the finest varieties is the Indian *Mangifera indica*, which has been cultivated since 2000 BC and is a descendant of a wild-growing variety that still thrives in the forests of India. The Indian mango has always been surrounded by myth and legend, one being that Buddha himself was so fond of the fruit that he had his own mango grove to meditate in. The Hindu scriptures, known as the Vedas, refer to the mango as 'food of the gods', and for centuries mangoes were prestigious status symbols among rajahs and other Indian nobles, who planted countless mango trees as proof of their affluence. The mango — fruit, leaves and blossoms — still forms a significant part of Indian rituals and ceremonies to this day.

At first, mango was only cultivated in Asia, but Portuguese explorers took the fruit to Africa in the 1700s, and from there it eventually spread to Brazil and the Caribbean. These days, large-scale producers of mango include Mexico, Venezuela, Australia and the United States.

Left, clockwise from top: Mangoes on a branch in India; A perfectly ripe mango should have silky smooth flesh; Mangoes in boxes at a Brazilian market; Three perfect mangoes

red, yellow or tart green mangoes

Mangoes can vary greatly in shape, colour and flavour. There are beautifully blushed mangoes, as well as red, yellow, green and almost purplish-pink ones. Certain varieties are nearly round while others are flat and pointy; some are sweeter and others quite tart... A perfectly ripe mango should have silky smooth flesh that is almost slippery to the touch.

TO DICE OR SLICE A MANGO: The mango flesh is attached to a large, oblong stone in its centre. To get around it, cut the unpeeled mango in half lengthwise as close to the stone as possible. Next, cut the flesh of each 'cheek' in a crisscross pattern, but not all the way through the skin. Turn the skin inside out so that the flesh opens up, separating the pieces. Serve the mango as is (as shown on the left), or carefully cut off the squares into little cubes.

   Another way is to neatly peel the entire mango with a sharp knife, and then cut off each 'cheek' as close to the stone as possible. Cut the remaining flesh from the stone and then slice or cut the mango as desired.

GREEN MANGOES: These are simply firm, unripe mangoes, which are very popular in India and Southeast Asia. Green mango is often pickled or preserved, and frequently used fresh in salads or served as a snack with salt, fish sauce or dried chilli powder. Green mango is crunchy and quite tart compared to the lush sweetness of ripe yellow mango.

AMCHUR: An Indian powder made from dried mango, used in traditional cooking to provide a certain acidity. It is used in spice mixes or sprinkled over the Indian lentil stew, dal.

MANGO CHUTNEY AND PICKLE: Two lovely accompaniments to Indian food. The chutneys in India are often made with fresh mango, and seldom as sweet as the ones we buy in jars. Pickled mango is frequently quite spicy, with lots of chilli.

DRIED MANGO: A soft piece of dried natural mango is a tropical delight, and a healthy sweet snack. The variety from the Philippines is a firm favourite with us.

Quick pickled mango

This lovely Indian-style pickled mango is very tasty alongside rice dishes, ideally with chicken or shellfish. Sometimes we make it with still green mangoes for a tangier result, but mostly we use ripe yet firm fruits to get that sweet, spicy flavour.

YOU WILL NEED:
2 medium mangoes
1 teaspoon fenugreek seeds
½ garlic clove
2 tablespoons vegetable oil
2 teaspoons mustard seeds, whole
  brown or yellow (or half of each)
¼–½ teaspoon ground turmeric
1 teaspoon chilli flakes, or to taste
sea salt

· Peel and chop the mangoes into fairly small pieces. Set aside. Crush the fenugreek seeds in a mortar, and peel and mince the garlic.

Gently heat the oil in a frying pan over medium heat. Add all the spices and garlic and sauté, while stirring, until the mustard seeds start to pop. Fold in the mango pieces and stir carefully to coat the fruit with the seasoning. Add sea salt to taste and perhaps a touch more chilli.

Transfer the pickle to a dish and leave to cool. Use it freshly made, and store for no more than a few days in the fridge.

Right, clockwise from top: Mango lassi, page 323; Dried sweet mango; Store-bought Indian mango pickles; Mango salsa with lime

Mango salsa with lime

YOU WILL NEED:
2 mangoes
1–2 shallots
1 fresh red chilli
juice and finely grated zest of 1 lime
fresh coriander leaves
a pinch of sea salt

· Start by peeling and dicing the mango, and finely chopping the shallots. Deseed and chop or finely slice the chilli. Grate the lime zest, being careful not to include any white pith. Chop a bit of fresh coriander.

Place everything in a bowl and gently toss to combine. Squeeze the lime juice on top, season lightly with sea salt and serve at once. This salsa is excellent with fish or meat, and is particularly good with anything barbecued.

Mango chutney dip

YOU WILL NEED:
300 g thick Greek yoghurt
3 tablespoons mango chutney
¼ teaspoon chilli powder or
  cayenne pepper, or to taste
a pinch of sea salt

· Combine all the ingredients in a bowl and season with a touch of salt. Great with chicken, fish or barbecued meat. Also a very tasty dip for carrot sticks and other crudités.

VARIATION WITH CURRY: Replace the chilli powder or cayenne pepper with 1½ teaspoons curry powder, or to taste. Delicious!

Green mango salad

This crunchy salad with tart green mango is fabulous with barbecued chicken or beef skewers, or a superb little starter on its own.

YOU WILL NEED:
75 g cashew nuts or peanuts
1 green mango
3 small Asian shallots
½–1 fresh red chilli
a handful of fresh coriander leaves, chopped

DRESSING:
2 teaspoons grated palm sugar
 or brown sugar
1 tablespoon fish sauce
2 tablespoons fresh lime juice

· First combine the ingredients for the dressing, stir to dissolve the sugar and set aside. Chop and then lightly toast the cashews or peanuts in a dry frying pan, and set them aside as well.
 Peel and cut the mango into thin strips. Finely chop the shallots, and then deseed and finely slice the chilli. Place everything in a bowl, add almost all the nuts and gently stir to combine. Spoon over the dressing and top with the rest of the nuts and the chopped coriander.

Indian mango and mint raita

Peel and roughly chop one sweet and perfectly ripe mango. Mash the flesh with a fork until fairly smooth.
 Combine the mango with 300 g thick Greek yoghurt, a pinch of chilli powder or cayenne, sea salt and 10–12 finely chopped fresh mint leaves.
 Serve the raita as a side to chicken, barbecued meat or spicy Indian dishes.

Prawn and mango cocktail

Try this fresh little starter: prawns piled on top of pieces of mango and avocado, drizzled with a tasty dressing.

SERVES 6–8:
1 ripe mango
2 avocados
200 g cooked peeled prawns
fresh coriander leaves or lime wedges, to serve

DRESSING:
3 spring onions, finely shredded
3 tablespoons lime juice
2–3 tablespoons Thai sweet chilli sauce
3 tablespoons finely chopped fresh coriander leaves
sea salt
a splash of water

· Combine all the ingredients for the dressing, then set aside.
 Peel and dice the mango and avocados, and arrange the pieces on individual plates or in glasses. Place a small pile of prawns on top. Give the dressing a good stir, then spoon it over the salad. Garnish with a few extra coriander leaves or lime wedges, and serve more or less at once.

Prosciutto with mango

Peel and cut perfectly ripe mango into neat wedges. Wrap a wafer-thin slice of prosciutto around each mango wedge, and serve with a glass of white wine or as finger food for parties. (Photo, page 312)

Right: Green mango salad

Chicken salad with mango curry dressing

A delightful, creamy salad flavoured with mango chutney and curry.

SERVES 4:
1 barbecued chicken
3-4 spring onions
4 celery stalks
½ cucumber, peeled
1 small mango, neatly cut
green lettuce leaves

DRESSING:
200 g thick Greek yoghurt
2½ tablespoons mango chutney, or to taste
1½ teaspoons curry powder, or to taste
½ garlic clove, minced
a pinch of sea salt
a splash of water if needed

· Remove the chicken skin and bones, cut the meat into pieces and transfer to a large bowl.

Finely shred the spring onions, cut the celery and cucumber into small pieces, and add them to the bowl. Peel and cut the mango into neat pieces, and add them too.

Rinse the lettuce leaves, spin them in a salad spinner or gently pat dry. Set aside, ideally in the fridge to make them extra crisp.

Combine the dressing ingredients (add a little water if too thick), season to taste and then fold the dressing into the ingredients in the bowl. You can prepare the recipe up to this point ahead of time.

Arrange the salad in the centre of a platter, decorating with crisp lettuce leaves around the edges. As a final touch, sprinkle the salad with a hint of extra curry powder.

Caribbean mango-glazed chicken

Mangoes are often used in Caribbean cooking. The sweet-and-sour tang of the roasted chicken goes well with beans, potato wedges or rice. Serve with a fresh green salad on the side.

SERVES 4:
1 chicken (about 1.4 kg),
    jointed into 8 pieces
2 medium onions
3 garlic cloves
3 medium tomatoes
2 tablespoons butter or oil
5 tablespoons mango chutney
2 tablespoons Worcestershire sauce
½ teaspoon ground allspice
½–1 teaspoon salt
freshly ground black pepper

· Preheat the oven to 200°C/400°F. Finely chop the onions, garlic and tomatoes.

Melt the butter or heat the oil over medium heat in a large frying pan. Sweat the onion and garlic until soft. Add the tomatoes and sauté for another minute or so, then stir in the mango chutney, Worcestershire sauce, allspice, salt and a little pepper. Cover and simmer for about 5 minutes, then remove the pan from the heat.

Put the chicken pieces in a greased ovenproof dish. Spread the mango mixture over the top, covering as much of the chicken as you can. Bake for 35-40 minutes. Increase the heat to 225°C/435°F towards the end of cooking time if the chicken needs a bit more colour.

Mango passionfruit drink

MAKES 3–4 GLASSES:
1 ripe and sweet mango
2–3 passionfruit
juice of 1 lime
sugar, to taste
sparkling mineral water
crushed ice or ice cubes

· Start by peeling and cutting the mango into pieces. Place the mango in a blender and mix until smooth. Halve the passionfruit and scoop out the pulp into a small sieve. Hold the sieve over the blender and press or rub the passionfruit pulp straight into the mango with the back of a spoon. Squeeze the lime juice in as well and pulse quickly. Season with sugar, to taste.

Pour into glasses, add sparkling mineral water and serve with ice.

Orange mango squash

MAKES 3–4 GLASSES:
1 ripe mango
juice of 3 sweet oranges
a touch of sugar (optional)
sparkling mineral water
crushed ice or ice cubes
a few strawberries

· Peel and cut the mango into pieces. Mix until smooth in a blender or food processor, together with the freshly squeezed orange juice. Taste to see if a touch of sugar is needed. Stir and pour into tall glasses, filling only halfway up each glass. Fill up with sparkling mineral water, lots of ice and garnish with finely sliced strawberries.

Mango lassi

LASSI FOR 3–4:
2 ripe and sweet mangoes
500 ml mild natural yoghurt
a pinch of sugar (optional)
50–100 ml cold water (optional)
ground cardamom (optional)

· Peel and cut the mangoes into pieces. Put the mango pieces in a blender with approximately half the yoghurt, and mix until smooth. Add the rest of the yoghurt, and a pinch of sugar and water if using. Stir, pour into glasses and serve right away, perhaps sprinkled with a touch of ground cardamom.

A cool and refreshing Indian yoghurt drink, perfect as a snack or as a great way to start the day. (Photo, page 319)

Sweet and hot fruit snack

SERVES 4–6:
1 large sweet mango
1 wedge watermelon
½ pineapple
1 rockmelon (cantaloupe)
juice of 1–2 limes
a pinch of mild sea salt (optional)
chilli powder for dusting

· Peel and cut all the fruit into neat cubes or pieces and place in individual serving bowls. Squeeze some lime juice over the fruit and sprinkle with a small pinch of mild sea salt, if using. Finish off with a light dusting of chilli powder. A spicy, sweet refreshing snack.

Rum–baked mango Caribe, page 326   *Olinda mango mousse, page 329*

Tropical yoghurt swirl, page 326

Mangoes, grapefruit and limes

Tropical yoghurt swirl

This is a smooth, fresh-tasting and rather light dessert. Very pretty when served in individual glasses. (Photo, page 325)

SERVES 4-5:
2 perfectly ripe mangoes
juice of ½–1 lime
500 g thick Greek yoghurt
60 g sifted icing sugar, or to taste
2 passionfruit

· Peel the mangoes, then cut one of them into neat pieces and set aside. In a food processor, mix the flesh from the other mango with the lime juice. Alternatively, mash the flesh by hand and use the back of a spoon to strain or press it through a sieve, then season with the lime juice.

Combine the yoghurt with the sifted icing sugar, and pour about half of the yoghurt into glasses or small bowls. Spoon over some of the mango purée and then dollop a bit of yoghurt on top. Give the yoghurt a brief stir to create a ripple of mango in the yoghurt.

Top with the mango pieces and then scoop out some passionfruit on top of each serving.

Sweet mango sauce

Drizzle this mango sauce over ice cream, Greek yoghurt or a piece of cheesecake.

· Peel and cut mango into pieces and mix until smooth in a food processor. Season to taste with icing sugar and a splash of fresh lime or lemon juice. Dilute with a little cold water if necessary.

Rum-baked mango Caribe

A Caribbean-style dessert where sweet, succulent mango wedges are baked with muscovado sugar, butter and a splash of rum. (Photo, page 324)

SERVES 4:
3 large, sweet mangoes
50 g butter + a bit more to grease the dish
4–6 tablespoons dark rum
4–5 tablespoons muscovado or caster sugar
vanilla ice cream, to serve
2 passionfruit (optional)

· Preheat the oven to 250°C/480°F. Peel and cut the mangoes lengthwise into wedges, as close to the stone as possible. Place the wedges in a greased ovenproof dish, add a few knobs of butter here and there, pour over the rum and, last of all, sprinkle the sugar on top. Bake for roughly 10 minutes, or until the mango pieces are nice and golden.

Serve the mango wedges slightly cooled or even lukewarm, with vanilla ice cream and some scooped-out passionfruit on top, if desired.

Toasty coconut mango

Toast 100 g desiccated coconut in a dry frying pan until lightly golden. Add 1–2 tablespoons muscovado sugar and 100 ml water, then stir vigorously and quickly let the sugar bubble and melt. Set aside. Cut 1 large perfectly ripe mango into pieces and arrange on a platter. Sprinkle with the toasted coconut and garnish with lime wedges.

Mango cheesecake

An elegant mango dessert that is quite easy to make with a food processor. To get the perfect consistency, make the cheesecake one day in advance. (Photo, page 409)

FOR 10-12 PIECES:
200 g (about 14) plain sweet biscuits,
  such as Marie or digestives
100 g butter, in cubes
3 tablespoons muscovado or caster sugar

FILLING:
3 large mangoes (you need 800 ml purée)
400 g Philadelphia cream cheese, at room temperature
175 g caster sugar
2 tablespoons fresh lemon or lime juice
4 medium eggs

TOP LAYER:
4 gelatine leaves
100 ml hot water
3 tablespoons caster sugar
300 ml of the mango purée above

• Preheat the oven to 175°C/345°F. Line a baking tray with non-stick baking paper.

Break the biscuits into large pieces and crumble them in a food processor. Add the butter and sugar and mix to combine. Pour the crumbs into a 24 cm springform tin. Using your fingers, gently press the crumbs into the base of the tin. Bake for 12-15 minutes, remove from the oven and set aside.

Reduce the heat to 160°C/320°F. Wash and set up the food processor. For the filling, peel and cut the mango from the stone, and put the pieces in the processor. Mix the mango into a smooth purée. Set aside 300 ml of the purée.

Return the remaining mango purée to the food processor, add the cream cheese, sugar and the lime or lemon juice and mix again. While the machine is running, add one egg at a time. Pour the mixture into the prebaked biscuit base.

Bake in the middle of the oven for 1 hour, or for 5-10 minutes more until set. Allow the cheesecake to cool down completely.

Prepare the top layer by soaking the gelatine leaves in cold water for 5 minutes. Remove the leaves and melt them in 100 ml hot water in a small saucepan. Stir the melted gelatine and sugar into the reserved mango purée until combined, and then pour it on top of the cheesecake. Allow to set, then cover the tin with plastic wrap and refrigerate until the next day.

Serve the mango cheesecake in slices, drizzled with fresh passionfruit pulp.

Mango and strawberry salad

SERVES 4-6:
2 perfectly ripe mangoes
500 g sweet strawberries
finely grated zest of 1-2 limes
a pinch of sugar

• Peel and then cut the mangoes into pieces and place them in a serving bowl. Hull and halve the strawberries and arrange them on top of the mango.

Zest the lime, being careful not to include any white pith. Sprinkle the lime zest over the fruit. Add a touch of sugar and serve at once. A tangy, summery dessert that is easy to make for a large gathering.

Mango sorbet

When making mango sorbet, having an ice-cream maker is a bonus as the consistency becomes a bit too icy in the freezer.

SERVES 5-6:
200 ml water
180 g caster sugar
1 gelatine leaf
3 ripe mangoes
juice of 1 lime

· Prepare a sugar syrup by bringing the water and sugar to the boil and letting it simmer, uncovered, for 3-4 minutes. Set aside to cool.

Soak the gelatine leaf in a bowl of cold water for 5 minutes. Remove the gelatine and let it dissolve in the hot sugar syrup, stir and then allow the syrup to cool a bit.

Peel and cut the mangoes using a sharp knife. Put the mango flesh and lime juice in a food processor, and process until everything is smooth. While the machine is running, pour in the cold sugar syrup and stop the machine.

Freeze the mixture in an ice-cream maker (it may take 45 minutes or so until the sorbet is done). Serve the mango sorbet straight away, or keep it in the freezer until you are ready to serve. Delicious with a few raspberries or some sliced strawberries and a mint sprig for garnish.

Left: Mango sorbet

Olinda mango mousse

During a trip to Olinda in Brazil, we were once treated to a delectable mango and lime mousse. We think the recipe went something like this. (Photo, page 324)

MOUSSE FOR 6-8:
2 sweet, ripe mangoes
400 g tin sweetened condensed milk
juice and finely grated zest of 1 lime
3 gelatine leaves
300 ml pure (whipping) cream
500 g strawberries
+ extra lime zest for garnish

· Peel and cut the mangoes into pieces, put them in a food processor and purée until smooth. Pour the purée into a bowl and stir in the condensed milk. Season with the lime juice and grated zest, then set aside.

Soak the gelatine leaves in a bowl of cold water for 5 minutes. Whip the cream in a separate bowl. Remove the gelatine leaves from the water and melt them in a small saucepan with 50 ml water over low heat. Stir the dissolved gelatine into the mango and condensed milk mixture. Fold the whipped cream, a little at a time, into the mango purée.

Pour the mousse into serving bowls or a single large dish. Cover well with plastic wrap and allow the mousse to set in the fridge for at least 3 hours. To serve, top with sliced strawberries and sprinkle with a bit of extra lime zest.

raspberries

the delicate flavour of raspberries

One of the highlights of summer, at least to us, is enjoying a bowl of freshly picked raspberries, dusted with a little sugar and served with creamy milk or a scoop of vanilla ice cream. Fresh raspberries are just heavenly, especially the older varieties as these often have smaller but more aromatic berries. A cool glass of fresh raspberry juice is also hard to beat. We are lucky to have lots of old-fashioned raspberry cultivars in the garden and, in season, we often keep a jug of chilled raspberry juice ready in the fridge. It's a truly delightful thirst-quencher, appreciated by grown-ups and children alike.

Raspberries, *Rubus idaeus*, are related to blackberries, dewberries and cloudberries. They are stone fruits or drupes, and each raspberry is essentially a whole bunch of drupelets stuck together to form a single berry. Red raspberries are the most common, but there are also yellow, black and purple varieties, and new cultivars are constantly being developed through cross-cultivation. Raspberries are bursting with vitamins and antioxidants, and are classified as one of the 'superfoods' due to their many nutrients and health benefits. Of course, freshly picked raspberries are tastier and more nutritious, but raspberries can easily be frozen as well (we sprinkle 1-2 tablespoons of caster sugar per 500 g over the raspberries before freezing them, as this helps to retain their flavour). And in the winter, having a freezer stocked with raspberries will give you countless possibilities to bake and make desserts with a real summery feel. Until raspberry season comes around again...

Left: Raspberries and ice cream — always delicious

Fresh raspberry juice, page 336

Garden raspberries

Freshly picked raspberries

Late summer crumble, page 341

Fresh raspberry juice

If you have plenty of raspberries, make a large jug of this sweet, fresh juice. (Photo, page 334)

• Carefully pick over the raspberries, or thaw frozen berries. Mix them in a blender, sweeten with sugar to taste and dilute with a bit of water. (If you wish, strain the raspberry mix through a fine sieve to remove the small seeds.) Enjoy the juice chilled or with crushed ice.

Raspberry punch

This is one of our favourite welcome drinks for summer parties. It's easy to double or multiply the recipe, and a few slices of ripe peach add a nice touch.

• Carefully pick over the berries: 250 g perfectly fresh raspberries will be enough for 1 bottle (750 ml) of dry white wine. Place the berries in a jug or bowl, sweeten with sugar to taste and stir carefully. Cover with plastic wrap and refrigerate for 2 hours. Add the wine, perhaps a few sliced peaches and chill for 1-2 hours before serving.

Raspberry smoothie

Mix 500 g vanilla yoghurt with 200 g fresh or frozen raspberries in a blender or food processor. Sweeten with a little icing sugar and serve in tall glasses. Serves 2

Swedish summer cordial

This is an old-style raspberry cordial, full of summer flavour. The raspberries aren't cooked, which means you should only use nice, fresh berries. This method also shortens the cordial's shelf life, so store it in the fridge for up to 1 month or freeze it right away to save for a wintry day.

YOU WILL NEED:
1.5 litres water
about 2 kg raspberries
2 tablespoons citric acid
  + 100 ml boiling water
850 g caster sugar

• Bring the water to the boil and let cool. In the meantime, rinse and pick over the raspberries. Mash the berries by hand in a large bowl or jug, preferably using a potato masher — a blender or a food processor will make the raspberries far too mushy.

Pour the pre-boiled cold water over the berries. Dissolve the citric acid in 100 ml boiling water and stir it into the cordial. Cover with plastic wrap and chill for 24 hours, stirring now and again.

Strain the cordial through a muslin-lined colander into a bowl. Next, stir in a little bit of sugar at a time and keep stirring until the sugar dissolves. Skim the cordial (if needed) and pour it into sterilised glass bottles, filling all the way to the top. Close with a lid or cork, or freeze the raspberry cordial in plastic freeze-proof containers.

Note! To serve, dilute a small amount of the cordial with cold water — about a fifth of a glass of cordial to four-fifths cold water, or to taste.

Sugar-stirred raspberries

In all their simplicity, sugar-stirred raspberries are a delicacy on top of ice cream or Greek yoghurt flavoured with vanilla. Use them frozen for baking, in smoothies and more.

• Carefully pick over the raspberries and mash them by hand, ideally with a potato masher. Sweeten with a bit of caster sugar and enjoy the raspberries pretty much immediately. You can also freeze them in small freeze-proof containers.

   Note! Mashed raspberries can also be frozen unsweetened, but won't maintain the exquisite berry flavour as well.

Nostalgic raspberry compote

An old-fashioned Scandinavian raspberry compote, lovely when served with full-fat milk and a biscuit (such as the sweet cardamom rusks on page 293) on the side.

SERVES 4:
500 g raspberries
600 ml water
3-4 tablespoons caster sugar, or to taste
1 tablespoon fresh lemon juice
2½ tablespoons potato starch
   + 50 ml water

• Carefully pick over the berries. Place half the berries in a saucepan and pour over the water. Add the sugar and lemon juice, bring to the boil and simmer for 2 minutes. Whisk together the potato starch and water and stir into the compote, stirring until it thickens. Add the reserved berries, taste and sweeten if necessary.

   Let the compote cool a little before covering it with plastic wrap to avoid a skin forming. Chill until ready to serve.

Warm vanilla raspberries

We often had this comforting dessert for Sunday dinner at Grandma's house. Serve the warm raspberries with vanilla ice cream and a spoonful of lightly whipped cream.

• Place 500 g fresh or lightly sugared frozen raspberries and 2 tablespoons water in a pan. Slice half a vanilla pod lengthwise, scrape out the seeds and put the seeds and pod in the saucepan. Bring to a quick boil, and stir until the raspberries are slightly mashed. Remove the vanilla pod and add icing sugar to taste.

   Serve the raspberries warm as above, or alongside the poached saffron pears on page 311.

Raspberry coulis

This dainty raspberry sauce is excellent for cheesecakes, poached pears, Peach Melba or individual servings of elegant fruit salad on a pool of raspberry coulis.

• Mix fresh or thawed raspberries with icing sugar in a food processor or blender. You will need about 3-5 tablespoons icing sugar for 500 g raspberries, depending on how sweet the berries are.

   Pour everything into a fine sieve placed over a bowl. Use the back of a spoon to rub the raspberries back and forth until only the seeds remain in the sieve. Discard the seeds, flavour the sauce with 1-2 teaspoons fresh lemon juice and pour into a small jug.

   Raspberry coulis can be prepared a day ahead and stored in the fridge, or frozen for later use.

Marsala raspberry soup

A refreshing dessert soup flavoured with a splash of Marsala. Serve the soup chilled in small bowls, ideally with a few biscuits on the side, such as the Mallorcan almond chews on page 253, or top with a few melon cubes and thinly sliced strawberries.

SERVES 4:
700 g fresh raspberries
  (or 500 g frozen + 250 g fresh raspberries
  for serving)
60 g sifted icing sugar, or to taste
3 tablespoons Marsala
  or other sweet dessert wine
1 wedge ripe, green melon (optional)
4–5 strawberries (optional)
fresh mint or lemon balm leaves

• Set aside about one-third of the raspberries. Mash the rest with the icing sugar and strain through a sieve, using a rubber spatula or the back of a spoon. Flavour with the Marsala and taste to see if more sugar is needed. Chill for 1 hour.

Pour the soup into small bowls, top with the reserved raspberries, and perhaps a few cubes of green melon and some thinly sliced strawberries. Garnish with a couple of small fresh mint or lemon balm leaves.

Lemon pavlova with berries

Tiny pavlovas topped with a rich lemon curd cream, raspberries and redcurrants.

FOR 12 MINI PAVLOVAS:
soft butter + flour for the baking paper
4 medium egg whites
200 g caster sugar
1 tablespoon cornflour
1 teaspoon white wine vinegar
300 g thick Greek yoghurt
about 100 ml lemon curd, or to taste
sifted icing sugar, to taste
about 500 g fresh raspberries
  + a few redcurrants

• Draw 12 small circles (7 cm in diameter) on two pieces of non-stick baking paper. Grease the circles, then place the paper on baking trays. Sift a bit of flour on top of the circles and shake off any excess flour. Set aside.

Preheat the oven to 130°C/260°F. Whisk the egg whites using a hand-held electric whisk, slowly at first and gradually increasing the speed. Add the sugar a little at a time, and keep whisking until you can pull long 'peaks' of shiny meringue from the whisk. Fold in the cornflour and vinegar. Spoon the meringue onto the circles and spread it out just a bit.

Bake for 35 minutes, or until the meringues are dry to the touch, swapping the trays once. Turn off the oven and leave the pavlovas inside until cooled.

Combine the yoghurt and lemon curd with sifted icing sugar to taste. Just before serving, dollop the lemon cream on top of the pavlovas and decorate with the fresh raspberries and a few redcurrants.

Raspberry mousse gateau

This sumptuous and festive mousse cake is quite elegant yet very easy to make. It serves up to 10, and can be prepared a week in advance and then frozen. Just remember to let the mousse thaw in the fridge for about 3 hours before serving. Decorate with finely sliced fruit and fresh berries, and serve with raspberry coulis. (Photo, page 343)

SERVES 10–12:

1 litre mashed raspberries from 1 kg fresh
  or frozen raspberries
120 g icing sugar
8 gelatine leaves
5 egg yolks
150 g sifted icing sugar
1 litre pure (whipping) cream
mixed fresh berries and raspberry
  coulis (page 337), for serving
fresh lemon balm or mint leaves for garnish

· Purée the raspberries and icing sugar in a food processor. Strain the mixture through a sieve, rubbing the raspberries with the back of a spoon to remove the seeds from the purée. This may take a little while, but it's the recipe's only time-consuming step.

Soak the gelatine leaves in plenty of cold water for at least 5 minutes. Take out a large springform tin, 22–24 cm. Whisk the egg yolks and icing sugar until nice and fluffy. In another large bowl, lightly whip the cream.

Remove the gelatine leaves and dissolve them in 3 tablespoons water in a small saucepan over medium heat. Once dissolved, carefully stir the gelatine straight into the cream.

Fold the raspberry purée into the cream, then fold in the egg yolks. Gently fold to combine, but stir no more than necessary. Pour the mixture into the tin straight away, and place in the freezer until the next day.

Once frozen, cover the tin with plastic wrap or foil and return to the freezer. Take it out 3–4 hours before serving and let it thaw in the fridge.

Just before serving, garnish with fresh fruit and berries, and perhaps a few fresh lemon balm or mint leaves.

Easy frozen yoghurt

TO MAKE 1 LITRE:

400 g frozen raspberries
60–90 g sifted icing sugar
½–1 teaspoon pure vanilla extract
500 g thick Greek yoghurt

· Partly thaw the berries and then purée them in a food processor or with a hand-held blender. Stir in the icing sugar and vanilla, then fold in the yoghurt last of all. Freeze the mixture in an ice-cream maker for the best results. Once frozen, transfer to a freeze-proof container and store in the freezer.

You can also pour the mixture straight into a freeze-proof container and freeze it right away. If so, give the raspberry yoghurt a good stir every 30 minutes while it freezes, which takes about 4 hours. The frozen yoghurt is best served the day it's made.

Peach Melba

This combination of raspberries and peaches is Master Chef Auguste Escoffier's timeless tribute to Australian soprano Nellie Melba, to celebrate her London performance in the 1890s.

SERVES 4:

4 perfectly ripe peaches, cooked
  with a vanilla pod (page 360)

RASPBERRY COULIS:

500 g fresh raspberries
3-4 tablespoons sifted icing sugar
1-2 teaspoons fresh lemon juice

SERVE WITH:

good-quality vanilla ice cream
3 tablespoons toasted almond flakes or
  crumbled amaretti biscuits

· Cook the peaches slowly, either whole or in halves, for about 8-12 minutes, depending on their type and ripeness. Gently pull the skin off the peaches and allow to cool.

Prepare the raspberry coulis following the recipe on page 337.

Arrange the peaches in small bowls or individual glasses. Add a scoop of vanilla ice cream and carefully spoon over the lovely raspberry coulis. Serve as is or sprinkle with a few almond flakes that have been toasted in a dry frying pan (and ideally lightly caramelised with a pinch of icing sugar towards the end). Or simply crumble an amaretti biscuit on top of each serving.

Late summer crumble

In late summer, we like to make this raspberry crumble with peaches or nectarines and serve it with vanilla ice cream. (Photo, page 335)

CRUMBLE FOR 6:

500 g raspberries
4-5 ripe peaches or nectarines
180 g plain flour
2 tablespoons caster sugar
1 teaspoon pure vanilla extract
150 g cold butter, in cubes
1 heaped tablespoon potato starch
100 g caster sugar for the fruit

· Pick over the raspberries to make sure all the berries are nice and fresh. Halve the peaches or nectarines, remove the stones and cut into thick slices.

Preheat the oven to 200°C/400°F. Measure out the flour, sugar, vanilla and butter in a big bowl. Use your fingertips to rub together the ingredients (or whiz in a food processor), leaving some visible pieces of butter in the mix.

Tip approximately half of the crumble mix into a 24 cm pie tin and flatten it with your hand to create a pie crust base. Dust the potato starch over the dough, and then arrange the sliced peaches or nectarines on top. Add the raspberries last, then sprinkle the 100 g of caster sugar over the fruit. Finally, sprinkle over the remaining crumble mixture.

Bake the crumble for 30-35 minutes, or until cooked through and nicely golden.

Overleaf: Peach Melba; Raspberry mousse gateau with fruit is a delightful summer cake

Raspberry Swiss roll

Swiss rolls are quick and easy to make, and very tasty when filled with sugar-stirred raspberries. Perfect with a cup of tea, or as a dessert topped with a dollop of whipped cream, mixed berries and flaked almonds. If you like, add a splash of amaretto or other liqueur.

YOU WILL NEED:
3 medium eggs
130 g caster sugar + extra for sprinkling
2 tablespoons milk
120 g plain flour
1 teaspoon baking powder
about 250 ml sugar-stirred raspberries,
  (page 337), or raspberry jam

· Preheat the oven to 250°C/480°F. Line two baking trays with non-stick baking paper.

Beat the eggs and sugar until nice and fluffy, preferably using electric beaters. Stir in the milk and, last of all, the flour (mixed with the baking powder). Stir the mixture as little as possible; it just needs to combine. Spread the mixture quite thinly into a fairly even, large square on one of the baking papers.

Bake in the middle of the oven for 5 minutes. Meanwhile, sprinkle a bit of sugar on the paper on the other baking tray.

Tip the baked sponge onto the sugared paper, and then carefully pull off the paper it was baked on. Immediately spread a thin layer of sugar-stirred raspberries or jam on top of the warm sponge. Roll into a Swiss roll starting from the longer side, pulling the paper a little as you go (from where you started rolling). Leave to cool, seam-side down, still wrapped in paper. Remove the paper, slice and serve.

Viennese almond squares

There are several steps to this recipe, but it's well worth it because these almond and jam squares are fabulous.

YOU WILL NEED:
200 g almonds, blanched and peeled
100 g caster sugar
½ teaspoon pure vanilla extract
200 g soft butter, in small cubes
260 g plain flour
about 200 ml raspberry jam
50 g flaked almonds

· Preheat the oven to 175°C/345°F. Use a food processor to make the dough. First grind the almonds using the shredding disc, then switch to the steel blade and mix/grate the almonds together with some of the sugar – this prevents the almonds from becoming too oily when ground. Add the rest of the sugar, the vanilla, butter and flour. Pulse for 15-20 seconds, or until the dough starts to form into a ball.

Turn out the dough onto a lightly floured work surface, gently knead it to combine, then flatten into a square. Place the dough between two pieces of non-stick baking paper and roll it into a large, 1 cm thick rectangle. Turn it onto a baking tray, peel off the top piece of baking paper but leave the bottom one on.

Bake in the oven for about 15 minutes. Meanwhile, gently heat the raspberry jam until slightly liquid. Remove the dough from the oven, spread the jam on top and sprinkle with the flaked almonds. Bake for a further 15-20 minutes, allow to cool and then cut into diamond shapes.

Alma's sweet catalans

Catalans are simply small almond pastries with a bit of raspberry jam in the centre and pale pink icing on top. Makes 10-12 catalans.

SHORTCRUST PASTRY DOUGH:
150 g butter, at room temperature
5 tablespoons caster sugar
2 egg yolks
1 tablespoon fresh lemon juice
180 g plain flour

ALMOND FILLING:
250 g almond paste
100 g butter, at room temperature
1 medium egg
10–12 teaspoons raspberry jam
  (1 teaspoon per catalan)

ICING:
about 100 ml raspberry jam
120 g sifted icing sugar
1–1½ tablespoons water

THE SHORTCRUST PASTRY: Cream the soft butter with the sugar, add the egg yolks, lemon juice, and then the flour. Quickly work into a dough. Use a floured thumb to press it into 10-12 small round or oval cake tins (6-7 cm diameter). Set them aside on a tray in the fridge. Preheat the oven to 190°C/375°F.

THE FILLING: Grate the almond paste and blend in the soft butter a little at a time. Add the egg and stir until smooth. Spoon about 1 teaspoon raspberry jam into each pastry shell, and then fill with the almond mixture until the tins are about three-quarters filled.

BAKE: Bake the catalans for 15-20 minutes. Turn them upside down and let cool slightly before you remove the tins, and then allow them to cool down completely.

THE ICING: Heat the raspberry jam in a small saucepan until almost liquid. Brush the top of the cold catalans with a thin layer of jam. Make the icing by combining the sifted icing sugar with a few drops of water, and spread it over the catalans. Allow the icing to set.

Raspberry jam

This reliable recipe works well for raspberries, which don't contain much pectin per se.

YOU WILL NEED:
1 kg fresh raspberries
150 ml water
500 g caster sugar
1½ tablespoons pectin
1 tablespoon citric acid
40 g extra caster sugar

• Simmer the raspberries with the water in a covered saucepan for 20 minutes or so. Gradually stir in the sugar and bring to a swift boil, just until the sugar dissolves.

Meanwhile, combine the pectin, citric acid and the extra sugar in a tea cup. Sprinkle the mixture over the surface of the jam and stir continuously. Once you add the pectin, only simmer the jam for 5 minutes at the most. Pour the jam into hot sterilised jars, cover and seal. Store in a cool pantry or the fridge.

vanilla

the scent of vanilla...

... is both subtle and intense. Opening the wrinkled, dark brown pods releases a multitude of aromas from the thousands of small seeds. Vanilla is such a wonderful ingredient, one of our most cherished flavours, and is used in sweets, baked goods and desserts all over the world. Sometimes the precious seeds are added to savoury dishes as well, often to accompany shellfish, which is considered a particularly good match with vanilla. We use vanilla often, but so far only in desserts, pastries and such. A few vanilla pods, ground organic vanilla powder and a large jar of homemade vanilla sugar are all staples in our pantry, as no artificial substitute can ever compare to the unique, mellow flavour of true vanilla...

Vanilla planifolia is a pale yellowish-green orchid originating from Central America. The plant grows wild on tall vines in the rainforests of Mexico. The Mayans and Aztecs used vanilla for centuries, among other things, for flavouring cocoa. The Spaniards eventually took both vanilla and cocoa back to Europe, where the new, exciting flavours became a huge hit. The French used vanilla to flavour sweets and tobacco, and in the 19th century they took the precious spice to their colonies in Réunion, Mauritius and Madagascar, where most vanilla comes from today.

The vanilla genus comprises a hundred or so varieties, but the species *V. planifolia* is the primary source of true vanilla. Fresh vanilla pods are bright green and have no vanilla scent at all. Extracting the lovely aroma is a lengthy process, which explains why vanilla is the second most expensive spice in the world, after saffron. The vanilla orchid blossoms only for a single day, and must be pollinated by hand with a small bamboo stick that same day. Several months later the pods are harvested, and then cured through an extensive drying and sweating process, followed by months of storage in airtight boxes. Once matured, the unique flavour has developed and the pods have turned a deep, dark brown. Finally, the vanilla pods are graded according to quality and length, before being packaged and sealed, and ready to be enjoyed in our kitchens.

Left, clockwise from top: Homemade vanilla sugar, page 352; Tahitian vanilla; Store-bought vanilla sugar; Fresh vanilla pods, Java

true vanilla and artificial vanillin

BOURBON VANILLA, or Bourbon-Madagascar vanilla, *Vanilla planifolia*, true vanilla, is primarily grown in Madagascar. Bourbon vanilla has narrow pods, with creamy, sweet flavour notes. Mexican vanilla is derived from the native *V. planifolia* plant.

TAHITIAN VANILLA, *Vanilla tahitensis*, is grown in Tahiti and other islands in French Polynesia. Tahitian vanilla has thicker, sturdier pods and a slightly floral, fruity aroma, which also makes it popular for perfume making.

WEST INDIAN VANILLA, *Vanilla pompona*, has a slightly lower content of vanillin compounds, and, as the name suggests, it is grown in the West Indies as well as in Central and South America.

GROUND VANILLA POWDER, or vanilla bean powder, consists of finely ground whole vanilla pods. You only need a small amount to get lots of lovely vanilla flavour.

VANILLA PASTE is a thick, syrupy paste based on true vanilla. It is very useful for baking and in desserts, with a much rounder flavour than vanilla extract.

PURE VANILLA EXTRACT is based on true vanilla infused in alcohol. To be on the safe side, though, always check to see whether it's true or artificial vanilla.

VANILLIN is the major flavour compound in the vanilla pod. Synthetic vanillin can be produced from wood and coal, and is commonly used in vanilla essence and artificial vanilla sugar.

a few vanilla tips

BUYING AND STORING: When buying vanilla, choose soft, moist pods. Store the pods in an airtight jar, ideally in a cool, dark place to preserve the flavour. A quick way to make a mild vanilla-infused sugar is to fill an airtight glass jar with caster sugar, pop in a couple of vanilla pods and store it in the pantry. If you want to make true, homemade vanilla sugar, you will find an easy recipe on page 352.

LIBERATE THE SEEDS: Split the vanilla pod lengthwise and scrape out the tiny black seeds onto a chopping board. Add 1 tablespoon of sugar and quickly rub the vanilla seeds and sugar back and forth with a blunt table knife to separate the seeds, making it easier to blend them into a panna cotta, crème caramel or sauce.

Right: Crème caramel, page 354

Creamy vanilla yoghurt

An utterly simple cream that we often serve with strawberries or other summer berries, sliced nectarines or a fruit salad. Alternatively, replace the yoghurt with crème frâiche for a richer cream, which is perfect with compotes, poached fruits or a pie.

• Put 250 g thick Greek yoghurt in a bowl and combine with ¼ teaspoon ground vanilla powder or ½ teaspoon vanilla paste, or use 1 tablespoon vanilla sugar (see recipe below) dissolved in 2 teaspoons hot water. Sweeten with 3-4 tablespoons sifted icing sugar, or to taste. Serves 4-5

Vanilla pouring custard

MAKES 350 ML:
300 ml pure (whipping) cream
½ vanilla pod, split lengthwise
2 egg yolks
3 tablespoons caster sugar
2 teaspoons cornflour

• Bring the cream and vanilla pod to the boil, and then gently simmer for 2-3 minutes. Set the saucepan aside and leave the cream to cool. Remove the vanilla pod and scrape out the seeds into the cream.

  Add the egg yolks, sugar and cornflour. Return to a low heat and simmer very carefully while stirring, *without boiling*, until the mixture thickens. Taste, add a touch more sugar if desired, then strain and pour the custard into a container and leave to cool. This pouring custard, or crème anglaise, is superb with rhubarb pie, apple crumble and much more.

Right: Vanilla custard

Vanilla custard

MAKES ABOUT 500 ML:
300 ml full-fat milk
200 ml pure (whipping) cream
2 tablespoons cornflour
3 tablespoons caster sugar
2 egg yolks
½ vanilla pod, split lengthwise

• Measure out the milk, cream, cornflour, sugar, and egg yolks in a small saucepan. Scrape the vanilla seeds into the pan and add the pod as well. Slowly simmer over low heat without boiling, and stir continuously until the custard thickens. Remove from the heat, strain quickly and let cool. The custard will thicken even more when it cools.

  Delicious as a filling in pastries and other baked goods.

Homemade vanilla sugar

With a jar of this fragrant vanilla sugar in the pantry, you can easily make delicious desserts even better. It's terrific with summer berries, sprinkled over fruits for oven-baking, and in pastries, pies and crumbles. Making your own vanilla sugar is easy if you have a food processor. (Photo, page 348)

• Measure out about 500 g caster sugar into the bowl of the food processor. Split 2 vanilla pods lengthwise, cut them into smaller pieces and place them in the processor. Whiz for about 3 minutes, or until the vanilla pod is finely ground and the sugar turns grey with little black dots. Sift the sugar through a fine sieve, pour it into an airtight jar and seal.

  Note! If you prefer even finer sugar, whiz and sift the vanilla sugar a few more times.

Crème caramel

Is there a more delectable dessert than this French classic? To us it's the ultimate dessert. Crème caramel benefits from being prepared one day in advance to achieve the perfect consistency. (Photo, page 351)

SERVES 8:
1 litre full-fat milk
290 g caster sugar
½ vanilla pod
5 tablespoons water
6 medium eggs

· Gently bring the milk and 90 g of the sugar to the boil in a heavy-based saucepan. Split the vanilla pod lengthwise, scrape out the seeds and add both the seeds and pod to the milk. Simmer for 3 minutes, then remove the pan from the heat and let the flavours infuse for 40-60 minutes.

THE CARAMEL: Put the remaining 200 g of sugar and the water in a heavy-based saucepan or sturdy frying pan. Stir while the sugar is melting but *do not stir* once it has started to bubble. Cook, uncovered, for 7-8 minutes, or until large bubbles appear and the caramel turns a light golden colour. At this point, *immediately* pour the very hot caramel into small individual ramekins or one large mould. Quickly tilt the ramekins to coat the base and sides with caramel, and set aside.

THE CUSTARD: Take out a roasting tin or dish. Place a folded thin tea towel in the base of the tin, then arrange the caramel-glazed ramekins or mould on top of the tea towel. Set the tin aside.

Preheat the oven to 160°C/320°F. Remove the vanilla pod from the cooled milk.

Crack the eggs into a bowl, whisk lightly and then pour them into the vanilla milk and stir to combine. Strain the mixture straight into a jug and pour the mixture into the ramekins or mould. Carefully pour a little bit of water into the roasting tin, until the water is about 2 cm deep.

BAKE AND SERVE: Baking times vary depending on the size of the ramekins or single mould. Bake small ramekins for 40-50 minutes or a single larger mould for 60-70 minutes, or until set. Be very careful when removing the tin from the oven as the water is hot; we often use kitchen tongs to lift out the moulds, leaving the water to cool in the oven.

Allow the crème caramels to cool completely and then refrigerate until the next day.

To unmould, slide a thin, flexible knife around the edge and tip onto individual plates. A larger crème caramel can also be served straight from the mould, spooning some of the luscious caramel sauce on top.

Crème brûlée

A true crème brûlée should be made with only cream, but we prefer this somewhat lighter version. Try flavouring the smooth vanilla cream with a bit of freshly ground cardamom for a nice variation.

SERVES 6:
6 egg yolks
300 ml pure (whipping) cream
200 ml full-fat milk
70 g caster sugar for the cream
½ vanilla pod, split lengthwise
about 60 g raw (demerara) sugar or caster sugar
  for the caramel crust on top

· Preheat the oven to 150°C/300°F. Place the egg yolks in a bowl and set aside.

Measure out the cream, milk and caster sugar in a heavy-based saucepan, and add the vanilla pod. Bring to the boil and simmer over low heat for a few minutes while stirring.

Take out a small roasting tin, place a folded tea towel in the base of the tin, then arrange 6 small ramekins on top. Set aside.

Lightly whisk the egg yolks in the bowl. Remove the vanilla pod from the hot milk and scrape the seeds into the milk in the saucepan. Pour a bit of the hot creamy milk over the egg yolks in the bowl while whisking vigorously, and then gradually stir in the rest. Strain the mixture straight into a jug and pour it into the ramekins in the roasting tin.

Place the roasting tin in the middle of the oven, then pour a bit of warm water into the tin, without splashing any into the ramekins. Bake the custards for about 40-50 minutes, or until set.

Carefully remove the ramekins (mind the hot water in the roasting tin) and let cool before placing the ramekins in the fridge. You can prepare the recipe up to this point the day ahead, for best results.

TO SERVE: Sprinkle an even layer of sugar over the top of the custards. Either use a chef's blowtorch to caramelise the sugar, or place the ramekins under a hot oven grill for about 2-3 minutes until the sugar is nicely golden but not burnt. The sugar should be caramelised, just enough to melt and start to bubble, and once it sets it will create a golden caramel crust. Serve at once.

VARIATION WITH CARDAMOM: Let I teaspoon freshly ground cardamom simmer in the creamy milk together with the vanilla pod.

This book also contains a recipe for Crema catalana, crème brûlée's Spanish cousin, which is flavoured with a bit of grated citrus zest. See page 215.

Vanilla-poached peaches, page 360

Vanilla rice pudding, page 359

Panna cotta with berries, page 358

Simple panna cotta, page 358

Panna cotta with berries

Vanilla panna cotta is a delightful dessert that is easy to make for a crowd. Serve it with fresh summer berries and perhaps a bit of raspberry coulis. (Photo, page 357)

FOR 10-12 SMALL SERVINGS:
600 ml pure (whipping) cream
400 ml full-fat milk
5 tablespoons caster sugar
½ vanilla pod, split lengthwise
4 gelatine leaves

TO SERVE:
400 g fresh berries, lightly sugared
raspberry coulis (page 337) (optional)

· First bring the cream to the boil with the milk, sugar and vanilla pod. Cover and simmer slowly for 15 minutes. Meanwhile, soak the gelatine leaves in cold water until soft.

Remove the gelatine leaves, add them to the warm cream mixture and melt while stirring. Remove the vanilla pod, scrape out the seeds and return them to the milk in the pan. Stir well to combine. Strain the mixture straight into a jug. Leave to cool until just lukewarm, stirring occasionally.

Pour the mixture into 10-12 small ramekins. Allow to cool and then refrigerate until set.

Just before serving, quickly dip the bottom of the ramekins in hot water and unmould the panna cottas onto individual plates. Garnish with lightly sugared berries and serve with some raspberry coulis, if desired.

Simple panna cotta in a glass

This is a slightly simpler panna cotta that we like to serve in small glasses, topped with lime-marinated strawberries and blueberries. (Photo, page 357)

FOR 8-10 SMALL SERVINGS:
600 ml pouring (single) cream
200 ml full-fat milk
3 tablespoons caster sugar
4 gelatine leaves
1-2 teaspoons pure vanilla extract or paste

TO SERVE:
strawberries and blueberries (400 g)
2 tablespoons caster sugar
finely grated zest of ½-1 lime

· Put the cream, milk and sugar into a pan. Soak the gelatine leaves in cold water.

Slowly simmer the creamy milk, uncovered, for 10 minutes. Remove the gelatine leaves from the water, and let them melt in the warm creamy milk. Stir in the vanilla, remove from the heat and strain into a jug.

Allow the mixture to cool for 15 minutes. Stir gently and then pour the mixture into 8-10 small glasses. Place them on a tray in the fridge to set.

Hull and slice the strawberries, and put them in a bowl with the blueberries, a little sugar and the grated lime zest. Let the flavours mingle for about 30 minutes before topping the panna cotta with the berries.

Vanilla rice pudding

We enjoy this creamy vanilla rice with assorted berries, finely cut mango, rhubarb compote or poached peaches. Or the old-fashioned way, with a bit of cherry or blackberry jam, diluted with a little water and gently heated in a small saucepan. (Photo, page 356)

SERVES 6:
180 g short- or long-grain rice
400 ml water
a tiny pinch of salt
½–1 vanilla pod
1 litre full-fat milk
3–4 tablespoons caster sugar
200 ml pure (whipping) cream

· Boil the rice and water with a bit of salt for 10 minutes in a heavy-based saucepan. Cover with the lid.

Split the vanilla pod lengthwise, pop it in the rice and pour in the milk. Bring to the boil, lower the heat, cover and simmer over the lowest possible heat for about 40 minutes, stirring occasionally. Remove the vanilla pod, scrape out the seeds and return them to the rice. Sweeten with the sugar and give it a good stir. Allow the rice to cool.

Lightly whip the cream. Fold it in once the rice has cooled, and taste to see if you need a bit more sugar. Leave the rice to cool completely and then refrigerate.

Our vanilla ice cream

This homemade vanilla ice cream is easy to make, amazingly good and is entirely free from artificial additives. The recipe doesn't require an ice-cream maker, and can be used as a base if you want to flavour the ice cream with a little ground cardamom, some almond brittle (see page 257) or a small splash of rum.

TO MAKE ABOUT 1 LITRE:
½–1 vanilla pod
5 tablespoons water
3 eggs
300 ml pure (whipping) cream
60 g sifted icing sugar

· Split the vanilla pod lengthwise. Put the water and vanilla in a small saucepan, cover and boil for about 5 minutes. Remove the lid and allow to cool. Separate the egg yolks and egg whites into two bowls. Pour the cream into a third bowl.

Whisk the egg whites until slightly foamy using a hand-held electric whisk at low speed. Increase the speed and continue whisking until the egg whites are stiff enough to allow you to turn the bowl upside down without the contents falling out. Set aside.

Whip the cream (but not too much) and set it aside as well. Whisk the egg yolks and icing sugar until nice and fluffy.

Remove the vanilla pod from the water, scrape out the seeds and add them to the egg yolks. Gently fold in the whipped cream using a spatula, then stir in about half of the egg whites. Gently fold in the rest of the egg whites. Pour the mixture into an airtight, freeze-proof container and freeze.

Vanilla-poached peaches or plums

You can never go wrong poaching plums, nectarines or peaches with a vanilla pod and a bit of sugar. A nice, simple seasonal dessert. (Photo, page 356)

SERVES 4:
½–1 vanilla pod
1 tablespoon caster sugar
800 ml water
90 g caster sugar
1–2 tablespoons fresh lemon juice
4–6 peaches or nectarines
  or 8 large, ripe plums

• Split the vanilla pod lengthwise and scrape out the seeds. Place the seeds on a chopping board and sprinkle over the tablespoon of sugar. Rub the sugar and vanilla back and forth with a blunt table knife, and then place the paste in a large stainless steel saucepan. Add the vanilla pod, water, sugar and lemon juice. Bring to the boil and let the syrup simmer, uncovered, for a few minutes.

Meanwhile, rinse the fruits and either leave them whole, or halve and stone them. Place the fruit in the saucepan and lower the heat, cover, and let simmer *very slowly* until just soft. Peaches and nectarines take about 8 minutes if halved, and 10–12 minutes if whole, while plums may only need 5 minutes. The skin from the peaches and nectarines can easily be removed once the fruit is cooked.

Serve the poached fruit either just slightly cooled or cold, with lightly whipped cream or ice cream.

Oven-baked stone fruits with mascarpone

Baked fruits sprinkled with muscovado sugar and vanilla turn out really flavourful. Choose assorted stone fruits such as plums, nectarines or apricots, and perhaps a handful of sweet cherries as well.

SERVES 4:
4 sweet nectarines or peaches
5 nice apricots or plums
a large handful of ripe cherries
3–4 tablespoons muscovado sugar
  + the seeds from ½ vanilla pod
  or homemade vanilla sugar (page 352)
2 tablespoons butter + a bit more for the dish

TO SERVE:
150 g mascarpone mixed with
  2 tablespoons sifted icing sugar
1 tablespoon amaretto (almond liqueur)

• First preheat the oven to 200°C/400°F. Generously grease an ovenproof dish with soft butter and then set it aside.

Cut the fruit into halves or large wedges, and remove the stones. Leave the cherries whole. Arrange the fruit quite snugly in the greased dish, sprinkle with the muscovado sugar mixed with the seeds from the vanilla pod, or with a bit of homemade vanilla sugar. Dot with the butter. Place the dish in the middle of the oven and bake for 25–30 minutes.

Serve the baked fruit while still warm, with the mascarpone combined with the sifted icing sugar and a small splash of amaretto, or just with some lightly whipped cream. Ideally with a small biscuit on the side as well…

Apple and vanilla compote

An old-fashioned apple compote may be quite modest, but it's lovely nonetheless. Firm, flavourful pears can be prepared the same way.

SERVES 4–5:
½ vanilla pod
1 kg ripe, tasty apples
800 ml water
juice of ½ lemon
90 g caster sugar
3 tablespoons potato starch dissolved in
  3 tablespoons cold water

• Split the vanilla pod lengthwise, scrape out the tiny black seeds and place both pod and seeds in a saucepan.

Quarter and core the apples and then cut them into thick wedges. Place the apple wedges in the saucepan with the water, lemon juice and sugar.

Slowly cook the apples, removing the pan from the heat as soon as the pieces are soft but not yet mushy. Gently stir in the potato starch dissolved in the cold water. Return the pan to the heat and simmer the compote for just 1 minute, stirring gently. Allow to cool.

Pour the compote into a bowl, cover with a plate and then store in the fridge until you are ready to serve.

Serve the apple compote with a small biscuit (the vanilla cornets in the recipe on the right are perfect), and a dollop of lightly whipped cream, or simply enjoy it on its own.

Aunt Mimi's vanilla cornets

Ground hazelnuts and vanilla make these Austrian biscuits extra special. Dredge the newly baked cornets with sifted icing sugar while still warm.

FOR ABOUT 40 CORNETS:
100 g hazelnuts
200 g butter, at room temperature
2 teaspoons vanilla paste
  or 2 teaspoons pure vanilla extract
90 g caster sugar
200 g plain flour
75 g potato starch
about 60 g sifted icing sugar

• Begin by finely grinding the nuts (if using a food processor, add some of the sugar when grinding) and set aside.

Cream the butter with the vanilla and sugar until nice and fluffy. Add the flour, potato starch and, finally, the ground hazelnuts.

You can easily make this dough in a food processor, but just before it comes together, turn it out onto a lightly floured work surface and knead the last bit by hand.

Preheat the oven to 150°C/300°F. Shape the dough into lengths and cut them into small pieces. Roll each piece into a walnut-sized ball, roll it into a 'finger' about 7 cm long, then bend into a crescent. Transfer to a baking tray lined with non-stick baking paper. Bake the biscuits for 20–25 minutes until cooked through but still fairly pale.

Sift the icing sugar onto a deep plate and turn the biscuits in the sugar while still warm. Leave the cornets to cool and then store them in an airtight container.

A cake from Tuscany

During a stay in Tuscany, we came across an exquisite cake at the bakery in San Gimignano. It was filled with smooth vanilla custard, raisins and almonds, and inspired us to make this luscious cake.

DOUGH:
150 g butter, at room temperature
4 tablespoons caster sugar
1 egg yolk (reserve the egg white)
175 g plain flour

FILLING AND TOPPING:
200 ml vanilla custard (page 352)
2 tablespoons raisins (optional)
2 tablespoons amaretto (almond liqueur) (optional)
1 tablespoon cornflour
1 teaspoon sugar
  + the reserved egg white for brushing
75 g almonds, blanched and peeled
3 tablespoons sifted icing sugar

· Prepare the vanilla custard and leave to cool.
  To make the dough, cream the butter with the sugar and egg yolk, and then stir in the flour. Work into a dough, then divide it in half and shape into two rounds. Refrigerate for 30 minutes. Meanwhile, soak the raisins in a bit of amaretto, if using.
  Preheat the oven to 180°C/350°F. Roll out one of the dough pieces into a circle, flouring lightly while rolling. Line the base of a small 18-20 cm pie tin with the dough, and bake it in the oven for 15 minutes.
  Combine the vanilla custard with the cornflour, and spread this on the pie crust, leaving the edges unfilled. Scatter the amaretto-soaked raisins over the top.

Roll out the other dough piece to fit the tin, and cover the filling completely. Press lightly around the edge to pinch the dough pieces together. Brush the top of the dough with the reserved egg white mixed with the sugar, then sprinkle the almonds over the top.
  Bake at 180°C/350°F for about 30 minutes, or until golden. Allow the cake to cool and then dust generously with the sifted icing sugar.

Eva's rhubarb pastries

FOR 10 PASTRIES:
6 thin stalks tender rhubarb
300 ml water
90 g caster sugar
250 ml vanilla custard (page 352)
375 g puff pastry
1 egg, lightly beaten
about 50 g flaked almonds
sifted icing sugar for dusting

· Trim and cut the rhubarb into 5 cm pieces. Gently cook the rhubarb in the water and sugar until just soft; this only takes a few minutes. Leave to cool. Prepare the vanilla custard.
  Preheat the oven to 200°C/400°F. Lightly roll out the puff pastry and cut it into 8 cm squares. Score a 1 cm edge around each square. Spoon a dollop of custard in the centre of each square, and top with a row of drained rhubarb, leaving the scored dough edge unfilled. Brush the edges with beaten egg, and sprinkle the flaked almonds over the rhubarb.
  Bake for about 15 minutes, or until puffed up and golden. Allow to cool before dusting with sifted icing sugar. (Photo, page 363)

Vanilla walnut turnovers

We are very fond of puff pastry turnovers, with all kinds of fillings. These are filled with silky vanilla custard, walnuts and caramel sauce, and we find them simply irresistible. Sometimes we make them half the size for a dessert table.

FOR 6 CRISPY TURNOVERS:
50 g walnuts
200 ml vanilla custard (page 352)
250 g puff pastry
2 tablespoons water
5-6 tablespoons sugar
1 egg, lightly beaten
sifted icing sugar for dusting

· Roughly chop the walnuts and set aside. Prepare the vanilla custard, let it cool and set it aside as well.

Lightly roll out the puff pastry and cut it into six 10 cm squares. Place a dollop of vanilla custard and some walnuts on each square.

Preheat the oven to 200°C/400°F. Line a baking tray with non-stick baking paper.

Put the water and sugar into a warm frying pan. Melt the sugar while gently stirring, but do not stir once it has started to bubble. The sugar should only be lightly caramelised and not too dark. Carefully pour 1 teaspoon of the extremely hot caramel over the walnuts on each pastry.

Brush the edges around the filling with beaten egg, fold into triangles and press the edges together with a fork to seal. Transfer to the baking tray and then brush the turnovers with the rest of the egg.

Bake in the middle of the oven for 20 minutes, or until golden. Lightly dust with sifted icing sugar when cooled.

Portuguese custard pastries

You will find these small, particularly good pastries, *pastéis de nata*, in nearly every coffee shop or bakery in Portugal. Delicate puff pastry shells filled with custard, flavoured with a bit of lemon and lightly dusted with cinnamon.

FOR ABOUT 20 SMALL PASTRIES:
1 batch vanilla custard (page 352)
2 teaspoons finely grated lemon zest
250 g puff pastry
sifted icing sugar + ground cinnamon for dusting

· Start by making a batch of the custard. Flavour with the grated lemon zest and leave to cool. Preheat the oven to 200°C/400°F.

Lightly roll out the puff pastry to about a 6-7 mm thickness, then use a glass to cut out 5-6 cm circles. Use your thumb to press the pastry dough into lightly greased small, round metal tartlet tins or into the holes of a muffin tin. Spoon the vanilla custard into the pastry shells, filling them up about three-quarters of the way.

Bake the pastries in the middle of the oven for 20 minutes, or until golden. Lightly dust the warm pastries with sifted icing sugar and a little cinnamon, and leave to cool.

Berry tartlets

Small, elegant tartlets filled with vanilla custard and topped with berries. We often use assorted berries, such as small, halved strawberries and a few blueberries or blackberries. You can bake the pastry shells in advance, but don't fill them until the day you serve them.

8 LARGE OR 16 MINI TARTLETS:
180 g plain flour
2 tablespoons caster sugar
150 g fridge-cold butter, in cubes
1 tablespoon cold water

FILLING:
300 ml vanilla custard (page 352)
about 600 g fresh berries
200 ml redcurrant jelly or
  apricot jam + 2 tablespoons water

• Measure out the flour and sugar in a bowl and rub in the butter with your fingers until the mixture resembles breadcrumbs. Add the water towards the end, and quickly work into a dough. Let it rest for about 15 minutes.

Grease small metal tartlet tins, 6 or 10 cm in diameter, or muffin tin holes. Preheat the oven to 180°C/350°F.

Divide the dough into 8 or 16 pieces, and use a floured thumb to press the dough into the tins. Bake the shells for 12-15 minutes, or until golden. Let them cool.

Prepare the vanilla custard and leave to cool as well. Fill the tartlets with custard and top with the berries.

To glaze the tartlets, melt the jelly or jam with the water in a small saucepan over low heat, and then let the jelly cool slightly until partly set. Quickly spoon it over the berries in the tartlets and allow to cool completely.

Vanilla cheesecake

This plain cheesecake can be varied in an infinite number of ways. Top it with lightly sugared blueberries or raspberries, and serve with a fresh raspberry sauce, or with sliced strawberries seasoned with a bit of sugar and finely grated lemon zest. Cheesecake is at its best if made a day in advance, but don't add the berries until just before serving.

SERVES 8-10:
10 digestive biscuits
80 g butter, melted

FILLING:
400 g Philadelphia cream cheese,
  at room temperature
3 medium eggs
90 g sifted icing sugar
2 teaspoons pure vanilla extract or paste
  or ½ teaspoon ground vanilla powder

• Preheat the oven to 200°C/400°F. Line a baking tray with baking paper.

Put the biscuits and melted butter in a food processor and combine until crumbly. Press the crumbs into a loose-based, 22-24 cm pie tin to create a thin base. Place the tin on the baking tray and bake in the middle of the oven for 5-10 minutes. Leave to cool.

Gently mash the cream cheese with a fork until fairly smooth. Or simply whiz it in the (cleaned) food processor. Add the eggs, icing sugar and vanilla, and mix until combined. Pour the mixture over the base.

Bake at 180°C/350°F for about 30 minutes, or until the filling starts to pull away from the edge of the tin. Allow to cool completely before adding the topping of your choice.

tea

中国福建乌龙茶

海堤牌

SEA DYKE BRAND

CHINA FUJIAN OOLONG TEA

JAPAN GREEN TEA
"SEN-CHA"
INGREDIENTS: GREEN TEA
DAIGO SHOTEN PA & CO.
MADE IN JAPAN
NET WT:100 g (3.5 OZ.)

On the package: 12 saquinhos · INDÚSTRIA BRASILEIRA · *Chá Preto Royal Blend®* · **Royal Blend®** · Royal Blend® · **Royal Blend.** O Tender Leaf que você já conhece. · *Orange Pekoe Tipo Assam*

a nice cup of tea warms the soul

Tea has a calming, soothing effect. It touches upon something primordial, or at least very old, inside of us. Maybe because we have been drinking tea for thousands of years, or because it is so closely linked to solemn, peaceful ceremonies like those in Japan or China. But also because of the comforting, everyday ritual of brewing your own cup of tea, just the way you like it. All across the globe, people drink tea at all hours of the day. Tea is something we have in common, and life happens around the teapot. A nice cup of tea can bring us closer, in conversations and friendly get-togethers. Tea is the world's most common beverage, second only to water.

Legends tell of the Chinese Emperor and herbalist Shennong, hailed as the Father of Chinese medicine, who always boiled his drinking water for reasons of health. One day, in the year 2737 BC, as the Emperor sat under a tree, a leaf floated into his kettle and coloured the water green. He was delighted, and found the beverage both refreshing and relaxing. The tree was a *Camellia sinensis*, which in the wild can grow up to 15 metres or more. When cultivated, these tea plants are kept waist-high, making it easier to harvest the young shoots that are used for tea. A single shrub can produce tea crops for over a hundred years, which is truly amazing.

Above: Assam tea; Tea harvest in southern India. Left, clockwise from top: Genmaicha, Japanese green tea with roasted brown rice; Cast-iron teapot from Japan; In Chinese, black tea is actually called red tea because of the colour of the brew; A package of Oolong tea. Previous page: A small teapot with Vietnamese lotus tea; Hand-tied jasmine tea that unfolds into a flower in your cup

oolong, green, black and white tea

Tea is primarily grown in China, Sri Lanka and Kenya, as well as in Japan, Indonesia, Turkey and Iran. There are thousands of different types of tea, all originating from the tea plant. Once harvested, the leaves are treated to obtain their different characteristics. Tea is usually divided into three main groups: green tea, oolong and black tea, depending on whether the tea leaves are fermented or not.

GREEN TEA is made with fresh tea leaves that are dried immediately after being harvested, without being fermented. This way the leaves maintain their lovely green colour and don't oxidise. Green tea contains antioxidants and flavonoids, which are very beneficial to your health. When brewing green tea, the water should be around 80°C/175°F (let the water cool for about 3 minutes after it has boiled). Steep the tea for 1-2 minutes, no longer, as green tea can quickly turn bitter.

OOLONG OR WULONG is a mild, partly fermented tea, which means that it is only fermented to a certain point in order to develop its unique flavour. These teas are quite fragrant, often with flowery, fruity notes and a slightly sweet aroma. Oolong, meaning 'black dragon' in Chinese, is graded according to quality and can be very expensive. The quality assessment not only considers how the tea leaves were treated, but also where and at what time of year they were harvested, and which part of the tea plant was harvested from.

BLACK TEA leaves have been entirely fermented and oxidised after being picked. The tea leaves are left to soften after the harvest, and then cut into smaller pieces that are rolled in large presses to squeeze out the liquid. During fermentation, the moisture in the leaves oxidises when it comes in contact with air, and the tea turns black during the final drying process. Black tea is brewed by pouring over some boiling water that has *only just* been brought to the boil. Steep the tea for 3-5 minutes, ideally in a preheated teapot.

WHITE TEA is made with the outermost, silver-coloured shoots at the bud stage. The tea leaves are then lightly steamed and dried. White tea has a pleasant, mild flavour and is considered very wholesome. Brew white tea in the same way as green tea, but let it steep a little bit longer.

Right, from top: Earl Grey tea; Gunpowder tea is Chinese green tea; Tea gardens in Nilgiri, southern India

darjeeling, gyokuro and yunnan...

Magnolia-scented tea from China, Darjeeling from the misty mountains of India, or green pearly dew from Japan. The softly poetic tea names evoke places far, far away, and, in a sense, to drink a cup of freshly brewed tea can be to travel for a moment...

KEEMUN TEA is a famous, black Chinese tea that is soft and mildly refreshing with a gentle aroma. The small, rolled black leaves make a reddish tea.

PU'ER, a black, post-fermented tea with an earthy quality, originates from the Chinese Yunnan province. It is often sold compressed into bricks, and is considered very beneficial to your health. Pu'er tea can be stored for a very long time: 40-50 years is not unusual.

GUNPOWDER is a Chinese green tea, and its leaves are rolled into tiny pellets that unfold when brewed. In Chinese, it is called 'pearl tea' or 'bead tea', and Gunpowder is made with young tea shoots and buds.

YUNNAN TEA comes from the Yunnan province, a famous tea-growing region in China, thought to be where all teas originated. Yunnan tea is a Chinese green tea with lots of flavour.

LAPSANG SOUCHONG, a Chinese black tea, obtains its characteristically smoky flavour from letting the tea leaves wither before drying them over burning pine wood.

BRICK TEA is the name given to teas compressed into bricks to simplify transportation. Used widely in Tibet and Mongolia, where the tea is brewed with yak butter and salt, and is known as 'butter tea' or *po cha*.

JASMINE TEA is a type of Chinese green or oolong tea that is stored with budding jasmine flowers. When the flowers unfurl, the tea leaves absorb the jasmine fragrance. This procedure is repeated several times until the tea acquires a delicate jasmine flavour. Sometimes a few dried jasmine flowers are added to the tea leaves.

LOTUS TEA is Vietnamese tea flavoured with lotus flowers. Lotus tea is considered very healthy, and is also used in certain Vietnamese dishes.

DARJEELING, often called the Champagne of teas, is an Indian black tea that grows in the foothills of the Himalayas. The high altitudes and cool climate cause the tea plants to grow very slowly, developing a unique flavour, with notes of rose, citrus and fruit. Darjeeling teas are often given the name of the plantation, which are usually small, family-owned farms, and just like wines from different vineyards, these teas vary in character and taste. Darjeeling tea harvested during the first spring harvest is especially light and considered to be the very finest.

ASSAM TEA, harvested from the domestic Indian tea plant variety, *Camellia sinensis var. Assamica*, is a black, robust and sometimes even rather spicy tea. Assam tea is grown in India, Malaysia and Indonesia.

CEYLON TEA is the collective name given to the best teas from Sri Lanka. These unadulterated, aromatic teas are cultivated in the mountainous inland.

EARL GREY is a black tea flavoured with bergamot oil from the small citrus fruit bergamot, *Citrus bergamia*. This is one of the classic, well-loved teas.

ENGLISH BREAKFAST is actually a mixture of black teas, often containing the robust Indian Assam tea and fruitier, more flavourful teas from Sri Lanka.

SENCHA is the most commonly grown green tea in Japan. The first harvest of the season is of a particularly high quality, and later on, the tea becomes more full-bodied in flavour.

GYOKURO ('jade dew' or 'precious dewdrop') is a very fine Japanese green tea. The tea plants are grown in the shade, only the uppermost buds are picked and the leaves are subsequently rolled by hand. Gyokuro teas are fresh and somewhat sweet in flavour. The tea used in the Japanese tea ceremony is green powder tea, matcha, and is made with gyokuro leaves. The tea is ground into a fine powder, then whisked in warm water with a small bamboo whisk.

GENMAICHA is a Japanese green tea flavoured with roasted brown rice. A light, tasty tea with a slightly nutty flavour that goes very well with Japanese food.

KUKICHA, or twig tea, is a unique-flavoured Japanese tea containing both leaves and tender stalks and twigs from the tea plant.

Sunflower

茉莉花茶

Jasmine Tea

福建茶叶进出口有限责任公司

中華人民共和國產品
PRODUCE OF THE PEOPLE'S REPUBLIC OF CHINA

Moroccan mint tea, page 380   *Tisane — fresh herbal tea, page 380*

Earl Grey punch with citrus, page 381

Jasmine tea with peaches, page 381

Moroccan mint tea

Sweet green tea with fresh mint is always lovely. We use less sugar than the original, but you can add more if you wish. Use Moroccan mint or spearmint, if available. (Photo, page 378)

FOR ONE TEAPOT:
1 litre water
90 g caster sugar
2 tablespoons green tea, such as Gunpowder
1 small bunch fresh mint leaves

• Bring the water and sugar to the boil, then add the green tea and mint leaves. Steep for 5-6 minutes. Serve the tea in small glasses with a little mint sprig in each glass, as shown in the photo on page 378.

Chai masala

An Indian spicy tea brew, both sweet and tasty. Just close your eyes and you are almost there...

FOR ONE TEAPOT:
500 ml water
1 tablespoon regular black tea
500 ml full-fat milk
3-4 tablespoons caster sugar
12 green cardamom pods
5 black peppercorns
1 cinnamon stick
4-5 whole cloves

• Start by bringing the water to the boil in a large saucepan. Add the tea, pour in the milk and add the sugar and spices. Bring to the boil again, and then reduce the heat to the lowest setting. Simmer for 4-5 minutes. Taste the tea, and strain through a fine sieve before serving.

Tisane – fresh herbal tea

It's delightful to brew a tisane, an infusion of fresh herbs. You can use mint, lemon balm, thyme, lemon verbena and many other herbs, and also add a piece of apple skin or lemon zest if you wish. Simply place the leaves in a teapot, pour over boiling water and allow the tisane to steep for 5 minutes or so. (Photo, page 378)

Another alternative is to first bring water to the boil in a saucepan, add the herbs and quickly transfer the saucepan to a wooden chopping board. Cover the pan and allow the tea to steep for 5-10 minutes. Strain through a sieve and pour into small glasses or a (heated) teapot.

Leaves from berry bushes can also yield a flavourful tea, but for this you need to bring the leaves and water to the boil together. Transfer the saucepan to a wooden chopping board, cover and steep for 5-10 minutes before you strain the tea. Tender blackcurrant leaves, preferably before the bushes bloom, make a particularly flavourful, delicious tea.

Drying herbs for tea

Pick the leaves and flowers from the herbs of your choice, and then let them dry in airy baskets out of direct sunlight. Spread out a fairly thin layer of herbs in the bottom of the basket, and shuffle the leaves once a day until the herbs have dried completely. It takes only a couple of days. The best way is to dry each type of herb separately, and then mix them to create your own blend of tea. A nice combination is blackcurrant leaves, spearmint and lemon balm. Another blend may include monarda (bee balm), apple mint and tender raspberry leaves.

Lemon iced tea

A cool, refreshing lemon iced tea, sweetened with a bit of sugar syrup. Keep a chilled jug in the fridge in the summertime.

SUGAR SYRUP:
200 ml water
200 g caster sugar

TEA FOR 4:
1 litre fairly strong, cold brewed tea
  such as Earl Grey or Earl Green
sugar syrup, to taste
1 washed organic lemon, thinly sliced
plenty of ice

· Start by making a sugar syrup by bringing the water and sugar to the boil. Allow it to boil gently, uncovered, for about 5 minutes, or until the mixture becomes transparent. Let cool. Pour the sugar syrup into a glass jug, cover and store in the fridge until you are ready to make the iced tea.

Brew 1 litre of black (tastiest in our opinion) or green tea, and allow to cool. Sweeten with the sugar syrup according to taste. Stir, add thin lemon slices and serve in tall glasses with plenty of ice.

Jasmine tea with peaches

Bring 1 litre of water to the boil. Add 1 tablespoon jasmine tea and steep for about 4 minutes. Strain and cool. Pour the tea into a glass jug, adding 4 ripe nectarines or peaches cut into pieces. Sweeten with a bit of sugar to taste, and stir. Let steep for 1 hour or so. Serve with ice and fresh mint. (Photo, page 379)

Earl Grey punch with citrus

The perfect non-alcoholic beverage at parties. (Photo, page 379)

FOR ABOUT 15 SMALL GLASSES:
1 litre fairly strong, cold brewed tea,
  such as Earl Grey or Darjeeling
1 litre diluted apple juice
sugar, to taste (optional)
1 lemon, 1 orange and 1 lime, thinly sliced
500 ml sparkling mineral water (or more)
plenty of ice

· Pour the cold tea and apple juice into a large glass jug or punch bowl, and sweeten with sugar if desired. Add thin slices of lemon, orange and lime. Chill and let the flavours mingle for 1-2 hours. Pour in the mineral water and lots of ice just before serving.

Peach and lime punch

FOR ABOUT 15 SMALL GLASSES:
1 litre fairly strong, cold brewed tea,
  such as Earl Grey or Darjeeling
1 litre peach juice
  or diluted apple juice
2 limes, thinly sliced
4 sweet peaches or nectarines, sliced
500 ml sparkling mineral water (or more)
plenty of ice
a handful of fresh mint leaves (optional)

· Pour the cold tea and peach or apple juice into a large punch bowl. Add the fruit slices, chill and steep for a few hours. Pour in the mineral water and plenty of ice cubes, and perhaps a few mint leaves, just before serving.

Afternoon tea

An invitation to friends for afternoon tea is always appreciated. Tiny sandwiches with tasty fillings can be quite irresistible with a cup of well-brewed tea.

TEATIME SANDWICHES should be made with thinly sliced bread. Use butter at room temperature and prepare the fillings beforehand.

Butter all the bread slices. Put the filling on one slice, place another slice of bread on top and press gently. Use a very sharp knife to trim the edges, and then cut the sandwiches into triangles or fingers.

Wrap the sandwiches in plastic wrap and refrigerate, preferably 3-4 hours in advance, for maximum flavour.

CUCUMBER SANDWICHES: Butter either white or brown bread. Add 2 layers of wafer-thin slices of peeled or unpeeled cucumber (sprinkle a little salt on the cucumber) between the bread slices.

CURRIED EGG: Chopped, hard-boiled eggs combined with a touch of whole egg mayonnaise, curry powder to taste and some finely chopped shallot. Use white or brown bread.

BLUE CHEESE AND RADISHES: Blue cheese, thinly sliced radishes and a dash of black pepper on brown bread.

CREAM CHEESE AND SMOKED SALMON: Use room-temperature Philadelphia cheese instead of butter. Top with thinly sliced smoked salmon, thinly sliced cucumber, a bit of dill and a wafer-thin lemon slice per sandwich. Best on white bread.

CHICKEN AND CELERY: Finely chopped cold chicken and a bit of celery. As a suggestion: use 2 celery stalks for 1 chicken breast fillet, which will be enough for 8 slices of bread (16 small sandwiches). Peel the celery with a potato peeler to remove the stringy bits. Cut the celery into thin strips, then into tiny pieces. Combine the celery and chopped chicken with a little bit of whole egg mayonnaise, and season with salt and pepper. Use white or brown bread.

MANGO CREAM CHEESE AND SMOKED TURKEY: Use room-temperature Philadelphia cream cheese flavoured with mango chutney, thin slices of smoked turkey breast and ideally a bit of garden cress. White or brown bread.

TURKEY AND ROCKET: A bit of Dijonnaise (whole egg mayonnaise flavoured with wholegrain Dijon mustard), smoked turkey or ham and a few rocket leaves. Use white or brown bread.

HAM AND WATERCRESS: Thin slices of ham, (spread a bit of Dijon mustard on the buttered bread if you like), plus a bit of watercress or snipped chives. White or brown bread.

SALTY RADISHES: Very finely chopped radishes and a touch of crumbled sea salt. Simple yet refined, delicious on buttered white or brown bread.

Right, clockwise from top: Tasty morsels with cream cheese and turkey; A freshly brewed cup of tea; Salmon sandwiches with lemon; Carrot cake, page 387

Scones the way we like them

Our favourite scones are made with yoghurt, and are quickly and easily thrown together in a food processor.

MAKES 16-20 SCONES:
375 g plain flour
¼ teaspoon salt
2 teaspoons baking powder
200 g thick Greek yoghurt
100 ml water

• Preheat the oven to 250°C/480°F. Line a baking tray with non-stick baking paper.

Combine the flour, salt and baking powder in a bowl or food processor. Add the yoghurt and water, and quickly work into a dough.

Turn out the dough onto a lightly floured work surface and divide into 4-5 pieces. Use floured hands to shape each piece into a fairly round scone, and place them on the tray. Flatten the scones slightly with your hand, then score each one crosswise with a blunt, floured knife to give 4 scones per piece.

Bake in the oven for 10-12 minutes. Break the scones apart and serve hot from the oven.

Raisin scones

Those of us who love raisins enjoy adding about 60 g raisins to the dough when making scones. Follow the recipe above, and only add the raisins when the dough is nearly combined. Shape into scones as usual and bake as above.

Top left: Scones and jam — a classic afternoon tea. Bottom left: Pitinga's creamy peach pie, page 386

Almond cinnamon galette

A thin French galette topped with chopped almonds, sugar and cinnamon is a real delicacy. Galettes are almost always tastier the day after, so we often make ours a day ahead.

YOU WILL NEED:
15 g fresh (compressed) yeast
2 tablespoons tepid water
100 g butter, at room temperature
2 tablespoons caster sugar
1 medium egg
200 g plain flour
  + 2 tablespoons for baking

TOPPING:
50 g fridge-cold butter
100 g almonds or hazelnuts, chopped
4 tablespoons raw (demerara) sugar
  or caster sugar
½–1 teaspoon ground cinnamon

• First dissolve the yeast in the tepid water in a tea cup, and set it aside.

Cream the butter and sugar in a bowl. Add the dissolved yeast, stir and then add the egg and the flour last of all. Work into a dough.

Cover and let the dough rise for 1-2 hours. Preheat the oven to 225°C/435°F.

Turn the dough out, quickly knead and then shape it into a large, very thin cake, about the size of a pizza. An easy way to do this is to place the dough between two pieces of non-stick baking paper on a baking tray and use a rolling pin; remove the top paper when you're done.

Thinly slice the cold butter, distribute it over the dough and then scatter with the chopped nuts. Sprinkle with sugar and a light dusting of cinnamon.

Bake for about 15 minutes, or until nice and golden. Serve the galette in thin wedges.

Pitinga's creamy peach pie

Our dear tía Pitinga often bakes this creamy pie, or *kuchen*, in her cosy kitchen in southern Chile. Sometimes she uses peaches, but the creamy pie is just as delicious with rhubarb or sour cherries. (Photo, page 384)

YOU WILL NEED:
5-6 peaches or nectarines
90 g caster sugar

DOUGH:
180 g plain flour
1 teaspoon baking powder
80 g butter, in 2 cm cubes
1 medium egg
1 tablespoon sugar
1 tablespoon white wine vinegar

YOU WILL ALSO NEED:
125 ml pure (whipping) cream
1 medium egg
90 g caster sugar
1 + 1 tablespoons cornflour
sifted icing sugar for dusting

· Rinse, halve and stone the peaches or nectarines. Cut the fruit into 2 cm thick slices and put them in a bowl with the 90 g of sugar. Set aside to allow the fruit to macerate.

For the dough, measure out the flour and baking powder in a bowl. Add the butter and rub together with your fingertips. When it starts to resemble rolled oats, combine the egg with the sugar and vinegar in a jug and pour the mixture into the dough. Work into a smooth dough.

Turn out the dough onto a lightly floured work surface and knead gently with floured hands. Shape the dough into a ball, cover with a tea towel and let it rest while you prepare the cream mixture.

In a small bowl, whisk the cream with the egg and sugar until combined.

BAKE THIS WAY: Preheat the oven to 225°C/435°F. On a lightly floured work surface, roll out the dough until nice and thin. Line the base of a large pie tin, 24-26 cm, with the dough, and trim the edges. Sprinkle a thin layer of cornflour (1 tablespoon) over the dough: this will soak up some of the moisture from the fruit later on.

Carefully drain the juice from the cut fruit in the bowl. Gently combine the fruit with the remaining 1 tablespoon of cornflour. Arrange the fruit evenly on the dough in the tin, ideally making a pretty, circular pattern. Give the cream mixture a final stir and pour it over the fruit.

Bake for 15 minutes at first, then reduce the heat to 175°C/345°F and bake for another 20 minutes, or until nicely coloured. Allow the pie to cool and dust with sifted icing sugar.

CREAMY PIE WITH RHUBARB: Trim 500 g tender rhubarb. Cut the stems lengthwise and then slice them into small pieces. Combine the pieces with 90 g sugar in a bowl. When making the pie with rhubarb, the cream mixture needs a bit more sugar, 140 g, but otherwise the pie is baked according to the recipe.

Our carrot cake

A moist carrot cake is perfect with a nice cup of tea. (Photo, page 387)

FOR A LARGE CAKE:
100 g walnuts
2-3 carrots (300 g)
200 ml sunflower oil
250 g caster sugar,
  ideally half brown/half caster
½ teaspoon salt
3 medium eggs
200 g plain flour
1 teaspoon ground cinnamon
1 teaspoon baking powder
1 teaspoon bicarbonate of soda

CREAM CHEESE ICING:
400 g Philadelphia cream cheese,
  at room temperature
100 g sifted icing sugar
3-4 tablespoons fresh lemon juice
toasted flaked almonds for garnish

· Line the base of a 22 cm springform tin with a circle of non-stick baking paper. Lightly grease and flour the side of the tin, and set aside. Preheat the oven to 175°C/345°F.

Roughly chop the walnuts, and peel and grate the carrots. Combine the oil, sugar and salt in a bowl, and then stir in one egg at a time. Add the walnuts and carrots. In a separate bowl, combine the flour, cinnamon, baking powder and bicarbonate of soda. Fold this into the carrot mixture and pour into the tin.

Bake for 50-55 minutes, or until cooked through. Leave the cake to cool completely and then take it out of the tin. Combine the cream cheese with the icing sugar and lemon juice, and spread the icing on the cake. Top with toasted flaked almonds.

Lemon cake with pine nuts

This is a soft, velvety cake with a delicate, lemony flavour. The pine nuts provide a pleasant crunch.

YOU WILL NEED:
125 g butter
finely grated zest of 2 organic lemons
5 tablespoons fresh lemon juice
4 medium eggs
240 g caster sugar
240 g plain flour
  (no baking powder)
30 g (about 4 tablespoons) pine nuts

· Slowly melt the butter and set it aside. Use some of the butter to grease a 22-24 cm round cake tin. Lightly flour the tin, shaking out the excess. Preheat the oven to 175°C/345°F.

Wash the lemons well in warm water, pat them dry and grate the outermost yellow lemon peel using a fine grater. Squeeze the lemon juice and measure the correct amount. *Note!* You won't need all the juice from the lemons for this recipe, only 5 tablespoons.

Beat the eggs and sugar until nice and fluffy, preferably using an electric whisk. Add the lemon zest, lemon juice and the cooled melted butter. Stir in the flour, then pour the mixture into the greased tin.

Bake the cake for 35-40 minutes all in all, but take it out after 10 minutes and sprinkle with pine nuts. Return to the oven and once the cake is done, allow it to cool in the tin.

chocolate

the sweet effects of chocolate

Many of us rejoice when we read all the findings confirming the positive effects of chocolate. Dark chocolate is actually good for you, albeit in moderate quantities… but still! The chocolate trend is here to stay, and the output of top quality chocolate is increasing by the day. Now, chocolate with different flavours and levels of cocoa content is available in practically every supermarket. Fortunately, more and more manufacturers have begun to use fairtrade ingredients, so do try to choose fairtrade chocolate whenever possible: it truly is important. Personally, we are among those who welcome a sweet ending to a meal, and sometimes a piece of really flavourful chocolate is just the thing. Chocolate is both comforting and satisfying at the same time. Possibly because it contains substances that stimulate the release of endorphins, which in turn increase our well-being, while not necessarily weighing down our conscience…

So it was quite fitting that botanist Carl Linnaeus gave cocoa the Latin name *Theobroma*, meaning 'food of the gods'. Throughout its extended history, chocolate has been closely linked to the Mayan and Aztec gods in Mexico, and was even used as a currency in the ancient Mexican civilisations. Chocolate eventually became incredibly popular in Europe, once Columbus, followed by Hernán Cortés, took it back from the New World. Chocolate soon became fashionable in higher circles, and special chocolate houses were popular meeting places among the aristocracy. Hot cocoa, apart from being so sweet and delicious, was believed to be an aphrodisiac and a general restorative for your health.

The cocoa tree, *Theobroma cacao*, is a small tropical tree with fruits growing directly on the trunk and the older branches. Each cocoa fruit or pod contains numerous cocoa beans, often between 30 and 50, surrounded by a white pulp that is considered a delicacy in many countries. Cocoa is currently grown in several tropical regions, but originated in Central America and the Amazon rainforests.

Left, clockwise from top: Chocolate-covered almonds; A few pieces of top-quality chocolate are perfect with a cup of coffee; Whole cocoa beans; Cocoa nibs, crushed cocoa beans, are used for cookies and more

the Mayans enjoyed hot chocolate long ago...

... and flavoured it with vanilla and chilli. How they discovered the chocolate aroma is something of a mystery though, as untreated cocoa beans are bitter and far from sweet. Legends tell that one day, long ago, a man found a cocoa pod in the rainforest, enjoyed the juicy pulp and threw the leftover beans on the fire. A few moments later, a wonderful aroma wafted up from the fire, and he tasted one of the toasted beans...

Who knows, perhaps that is what happened after all, because the journey from raw cocoa beans to delectable chocolate is quite long. The cocoa pods must first be picked by hand, since they all ripen at their own pace, then the beans and pulp are removed and fermented, which is when the dramatic change in the cocoa beans' aroma takes place. Once fermented, the beans are dried, preferably for a couple of weeks spread out in the sun, and then roasted to fully release their flavour and aroma. The next step is to extract cocoa butter, cocoa mass and cocoa powder, to which sugar is added to make the final product – chocolate. The mixture is heated and mixed, or 'conched' in chocolate terms, in different proportions and for varying times, depending on the quality of the chocolate. Vanilla and soy lecithin are also added for the sake of flavour and consistency. In order to make 1 kilo of chocolate you need 300-600 cocoa beans, which means between 10 and 20 large cocoa pods. And a cocoa tree only produces about 50 pods a year. With that in mind, perhaps we should make sure to truly take pleasure in chocolate when we eat or drink it...

Right, clockwise from top: A cup of hot chocolate with lightly whipped cream; Chocolate buttons make hot chocolate quite heavenly; A Spanish chocolate bar for making hot cocoa

Chocolates Simón

COLL

SANT SADURNÍ D'ANOIA

French chocolate sauce

This dark, glossy chocolate sauce is just as good with poached ginger pears (page 311) as it is with ice cream. If you wish to make a larger batch, just multiply the recipe.

FOR ABOUT 250 ML:
100 ml water
100 g caster sugar
40 g cocoa, sifted

· Put the water and sugar into a small saucepan. Bring to a quick boil and simmer, uncovered, for 1-2 minutes. Remove the pan from the heat. Sift in the cocoa and stir the sauce until smooth. Strain the chocolate sauce, if necessary.

Rich chocolate caramel sauce

Serve this scrumptious caramel sauce with ice cream, poached pears or the dainty profiteroles on page 396.

FOR ABOUT 500 ML:
50 g butter
100 ml golden syrup
70 g caster sugar
4 tablespoons cocoa, sifted
200 ml pure (whipping) cream
200 ml full-fat milk

· Place all the ingredients in a heavy-based saucepan, bring to the boil and then slowly simmer, uncovered, for 20-25 minutes. Stir occasionally. The sauce is especially nice when served still a bit warm, although it can be made ahead of time and gently reheated.

A cup of hot cocoa

OLD-FASHIONED COCOA: Combine 1 tablespoon good-quality cocoa with 1-2 tablespoons caster sugar in a large cup. Pour in 2 tablespoons pouring (single) cream and stir to combine. Last of all, pour in boiling hot milk, stir once more and serve right away.

COCOA DELUXE: Finely chop quality chocolate with 60-70% cocoa content (or mix both dark and milk chocolate), or use chocolate buttons instead. Bring full-fat milk to the boil, add the chocolate and slowly melt it in the milk. Remove from the heat, stir and sweeten with a bit of sugar, if desired. Pour into a cup and serve the hot cocoa with a dollop of whipped cream and some chocolate shavings on top.

VANILLA COCOA: Simmer milk with a piece of vanilla pod (sliced lengthwise) in a saucepan for 3 minutes. Remove from the heat, add chopped top-quality chocolate and stir while the chocolate slowly melts. Discard the vanilla pod and sweeten to taste with sugar, if desired.

HOT CHILLI COCOA: Spicy chilli is a great addition to hot chocolate. Use 1 halved and deseeded fresh red chilli for about 500 ml milk. Simmer the chilli and milk with a piece of vanilla pod for 3-5 minutes. Remove from the heat, add 60 g chopped quality chocolate and stir while the chocolate melts. Strain and pour into cups.

AS A SMALL DESSERT: Prepare the Cocoa deluxe as above, let it cool down and flavour with a splash of cognac or rum. Pour into elegant glasses, and top with whipped cream and a few shavings of dark chocolate. (Photo, page 403)

Profiteroles

Profiteroles or petits choux are lovely, airy cream puffs made of a water-based dough that is quickly simmered on the stovetop. You can freeze unfilled pastries for up to 1 month and then thaw them in a 175°C/345°F oven for about 5 minutes. (Photo, page 399)

FOR 20 MINI PASTRIES:
300 ml water
100 g butter
120 g plain flour
3 medium eggs

FILLING:
200 ml pure (whipping) cream
½ teaspoon vanilla paste (optional)
rich chocolate caramel sauce (page 395)

· Preheat the oven to 200°C/400°F. Line two baking trays with non-stick baking paper.

Bring the water and butter to the boil in a small heavy-based saucepan. Lower the heat and add the flour. Stir *vigorously* with a wooden spoon until the mixture pulls away from the side of the pan. *Note!* Don't allow the mixture to boil or it will separate.

Take the saucepan off the heat and allow the mixture to cool slightly. Add the eggs one at a time, stirring thoroughly after each egg. Transfer the dough to a piping bag fitted with a fluted nozzle, and pipe the batter into walnut-sized balls on the baking paper, not too close together. Bake for about 25 minutes, or until the pastries have risen and are nicely coloured. Cool on wire racks without covering.

Split them just before serving, fill with vanilla-flavoured whipped cream and put the 'lid' back on. Drizzle with chocolate caramel sauce, about 1 tablespoon per profiterole, and serve more or less immediately.

Chocolate fondant

These rich chocolate puddings with a lush, runny centre should be served warm. Prepare the batter in advance, refrigerate until serving and then bake the fondants at the last minute. Lots of calories but extraordinarily tasty ones...

FOR 8-10 FONDANTS:
40 g soft butter for greasing
2 tablespoons sifted icing sugar
170 g dark chocolate (70%)
125 g butter, at room temperature
3 eggs
3 egg yolks + 90 g caster sugar
45 g plain flour

· Generously grease 8-10 individual ramekins or small metal tins with butter. Dust with the sifted icing sugar, give them a shake and pour off any excess sugar.

Break the chocolate into pieces and melt in a heatproof bowl placed over (not touching) a small saucepan of simmering water. Add the butter and let it melt as well. Stir in one egg at a time, stirring well after each egg, and then set the bowl aside.

In a separate bowl, beat the 3 egg yolks and sugar until fluffy. Use a spatula to gradually fold in the melted chocolate cream. Sift in the flour and blend, stirring as little as possible. Fill the ramekins or tins three-quarters full. Place on a tray, cover with plastic wrap and refrigerate for no more than 24 hours.

Bake the fondants just before serving in a 180°C/350°F oven for 9-12 minutes, or until the fondants puff up slightly but are still underdone in the centre.

Tip them onto individual plates and serve right away, either as they are, or with vanilla ice cream or whipped cream and perhaps a couple of fresh raspberries.

White chocolate panna cotta

A delectable panna cotta with white chocolate that we like to top with tangy lime-marinated strawberries or blueberries, or with plain, freshly picked raspberries. You will find two additional panna cotta recipes on page 358.

FOR 6-8 SMALL GLASSES:
3 gelatine leaves
100 g white chocolate
200 ml pure (whipping) cream
200 ml full-fat milk
2 tablespoons caster sugar

TOPPING:
lime-marinated strawberries (page 222)
  or other berries + a few fresh mint leaves
sifted icing sugar for dusting (optional)

· Soak the gelatine leaves in cold water for at least 5 minutes. Break the chocolate into large pieces and roughly chop them with a sharp knife.

Bring the cream, milk and sugar to the boil in a saucepan, take the saucepan off the heat and add the chopped chocolate. Let stand for a few minutes while the chocolate melts, stirring a couple of times.

Remove the gelatine leaves. Squeeze them gently with your hand, add them to the warm creamy milk mixture and stir.

Arrange small glasses on a tray, fill them with the mixture and chill until the panna cotta sets.

To serve, garnish with sliced lime-marinated strawberries and a few fresh mint leaves, or top with other summer berries and dust with a bit of sifted icing sugar.

Tiramisu

We never tire of this Italian classic. Not only is it easy to make, but it can be prepared ahead of time and is perfect for a crowd. Luscious layers of coffee-soaked ladyfingers and amaretto-flavoured mascarpone cream, dusted with cocoa. (Photo, page 398)

FOR ABOUT 8:
24 savoiardi biscuits
  (ladyfingers or sponge fingers)
300 ml strong coffee, cooled
2 large eggs, separated
5 tablespoons caster sugar
2-3 tablespoons amaretto (almond liqueur)
250 g mascarpone, at room temperature
about 2 tablespoons sifted cocoa

· Dip 12 of the biscuits in the coffee: they should just soak up a little coffee without becoming mushy. Arrange them in a dish that will fit two snug layers of biscuits.

Beat the egg whites in a bowl until stiff and then set aside.

Whisk the egg yolks and sugar in another bowl until light and fluffy. Stir in the amaretto and mascarpone. Gradually fold in about half of the egg whites, then fold in the rest and stir to combine.

Pour half of the mascarpone cream over the biscuits in the dish. Place another layer of coffee-dipped biscuits on top, and cover with the rest of the lovely cream. Cover with plastic wrap and place the tiramisu in the fridge for a couple of hours. Just before serving, dust the tiramisu with a generous layer of sifted cocoa.

Chocolate cake with walnuts

A delectable cake with walnuts, icing and lots of chocolate flavour. Prepare the cake a day in advance to get just the right consistency. (Photo, page 403)

YOU WILL NEED:
200 g walnuts
250 g butter
200 g dark chocolate (70%)
4 eggs, separated
225 g caster sugar
1 teaspoon vanilla paste
1 tablespoon cognac (optional)
60 g plain flour + extra for dusting
ganache (see next recipe)
about 20 walnuts for garnish

· Start by roughly chopping a quarter of the walnuts and setting them aside. Coarsely grind the rest of the walnuts in a food processor.

Melt the butter over low heat in a heavy-based saucepan, and use some of the butter to grease a 24-25 cm springform tin. Lightly dust the tin with flour.

Remove the saucepan from the heat and place it on a wooden chopping board. Break the chocolate into pieces and let them melt in the warm butter in the pan. The wood will keep the saucepan warm for longer.

Whisk the egg whites until stiff enough to allow you to turn the bowl upside down without the egg whites falling out. Set aside.

Whisk the egg yolks, sugar and vanilla until fluffy. Stir in the melted chocolate butter, as well as both the ground and roughly chopped walnuts, and maybe a splash of cognac as well. Fold in the flour and stir. Use a spatula to gently fold in about half the stiff egg whites, and then gradually, and very gently, fold in the rest.

Pour the mixture into the prepared tin. Bake the cake at 175°C/345°F for 10 minutes, then reduce the heat to 150°C/300°F and bake for another 45 minutes or so. Leave the cake to cool in the tin until the next day, then unmould and spread a nice, glossy ganache on top. Decorate with the walnuts once the icing has set.

Ganache

Ganache is a rich chocolate cream that can be used as icing, cake filling or for making truffles, and it can also be flavoured with cognac, rum or vanilla.

YOU WILL NEED:
200 g dark, semi-sweet chocolate (60%)
150 ml pure (whipping) cream
1 heaped tablespoon butter

· Finely chop the chocolate using a sharp knife and place it in a heatproof bowl.

Bring the cream and butter to the boil in a small saucepan, then pour the mixture over the chopped chocolate. Slowly and gently stir the mixture until the chocolate melts and combines with the cream into a thick, glossy cream. The ganache will thicken once cool.

TO ICE A CAKE: Brush off any crumbs from the cold cake. Place the cake on a wire rack on top of a tray covered with baking paper. First ice the cake with a thin base layer, using a palette knife if you have one. Then pour the rest of the ganache onto the centre of the cake and spread it out using sweeping motions, covering the sides as well. Any excess chocolate will fall onto the tray. Allow the icing to set while sitting over the tray.

Chocolate mousse

Chocolate mousse is quite intense and rich in flavour, so a little goes a long way. Use dark chocolate, but ideally under 70% or the mousse may become slightly bitter. If you freeze this mousse, it will turn into a lovely chocolate ice cream. (Photo, page 402)

FOR 8 SMALL SERVINGS:
100 g dark chocolate (62%)
300 ml pure (whipping) cream
2 egg yolks

· Break the chocolate into pieces and melt in a heatproof bowl placed over (not touching) a small saucepan of simmering water. The chocolate will melt within minutes.

Whip the cream, but not too much or the mousse will become grainy.

Remove the chocolate bowl from the heat and stir in one egg yolk at a time.

Take about a tea cup of the whipped cream and use a spatula to gently fold it into the warm chocolate mixture. Stir vigorously to combine, and then do just the opposite: fold the chocolate mixture into the bowl of whipped cream, now stirring with gentle, light motions.

Pour the mousse into small individual cups or glasses, place them on a tray and refrigerate until the mousse sets.

White chocolate mousse

This white chocolate mousse is delicious served with fresh berries on top. Sometimes we make a layered mousse with both dark and white chocolate. We start by filling individual glasses half-way with one of the mousses, letting them set for 1 hour in the fridge, and then we pour the second mousse on top and chill for another hour before serving. (Photo, page 402)

FOR 8 SMALL SERVINGS:
1 gelatine leaf
300 ml pure (whipping) cream
100 g good-quality white chocolate

· Soak the gelatine by rolling the gelatine leaf into a thin roll and placing it in a large glass of cold water. Take it out after 5 minutes. Whip the cream, but not too much — it should still be a bit runny.

Chop the chocolate into little pieces and melt them in a bowl placed over (not touching) a small saucepan of boiling water. The chocolate will melt within minutes.

Remove the gelatine from the water and add it to the warm chocolate. Take the pan off the heat and stir until the gelatine dissolves. Use a spatula to fold some of the whipped cream, a few tablespoons at a time (100-150 ml in total), into the chocolate, and stir vigorously until smooth. Next, do exactly the opposite: fold the chocolate mixture into the bowl of whipped cream. Gently stir just until smooth.

Pour into glasses or small individual dishes and chill until you are ready to serve.

Layered chocolate mousse, page 401

Frozen chocolate mousse turns into ice cream, page 401

Chocolate cake with walnuts, page 400

Chocolate drink as a dessert, page 395

Brownies

These moist, very chocolatey brownies are perfect when you have lots of guests, or want to make them beforehand and freeze. We like to make quite small squares, as the brownies are fairly sweet.

FOR ABOUT 25 BROWNIES:
200 g butter
150 g dark chocolate (60-70%)
4 medium eggs
290 g caster sugar
1-2 teaspoons vanilla paste
120 g plain flour
1 teaspoon baking powder
2 tablespoons sifted cocoa
100 g walnuts, roughly chopped (optional)

· Start by generously greasing and lightly flouring the sides of a baking tin, measuring about 30 x 24 cm. Line with non-stick baking paper and set it aside.

Melt the butter over low heat and then move the saucepan to a wooden chopping board to keep it warm. Break the chocolate into pieces and let them melt in the warm butter.

Meanwhile, preheat the oven to 175°C/345°F. Whisk the eggs and sugar until fluffy, and add the vanilla. Fold in the flour mixed with the baking powder and sifted cocoa. Fold the melted chocolate butter into the egg and flour mixture and stir in the walnuts, if using. Spread out the mixture in the baking tin.

Bake for about 30 minutes. Watch the brownies towards the end so that they don't overbake and become dry. Allow to cool and then leave for a few hours, or preferably until the following day. Cut the brownies into 5 cm squares.

Simone's chocolate cake

This exquisite yet rather delicate cake is one of our favourites. It should be baked a day ahead to get the perfect flavour. Serve Simone's cake with lightly whipped cream.

YOU WILL NEED:
3 medium eggs
75 g butter
100 g dark chocolate (60-70%)
130 g caster sugar
1 teaspoon vanilla paste
a pinch of sea salt
3 tablespoons plain flour

· Grease and then flour the side of a round, 22 cm loose-based cake tin. Line the base of the tin with a circle of non-stick baking paper and set aside.

Separate the egg yolks and egg whites into two bowls, and set aside.

Melt the butter in a small saucepan over low heat, then transfer it to a wooden chopping board. Break the chocolate into pieces and let them melt in the saucepan.

Preheat the oven to 180°C/350°F. Beat the egg whites until stiff peaks form and set aside.

Whisk the egg yolks with the sugar, vanilla and salt. Add the chocolate mixture and flour. Fold in about half of the whisked egg whites with a spatula. Carefully fold in the rest of the egg whites and then pour the mixture into the prepared tin.

Bake in the middle of the oven for 30 minutes. The cake will rise at first, but sink again once it cools. Don't worry, it turns out absolutely fabulous anyway. Let it stand until the next day. The cake is a bit fragile, so handle it with care when removing it from the tin.

Truffles from Gascogne

Dainty chocolate truffles flavoured with coffee and a splash of cognac or Armagnac, typical of the French province of Gascogne, where we first learned to make these truffles.

FOR ABOUT 30 TRUFFLES:
200 g dark chocolate (70%), in pieces
  + another 100 g chocolate for garnish
2 tablespoons butter
1 tablespoon crème fraîche
2 tablespoons strong coffee
  or 2 teaspoons instant coffee
    dissolved in 2 tablespoons hot water
90 g sifted icing sugar
1 tablespoon cognac or Armagnac
wooden toothpicks
about 40 g sifted cocoa

· Break the 200 g of chocolate into pieces and melt them in a bowl with the butter over a small saucepan of boiling water.

Stir in the crème fraîche, coffee, icing sugar and cognac or Armagnac. Take the saucepan off the heat and stir with a spatula. Refrigerate for 1 hour, or until the mixture sets and can be handled.

Shape the mixture into little round marbles. Place them on a tray lined with non-stick baking paper and put a toothpick in each one. Refrigerate the tray for at least 2 hours.

Next, melt the rest of the chocolate and brush the fridge-cold truffles with a layer of chocolate, holding them with the toothpicks. Dust with plenty of sifted cocoa and allow to cool. Remove the toothpicks, place the truffles in an airtight container and store them in the fridge. The delicious truffles will keep for around 3 weeks.

Chocolate toffee sweets

We make this wonderfully chewy toffee every Christmas. To test whether the toffee is done, pour a few drops of the hot mixture into a glass of cold water. The toffee is ready when you can easily shape it into a small ball, and should then be poured immediately into a greased ovenproof dish.

YOU WILL NEED:
100 g butter
200 ml pure (whipping) cream
250 g caster sugar
100 ml golden syrup
3 tablespoons honey
1 teaspoon vanilla paste
4 tablespoons cocoa

· Combine all the ingredients in a heavy-based saucepan. Bring the mixture to the boil, then reduce the heat and simmer, uncovered, over fairly low heat (the surface should be full of small bubbles that grow bigger towards the end). Carefully stir the caramel mixture at least once every 5 minutes. Continue cooking for about 35 minutes, or until the toffee passes the cold water test mentioned above.

When ready, immediately pour the mixture into a small, greased baking tray or ovenproof dish. Allow it to cool slightly before you use a blunt knife to score small squares into the mixture before it cools completely. Once cooled, cut the toffee pieces apart and wrap them in greaseproof paper. Store the chocolate toffee sweets in an airtight container.

on the menu

sharing a meal...

There are often many of us around the table in the kitchen under the walnut tree. We bring out the extra chairs, and the air is filled with good conversation and laughter. Food, talk, wine and music. Those are the evenings that leave a lasting impression, and they generate an energy that lingers even during other, quieter moments.

An evening spent in the company of just a few good friends also leaves a warmth behind long after they're gone. Getting together to share a meal is such an essential part of life. Sometimes the actual cooking provides a lovely opportunity for small talk, but when entertaining, it's often convenient to have most of the food prepared in advance. It could be a hearty autumn stew, a spicy Indian curry, or perhaps roast chicken with white wine and oven-roasted vegetables. Or platters with assorted finger foods that are pleasing to both the eye and the palate, while still being relatively easy to whip up.

In this chapter we have assembled a few menu ideas for all kinds of occasions, picking recipes from different chapters throughout the book. You will find menu suggestions for last-minute dinners for unexpected guests, or standing buffets for large parties, an Indian feast, summer evenings by the barbecue and much more. There are so many opportunities to get together with friends and family, and we should make the most of them.

Above: Mango cheesecake, page 327; A simple meal. Left: Limes and lemons decorate the table

A summer evening in the garden

Simple and delicious, perfect for an evening with friends around the garden table.

Ginger ale, page 166 or Barley water, page 196.
Jazzed-up feta with herbs, page 92.
Garlic and herb-roasted zucchini, page 92.
Roasted red capsicums, page 246.

Herb-crusted salmon, page 106,
  with a Simple summer sauce, page 85,
  and new potatoes with dill, or
Vitello tonnato, page 206,
  with new potatoes , or
Herb-crusted leg of lamb, page 113
  served with Salsa verde, page 84.
Creamy fresh yoghurt cheese, page 87.
Summertime bread, page 242.
A large mixed green salad.
Our vinaigrette, page 60.

Summer berries with lemon curd cream, page 221, or
Oven-baked stone fruits with mascarpone, page 360.

Fish on the menu

A light main course with fish followed by a rich dessert.

Honey-roasted goat's cheese on baby greens, page 66, or
Individual servings of Our easy salad deluxe, page 22.

Fish stew from Mariestad, page 106, or
A hearty fish soup, page 104
  served with Lemon aioli, page 198, or
Turbot in beurre noisette, page 154, or
Baked salmon on spinach, page 65.
Bread and cheese.

Torta della nonna, page 214, or
Martin's exquisite pears, page 309, or
Frangipane tart with fruit, page 251.

A buffet for a crowd

A larger buffet requires a bit of planning. In this case, the walnut nibbles, breadsticks, Nobis dressing and tiramisu can all be prepared the day before. The chocolate cake can be baked up to a week beforehand and frozen, and then thawed and glazed the day before serving. The almond biscotti can be baked 3-4 days in advance and stored in an airtight container.

Chèvre and walnut nibbles, page 236.
Assorted quality olives.
Poppy seed breadsticks, page 240.

A big birthday salad, page 65.
Nobis dressing, page 60.
Herb-crusted salmon, page 106.
Herb-marinated roast beef, page 107.
Crispy feta cheese pastries, page 69.
A mixed green salad.
Assorted cheeses, freshly baked bread.
Fresh figs and melon, in slices or wedges.

Tiramisu, page 397.
Chocolate cake with walnuts, page 400.
Panna cotta with berries, page 358.
A large platter with seasonal fruits.
Almond biscotti, page 250.

A small dessert buffet on a tray

A bit of this and that to end the meal on a sweet note.

Beautiful fresh fruit, perhaps melon in pieces,
  sweet cherries or apricots.
Good-quality dark chocolate.
Mallorcan almond chews, page 253, or
Almond biscotti (store-bought or see page 250).
Shrikand, a cardamom dessert from India, page 288.
Chocolate mousse, page 401.

South American-style barbecue

While waiting for the meat on the barbecue, serve pieces of spicy sausage, such as chorizo, in crusty bread with a bit of pebre, a fabulous tomato salsa. Make a large batch of pebre — it's delicious with the meat as well.

Grilled chorizo in a piece of baguette or other crusty bread.
Pebre — a fabulous tomato salsa, page 38.
Quality beef or lamb to barbecue, seasoned with sea salt.

Avocado mash from Chile, page 20, or Guacamole, page 20.
Sliced tomatoes with fresh coriander, sea salt,
  and a splash of olive oil.
Ají verde — green chilli mix, page 124.
Tito's avocado and celery salad, page 21.
A green mixed salad.
Roasted potato wedges.
Lemon aioli, page 198.

Olinda mango mousse, page 329, or
Creamy lime pie, page 214.
 Assorted seasonal fruits.

An autumn dinner

Hearty, comforting food and desserts using seasonal fruit.

Chicken and thyme pâté (on toast), page 107, or
Jerusalem artichoke soup, page 103.

Roast chicken with chorizo, page 141, or
Roast lamb in a lovely herb jus, page 112
  with Mushroom risotto, page 101, or
  Rosemary and carrot potatoes, page 103.
Our easy salad deluxe, page 22.

Pears in Marsala, page 309, or
Apple and vanilla compote, page 361, or
Apple wedges à la maison, page 258.

One-pot cooking

You really don't need much else, just a green salad, some tasty bread and perhaps a piece of cheese or two. Convenient cooking!

Casserole from Gotland, page 210.
Tarragon chicken with lemon and artichoke, page 208.
Lamb with spring vegetables, page 157.
Fanny's 'all-in-one' chicken, page 109.
One-pot Parma chicken, page 109.
Roast chicken with chorizo, page 141.
Fish stew from Mariestad, page 106.
Ethiopian doro wat (chicken stew), page 139.
An aromatic broth with noodles and whatnot, page 171.
Chilli con carne, page 141.
A hearty fish soup, page 104.
Red lasagne with green leaves, page 46.
Cannelloni with ricotta, page 247.

With a Scandinavian touch

A menu with flavours from the north…

Pernilla's smoked herring (on crispbread), page 152, or
Mini Danish smørrebrød (with roast beef and curry
  remoulade), page 148.

Creamy mustard potato salad with smoked trout, page 151, or
Fish stew from Mariestad, page 106, or
Herb-crusted salmon, page 106,
  with Simple summer sauce, page 85,
  and new potatoes with dill, or
Swedish Lindström patties (with beetroot), page 157, or
Turbot in beurre noisette, page 154.

Rhubarb compote with cardamom cream, page 289,
  with Sister Sara's biscuits, page 292, or
Swedish ginger pears, page 311,
  with a bit of lightly whipped cream.

A green menu

A few suggestions on how to combine some of the book's vegetarian recipes.

Baked baby beetroots with Chèvre and thyme dip, page 87, or
Warm lentil salad from Arles, page 97, or
Small mushroom quiches, page 69, or
Tourte de blettes chard pie, page 70, or
Pea, farro and avocado salad with mint, page 22.

Lentil and chilli soup, page 131, or
Feta and bean salad, page 98, or
A warming winter soup, (omit the chorizo), page 111, or
Asparagus and herb risotto, page 101, or
Red lasagne with green leaves, page 46, or
Cannelloni with ricotta, page 247, or
Eggplant pasta della casa, page 100.

A bowl full of crisp leafy greens.
Creamy fresh yoghurt cheese, page 87.
Bread from Sacré Cœur, page 242.

Dinner in an hour

Something quick and tasty for just a few...

Individual servings of avocado, rocket and walnut salad
with Our vinaigrette, page 60. Ideally with some crumbled
soft goat's cheese on top.

Baked salmon on spinach, page 65,
with baby potatoes and steamed snow peas, or
Alex's tomato chicken with basil, page 47,
with pappardelle pasta, or
Pasta puttanesca, page 100.
A green salad and crusty bread.

Dessert tray with good-quality chocolate, store-bought
biscotti and beautiful seasonal fruit.
Perhaps the Creamy vanilla yoghurt, page 352, with
nectarines in wedges.

Prepared in advance

A menu with everything conveniently prepared
a day ahead...

Lamb and apricot tagine, page 210.
Casserole from Gotland, page 210.
Osso buco, page 207.
Vitello tonnato, page 206.
Chilli con carne, page 141.
Lentil and chilli soup, page 131.
A hearty fish soup (base only), page 104.

Simone's chocolate cake, page 404.
Creamy lime pie, page 214.
Chocolate (or layered) mousse, page 401.
Crème caramel, page 354.
Frangipane tart with fruit, page 251.
Tiramisu, page 397.
Tosca pie with walnuts, page 251.

A Provençal dinner

A rustic menu with a hint of southern France.

Individual portions of Lentil salad from Arles, page 97, or
Chicken and thyme pâté (on toasted country bread,
with small cornichon gherkins), page 107.

Herb-crusted leg of lamb with anchovies, page 113,
with a green salad with Our vinaigrette, page 60, or
A hearty fish soup, page 104,
with bread and Lemon aioli, page 198.

Provençal pears in red wine (with cheese), page 311, or
Crème caramel, page 354, or
Granny's French pear and almond cake, page 307.

An Indian feast

While the food is cooking, set the table with lots of colourful flowers...

Indian chilli nuts, page 235.
Lemony chickpea salad, page 200.
Store-bought naan bread or papadums.

Tandoori chicken, page 284,
  served with Indian tomato kachumber, page 39,
  and Indian raita with mint, page 86.
Indian curry from Stockholm, page 175, or
Chicken korma with almonds, page 285.
Chickpeas Kerala-style, page 271, or
Dewi's potato curry, page 284.

Quick pickled mango, page 318.
Cardamom rice with nuts, page 283, or basmati rice.
A salad with mixed baby greens.

Shrikand, Indian yoghurt dessert, page 288, or
Rice pudding from Amritsar, page 288.
Nicely cut pieces of ripe mango.
Chai masala, spicy tea with milk, page 380.

Tapas and a glass of wine

Simple, appetising Spanish-style finger food, perfect with a glass of wine.

Pimientos de Padrón, page 130.
Chilli and garlic prawns, page 130.
Tuna tapas from Seville, page 130.
Roasted red capsicums, page 246.
Jamón serrano, lomo or other Spanish cold cuts.
Good-quality black and green olives.
Manchego cheese and crusty bread.
A variety of nuts and dried fruits.
Crema catalana, page 215.

Southeast Asian flavours

Beautiful Asian-inspired finger food with fresh tropical fruit for dessert.

Spring rolls from Hanoi, page 67,
  with crisp lettuce leaves and mint.
Chicken salad from Laos (with cashews and
  sesame seeds), page 245,
  served in small lettuce leaves.
Fiery steak skewers, page 129.
Thai fish cakes, page 129.
Coconut lime prawns, page 268.
Pomelo and prawn salad, page 201.
Green mango salad, page 320.
Nuoc cham dipping sauce, page 126
  and Thai sweet chilli sauce.

Pineapple with ginger and mint, page 178.
Papaya with lime wedges.
Lime and coconut ice cream, page 274, with tropical fruit.

Middle Eastern ideas

Wonderful food for entertaining, both savoury and festive.

A great hummus, page 199.
Fresh mint labneh, page 86.
Tabbouleh, page 93.
Toasted pita bread in wedges.
Citrus-marinated olives, page 199.

Lamb and apricot tagine, page 210, served with couscous, or
One-pot chicken with fragrant saffron rice, page 283.
A large green salad.
A small bowl of chilled yoghurt.

Moroccan oranges, page 217, or
Oranges with pomegranate, page 217.
Walnut baklava, page 256.
Moroccan mint tea, page 380.

There are two indexes in the book: an alphabetical one on page 422, and this one, which shows the contents of each chapter.

vanilla

tea

chocolate

on the menu

index

a

Afternoon tea 382
Aioli 198
Ají
  Roberto's indispensable 124
  verde 124
Alex's tomato chicken with basil 47
All-round fruit salad 272
Alma's sweet catalans 345
Almond(s)
  biscotti 250
  blueberry muffins 252
  brittle 257
  chews, Mallorcan 253
  cinnamon galette 385
  crisp parcels, with pears and
    cinnamon 307
  festive almond slices 253
  salted 235
  spicy with garlic 235
  Viennese almond squares 344
Anna's avocado soup 31
Antonia's roasted tomato and
  mozzarella salad 41
Apple(s)
  and carrot slaw 149
  and coconut crumble 275
  baked walnut 258
  vanilla compote 361
  wedges à la maison 258
Artichoke hearts with garlic, thyme
  and chilli 92
Asparagus and herb risotto 101
Aunt Mimi's vanilla cornets 361
Avocado
  baguette, with tuna 29
  Churrasco, Chilean steak
    sandwich 27
  club sandwich with chicken 28
  Completos, chorizo in
    bread 27
  Danish rye with rocket and
    mozzarella 29
  fresh salsa for barbecues 21
  Green Goddess dressing 20
  guacamole 20

mash from Chile 20
quesadillas 27
salad deluxe 22
salad, John's 24
salad, quick 20
salad, with celery 21
salad, with croutons and roasted
  Parma ham 22
salad, with grapefruit 21
salad, with peas and farro 22
salad, with tuna, from Mallorca 24
salsa, with prawns and lime 25
sandwich with turkey, sesame
  seeds and chilli 29
soup, Anna's 31
starter on crispbread 25
zesty dip 21

b

Baked salmon on spinach 65
Baked walnut apples 258
Baklava, walnut 256
Balinese sambal 126
Barley water 196
Bean salad
  a colourful 244
  lemony beans 199
  with feta 98
Beef
  Churrasco, Chilean steak
    sandwich 27
  curry, green 268
  roast beef, herb-marinated 107
  steak skewers 129
Beetroot salad 153
Berbere 125
Berries
  lime-marinated 222
  panna cotta 358
  tartlets 367
Big birthday salad 65
Biscotti
  almond 250
  hazelnut, Mette's 250
  with olives and almonds 239
Bok choy, braised 72
Bread
  breadsticks, poppy seed 240

from Sacré Cœur 242
Jean's thin savoury flatbread 90
nutty fruit 236
pear crostini with chèvre 304
summertime 242
sunday breakfast buns 241
tomato 51
walnut, from Gotland 241
Broth, aromatic with noodles 171
Brownies 404
Bruschetta
  Portobello, with pecorino and
    rocket 66
  tomato 51
Buns, our best vega 291
Butterscotch thins 252

c

Cabbage, tender with lemon 72
Caesar salad 64
Cake
  cardamom 292
  carrot 387
  chocolate, Simone's 404
  chocolate, with walnuts 400
  cinnamon carrot, Ginger's 181
  coconut, for Susanne 275
  from Tuscany 364
  lemon, with pine nuts 387
  pear and almond cake, Granny's
    French 307
  pear, teatime 308
  Raspberry Swiss roll 344
Cannelloni with ricotta 247
Capsicums, roasted red 246
Cardamom
  biscuits, Sister Sara's 292
  buns, our best vega 291
  cake, country 292
  Chicken korma with almonds 285
  chicken, with fragrant saffron
    rice 283
  Dewi's potato curry 284
  fruit compote, spicy dried 289
  rhubarb compote 289
  Rice pudding from Amritsar 288
  rice, with nuts 283
  rusks, from the farm 293

many thanks to all our friends who have contributed to this book in different ways...

To Roberto Jequier, who is the third party in all our projects and who works behind the scenes. To Susanne Lindh for providing every conceivable kind of assistance. To Charlotta Oljelund for trying out the recipes morning, noon and night. To Clara Garzón, Sebastien Boudet, Åsa Anderberg and Tobias Strollo for inspiration (and for Åsa's delicious saffron oranges!). To Linda Knutas and Kalle Edeus at Sudergarde. To Erik and Cornelia Sojdelius. To Pia Crafoord and Gunilla Appelqvist, our inspiring and encouraging friends. And also, for the edition in English: A warm thank you to Susanne Lomander, Lillemor Broni, Amy Oliver, Annika Hultman Löfvendahl and Ulla Wikström Schaeffer. And of course to all of you, beloved friends and family, who have contributed with your encouragement, support and warmth. Thank you!

Literature:

The Oxford Companion to Food, Alan Davidson. Oxford University Press, 1999.

The Cambridge World History of Food, K. F. Kiple and K. Coneè Ornelas. Cambridge University Press, 2000.

Larousse Gastronomique, Larousse Bordas, 2000.

The New Oxford Book of Food Plants, J. G. Vaughan and C. A. Geissler. Oxford University Press, 1997.

First published by Trio Förlag in Swedish in 2006

This edition published in 2012 by Hardie Grant Books

Hardie Grant Books (Australia)
Ground Floor, Building 1
658 Church Street
Richmond, Victoria 3121
www.hardiegrant.com.au

Hardie Grant Books (UK)
Second Floor, North Suite
Dudley House
Southampton Street
London WC2E 7HF
www.hardiegrant.co.uk

Photography and design by Fanny Bergenström
Translated by Susanne Lomander
Edited by Kim Rowney

Cataloguing-in-Publication data is available from the National Library of Australia.

ISBN 9781742702070

Printed in China by 1010 Printing International Limited